Potholes in the Road

Potholes in the Road

TRANSITION PROBLEMS FOR LOW-INCOME
YOUTH IN HIGH SCHOOL

Martín Sánchez-Jankowski

UNIVERSITY OF CALIFORNIA PRESS

University of California Press
Oakland, California

© 2022 by Martín Sánchez-Jankowski

Library of Congress Cataloging-in-Publication Data

Names: Sánchez-Jankowski, Martín, author.
Title: Potholes in the road : transition problems for low-income youth in high
    school / Martín Sánchez-Jankowski.
Description: Oakland, California : University of California Press, [2022] |
    Includes bibliographical references and index.
Identifiers: LCCN 2021046149 (print) | LCCN 2021046150 (ebook) |
    ISBN 9780520387102 (cloth) | ISBN 9780520387119 (paperback) |
    ISBN 9780520387126 (ebook)
Subjects: LCSH: Low-income high school students—United States—Case
    studies.
Classification: LCC LC208.4 .S26 2022 (print) | LCC LC208.4 (ebook) |
    DDC 373.1826/940973—dc23/eng/20211018
LC record available at https://lccn.loc.gov/2021046149
LC ebook record available at https://lccn.loc.gov/2021046150

31 30 29 28 27 26 25 24 23 22
10 9 8 7 6 5 4 3 2 1

To Three Extraordinary Educators:
Richard P. Young
Lewis I. Jeffries
Roger L. Dial

There is nothing in the single frame caterpillar
that tells you it's going to be a butterfly.

R. BUCKMINSTER FULLER
Integrity of San Francisco Lecture, 1983

CONTENTS

LISTS OF FIGURES AND TABLES

FIGURES

TABLES

PREFACE

Formal education has been seen as the keystone of all modern societies because it provides essential knowledge for advancing economic and social life. Yet, despite recognizing the importance of education, modern societies have had difficulty in providing equal educational opportunities for all segments of their societies, especially those from low-income families. Personally, I have understood the importance of education for improving the lives of individuals in society—I was a person from a low-income family who was able, through education, to be socioeconomically mobile. What is more, I have been an educator for my entire professional life, first as a junior and senior high school teacher in a number of Detroit inner-city schools, and finally as a university professor. Thus, this book carries both a personal and profession interest into understanding the problems encountered by both students from low-income families and educators in creating successful academic outcomes.

I turn now to that part of a preface which is the most enjoyable to me— the acknowledgment of the people and institutions that contributed to the book's completion. Let me begin by thanking the Spencer Foundation, the John D. and Catherine T. MacArthur Foundation, the Robert Wood Johnson Foundation, and the University of California's Faculty Research Program for their financial support that allowed me to carry out the twenty-three years of field research for this project.

Special thanks must be extended to those who directly aided the research part of the project. That starts with thanking the various school district officials, as well as the school administrators, staffs, teachers, counselors, and students, who allowed me to be involved in their lives over the time covered in the study. Also, I would like to express gratitude to all the parents who over the years invited me into their homes to share that part of their families' lives.

Next, I want to thank the people who aided in the completion of the book. Portions of the book were presented at various lectures I gave, and I so much appreciate those in the audience who provided substantive comments. I would also like to thank John Ferry of the Estate of R. Buckminster Fuller, who researched the exact source of the quote of Mr. Fuller's that I used as the lead epigraph for the book. In particular, I want to express my enormous appreciation to Claude S. Fischer, Corey M. Abramson, Gilberto Q. Conchas, and Lynn S. Chancer for reading all of the manuscript and providing detailed comments that have greatly improved it. Of course, having acknowledged their contributions, I also want to make very clear that all those who commented on the book and provided financial support for the book's research are not responsible for any errors or defects that may exist. That responsibility lies solely with me.

Over the years, I have been fortunate to work with the University of California Press and the professional staff associated with it. I thank Naomi Schneider for all that she has done for this book project. She continues to be a wonderful editor to work with. I also want to acknowledge the terrific help I received from Summer Farah for her logistical assistance in preparing the manuscript for production, as well as Francisco Reinking for efficiently managing the production process. Of course, I would be remiss if I did not thank Paul Tyler for the wonderful job he did in editing the manuscript and making it more clear and readable. This is the first time I have worked with him and it would be an honor to do so in the future. Last, but certainly not least, I want to thank Eileen Hout, the artist whose work graces the cover of the book.

Now, a word about the three educators to whom this book is dedicated. The late Lewis I. Jeffries was a junior high school teacher, principal, and district administrator in Detroit who supervised the student-teacher experience required for the secondary education degree, and Richard P. Young and Roger L. Dial were university professors. All three were special in sharing their knowledge and time with every student they had contact with. It would be hard to find a student from their courses who did not appreciate what each gave to them. I was fortunate and grateful to have all three.

Finally, I want to thank various family members who provided moral support during the research and writing of this book. The first expression of gratitude must go to my late wife, Carmen, who was so instrumental in all my research projects because she both encouraged me and maintained our home during the long periods of time I was away doing extended field research. She unfortunately passed away a few years ago, so there is emptiness associated with writing this part of the preface.

My second expression of gratitude goes to the other family members who tried their best to fill in for Carmen. A big thank you must go to my brother Mike and sister-in-law Sharon, brothers-in-law Frank and Luciano, sister-in-law Inga, Maria Martinez, and David Montejano for their continued support; as well as my three sons, Javier, Julián, and Andrés.

It has been my custom with other books I have written to discuss the title I selected for the book at the end of the preface. Usually I would take the opportunity to inform the reader how the title was chosen and in what ways it related to the argument developed in the book, but that is not necessary this time. Simply stated, the title of this book, *Potholes in the Road*, is a straightforward depiction of what is developed throughout the book. Nonetheless, I do have something to say regarding the title. As some readers will recognize, this is the third title of a book I have written that refers to a passageway, the other two being *Islands in the Street* and *Cracks in the Pavement*. Although all three titles capture the substantive argument in each book, I have promised myself that this is the last time I will use a roadway symbol for a book title. So, despite my affectionately referring to these three as the "Detroit Title Trilogy," undoubtedly others will be relieved by this commitment.

Introduction

> ... and I imagine that he shared the attitude, which I was to
> encounter so often later, toward the children who were helping
> to bring this future about: admiration before the general spec-
> tacle and skepticism before the individual case.
>
> JAMES BALDWIN,
> *"A Fly in Buttermilk," 1958*

AMERICANS HAVE LONG TAKEN PRIDE in the idea that their country provides everyone the opportunity to achieve a better life. No aspect of the American ideology has shaped economic life in the United States more force-fully than the premise that individuals can, through hard work and determi-nation, improve on their socioeconomic origins and create a better future for themselves. This idea has lured a constant stream of immigrants to the United States and governed a good deal of public policy.[1] It is fair to say that most Americans desire and hope that they and their children will improve their economic situation over time—and that most believe this is possible.

This norm is an integral part of the "American Dream" and has captivated current and aspiring citizens for at least a century and a half.[2] Significant disparities among individuals in talent and resources are generally acknowl-edged, but Americans commonly believe that most individuals can obtain the skills necessary to secure jobs that provide incomes associated with the American Dream—even when evidence suggests this is not the case.[3] In the American Dream, the United States is a meritocracy, and because skills can be taught, it has long been argued that with education and training, any individual can improve their economic chances; this is why so much emphasis in social policy has been devoted to schooling. Ever since education became compulsory through age 16, American society has relied on it to be the antidote to socioeconomic inequality.

No institution in society has been given more responsibility for reinforcing the American Dream than public schools, particularly for young people from families with low incomes.[4] However, public education has not been successful in improving the economic fortunes of significant numbers of students from low-income families, as many drop out before matriculating or they matriculate but cannot proceed to college because of their poor grades in high school or low scores on the standardized tests used to assess knowledge and competency for college admission.[5] This situation has elicited concern among education professionals, social scientists, and the general public that underlies many education policy initiatives.

Consider, for instance, President Bill Clinton's package of education reforms announced in 1999 as "Expanding Educational Opportunities"; President George W. Bush's promotion of still other reforms—and testing— in the "No Child Left Behind Act," which he signed in 2002; and President Barack Obama's "My Brother's Keeper," a public-private partnership launched in 2015 to address opportunity gaps, especially for young individuals of color. Despite these initiatives, barriers to successful transitions in education still challenge many low-income youth. Based on observations of low-income youth inside and outside of high school in five different studies covering parts of twenty-three years, this book focuses on factors that created difficulties for these students and how these difficulties created systemic problems that limited their chances of transitioning to the next stage of their education.

LOW-INCOME YOUTH AND THE EDUCATION PROCESS

While low-income youth face significant barriers to their progress through the education system, some make successful transitions through their education and are economically mobile. So why are some individuals from low-income families ineffective in their efforts to complete high school and go to college? Researchers have advanced a number of answers and they will be addressed more fully in the substantive chapters of this book. I will, however, briefly summarize them now and discuss the three broad categories they fall into: structure, culture, and agency.

One group of explanations offered by social scientists for the difficulty low-income youth face in transitioning to the next stage of their education concerns social structures that place these youth at an extreme disadvantage. Environmental conditions, a lack of material resources, various rules and regulations, and certain pedagogical approaches adversely impact learning for low-income youth.[6] In addition, the limited family resources available to low-income students also impose structures.

Another group of explanations centers on the profound influence that culture has on students' ability to advance. Researchers have focused on what they have seen as limited resources in the personal networks of low-income students (often referred to as their "social capital") and the norms of social decorum in their networks (known as "cultural capital") that negatively affect academic achievement.[7]

The third set of explanations researchers have forwarded is that low-income youth lack agency in achieving the skills they need to succeed in school. In other words, some lack the ability or desire to master the skills associated with the concept of "human capital."[8] Other researchers concerned with agency have argued that it is not the desire to accumulate "human capital" that separates low-income students from their middle-class counterparts. Instead, they maintain, low-income students' capacity to secure human capital is limited by their inability to acquire sufficient social and cultural capital[9] and their propensity to make one or more bad decisions.[10]

Prior research on educational transitions has had key limitations. First, there is often the merging of the concepts "advancing" and "transitioning." This leads to a conflation of two different outcomes involved in the educational process. When a student moves from one semester, grade, or high school to the next educational stage, they can either *advance* or *transition*. In the case of "advancing," the student is promoted from one level of education to the next, but when the student "transitions," they are both moving from one level of education to the next and are able to understand the new material and competently execute the concomitant operations associated with it—i.e., they are operating successfully in the new stage. I will use this definition of educational transitioning throughout this book. In addition, even though the definition I am using for "transition" means a successful move to the next level of education, in later chapters I will use the technically redundant phrase "successful transition" because some readers may not have read this introduction or read it and forgotten how I defined the concept.

Second, prior research has generally focused on isolating single factors that produce difficulties for low-income high school students. Although this research has identified factors that affect the academic performance of low-income youth, it has not investigated how these factors work in everyday life to produce academic underachievement and to inhibit the transition to college. Further, existing explanations based on aggregated administrative data and surveys are important but primarily inferential because they are not based on direct observation of how these factors influence students' behavior. In practice, by isolating the impact of certain variables, researchers have understated both the role and significance of others, as well as the interactional effects among variables.

A second issue in the existing literature has to do with the concept of transitions. There has been significant research concerning educational transitions, but most of it has focused on the factors affecting the transitions from primary school to high school and from high school to college.[11] Students experience many other strategic and meaningful transitions. Of particular importance are transitions from one grade level to another, because their cumulative effect ultimately determines the ability to transition from one school environment to the next. Remaining unaware of barriers that hamper intermediate transitions seriously weakens our understanding of what went wrong or right in a student's ultimate transition to the next major stage. Further, a significant amount of the previous research on transitions used econometric techniques to measure the degree to which various factors accounted for success and failure in educational attainment and transitioning.[12] This enabled researchers to measure the influence that each tested variable had on academic achievement, but it did not help them understand how these variables actually worked.

Thus, additional research is necessary in two key areas. The first is to identify additional factors that play a role in education transitions at all levels. Since these are grounded in organizational and individual practices, it is necessary to identify them empirically instead of simply using those advanced solely in theory. The second area where additional research is needed is in understanding how the identified factors work in everyday life and affect student behavior. Until we know more about how and under what conditions these factors affect individuals during high school, we will not be able to provide effective interventions to increase educational opportunities.

The present book aims to contribute toward addressing these gaps in the research. Throughout, I will separate the concept of "advancing" and "transitioning," and will use the definition of transitioning provided earlier. I will also focus on identifying the factors that create educational challenges for low-income youth during grades 9 through 12 in high school, how these challenges create transition problems for these youths even if they advance to the next grade, how the unsuccessful management of these challenges makes each transition from one grade to the next precarious, and how difficulty in making transitions during high school makes the transition to college more fragile.

UNDERLYING ISSUES IN THE TRANSITION PROCESS FOR LOW-INCOME YOUTH

Before delving into the analysis of problems that students from low-income families face during high school, it is useful to consider some issues underlying the transitions. Because there exists in the United States a strong belief that education can produce a better life for every individual in society, public policy has been concerned with providing students from low-income backgrounds the opportunity to achieve educational excellence—although it has not been so concerned with ensuring positive outcomes.[13]

Each student starts the school year not only with a backpack but with an array of personal traits that affect how they learn and acquire the skills, dispositions, and capital that enable mobility and future transitions. One trait most people think of immediately is intelligence, and students vary in their capability to understand information, process and store it (i.e., index it for cross references), recall it, analyze it, and articulate it. Students also vary in their physical capability, coordination, and psychological disposition, all of which affect their abilities to learn and to execute what they learn. Biologically based intelligence cannot be considered the sole determinant of success, however, given that environmental factors also significantly affect academic achievement. In other words, the biological assets or liabilities mentioned above have some impact, but they are found across ethnic and socioeconomic groups and cannot meaningfully account for the variance in the success experienced by students from low-income families.[14]

Students transport various social factors to the learning process such as the socioeconomic condition of their family, social network, and neighborhood. Further, there are cultural issues in play. Individuals come to school from homes where guardians (parents, relatives, and other officially authorized protectors), neighbors, and friends bestow on them a complex set of values, morals, beliefs, and etiquettes; and these aspects of culture provide individuals a window into the human condition generally and into their condition in particular. They also affect an individual's ability to perform well in school.

When students enter a campus, several environmental conditions impact their educational experience. These include the instructional quality of the school[15] and the official regulations students must abide by while on campus (clothing requirements, social guidelines, curriculum, and scheduling).[16]

Students also must integrate their personal capabilities and cultural orientations with the structure, culture, and professional capabilities of the school's staff. How well students integrate themselves in these three ways during various periods of high school goes a long way in determining how prepared they will be to transition to college. The process of education includes acquiring technical skills in language, calculation, and analysis, but during the process of education students construct social networks and adopt behavior etiquettes that can provide—or limit—opportunities for academic development and advancement.

It is best to understand that students in general are involved in a development process that includes a sequence of stages and transitions within primary school, high school, college, and postgraduate training. Thus, during high school, students may accumulate some of the educational assets available at that stage, but success occurs only when they accumulate a sufficient amount of the assets available before transitioning to the next stage. Any obstacle that impedes this accumulation process must be navigated so that the basket of accumulated assets is not so small as to compromise the effort to continue to the next stage. When the accumulation process is free of glitches, students can progress at the prescribed pace. When there is a glitch, they fall behind the prescribed pace and must either catch up or carry a limited amount of assets to the next educational stage. If there is a shortfall, the upshot is an increased unlikelihood of fulfilling their next stage goals.

Finally, it is important to point out that recent research has identified key factors that affect an individual's ability to accumulate the assets required for successful transitions. For example, in a very important book analyzing the transition question, Michelle Jackson and colleagues identified primary and secondary factors accounting for individual transition outcomes.[17] In their studies, a primary factor was an individual's performance in executing academic activities, while a secondary factor involved choices the individual made regarding postsecondary education. This model revealed that a student's social background directly influenced performance, which in turn influenced the process of choosing whether to attend college. Jackson et al. compared several societies and consistently demonstrated the importance of primary and secondary effects in the transition process. Their model did not, and perhaps could not given the compositional content of the aggregate data available, identify the variety of factors in an individual's social life that might have helped explain performance, nor was it able to consider how these factors acted and interacted to produce an individual's performance. Further, because it focused on an individual's social background and used statistical techniques to assess a factor's effect on an individual's performance, the model was not able to assess factors related to the school's daily operations that also played a role.[18] Finally, homing in on the final choice of whether to attend college missed all the choices made during a student's high school experience that affected their performance—and their ultimate decision.

With all of these issues in mind, and utilizing participant observation to directly monitor how students, teachers, and administrators navigated their respective everyday responsibilities, the present study had three objectives: (1) to identify environmental factors that created obstacles for youth from low-income families during high school; (2) to examine how these obstacles worked to create specific difficulties; and (3) to analyze how the interrelationship of obstacles and choices affected their educational decisions.

DATA AND METHODS

The data for this inquiry come from two primary studies—1991 to 1999 and 2000 to 2003—and four follow-up studies—2006 to 2008, 2007 to 2009, 2010 to 2011, and 2013 to 2014—of eleven schools over twenty-three years. Two of the studies were not specifically focused on education but involved the collection of participant-observation data in schools. The first (Study 1) assessed the dynamics of social change and stability in poor neighborhoods, and an important part of it included the functioning of the high schools in the five neighborhoods researched. This study, from 1991 through 1999, included five high schools: three in New York and two in Los Angeles.[19] The second study (Study 2), from 2000 through 2003, investigated ethnic violence in high schools and involved three schools in Los Angeles and three in Oakland, California (see table I.1 for a list of all eleven high schools that will be discussed in this book).[20]

TABLE 1.1 High Schools Included in the Study

Lanape High School, Bronx, NY
Van Twiller High School, Bronx, NY
Knickerbocker High School, Brooklyn, NY
Chester Himes High School, LA, Calif.
James K. Polk High School, LA, Calif.
Tongva High School, LA, Calif.
Chumash High School, LA, Calif.
De Neve High School, LA, Calif.
Miwok High School, Oakland, Calif.
Kaiser High School, Oakland, Calif.
Ohlone High School, Oakland, Calif.

The follow-up studies I refer to above involved the same schools included in the first two studies but with a narrower focus. Whereas I approached the first study from an institutional perspective with the intent to analyze schools' role in the social order of poor neighborhoods and the second study from the perspective of the dynamics in which neighborhood ethnic conflict entered a school's confines, my focus in the follow-up studies (in 2006 through 2014) was on understanding *how* educational problems that low-income students encountered in high school affected whether they were able to transition to college. Thus, in the follow-up studies I more narrowly focused on the interaction of students, family members, peers, politicians, administrators, and teachers in the everyday business of high school. In sum, the first two studies accumulated data on educational issues but in the context of a broader question, whereas the subsequent follow-up studies focused exclusively on educational issues.

For a list of the schools in the present book that includes the schools' locations and the time periods when each was studied, the reader should consult table MA.1 in the methodological appendix.

Because all of the studies utilized participant-observation methodology, it is helpful to review the nature of the resulting data. Each study compared multiple neighborhoods so these sites needed to be representative of poor or socioeconomically changing neighborhoods in different cities.[21] New York, Los Angeles, and Oakland, California, were selected to provide variation in factors such as administrative context and climate, but the exact neighborhoods were selected at random from a stratified list of potential sites. A detailed discussion of this selection process can be found in the methodological appendices of my previous books, *Cracks in the Pavement: Social Change and Resilience in Poor Neighborhoods* and *Burning Dislike: Ethnic Violence in High Schools*.[22]

The first two studies were comparative and involved high schools in each of the selected neighborhoods, although the first study also included an array of other institutions. Even though the reader can find detailed descriptions of the research sites in the methodological appendices of the two books mentioned above, I will provide an abbreviated description of the neighborhoods and schools that constitute data for the current book.

Among the three studies just mentioned, nine neighborhoods and eleven schools were researched over a period covering twenty-three years. There were five neighborhoods in Los Angeles, three in New York, and three in Oakland. Nine of the neighborhoods were primarily inhabited by low-income families, while two neighborhoods and schools, one each in Los Angeles and Oakland, were inhabited by middle-income families. A low-income neighborhood was defined as one in which more than 50 percent of the families living in them had low incomes. The following criteria was used to assess whether the neighborhood was low or middle income: the median income for an area reported by the Current Population Survey (jointly produced by the US Census Bureau and US Bureau of Labor Statistics); the median housing price of the area; and the number of families who were eligible for the US government's Federal School Nutrition Program for needy families. Thus, for the current study, this generally meant that "low-income" families with four members had incomes at or below 250 percent of the official poverty line (meaning, for example, at or less than $34,810 in 1991 and at or less than $44,007 in 2000). "Middle-income" families were those who had incomes of $75,000 or more a year.

The schools in this study included students from a variety of ethnic groups that constituted the neighborhoods in which they were located. In the New York schools, the students primarily included the following ethnicities: African American, Puerto Rican, Dominican, Afro-Caribbean (Jamaican, Haitian, Barbadian, Trinidadian-Tobagonian), and small numbers of South Asian and Middle Easterners. In Los Angeles, the students included the following ethnicities: African American, Mexican American, Central American (Salvadoran, Nicaraguan, Guatemalan), as well as various European ethnicities who primarily attended the "middle-class" school. In Oakland, the students came from the following ethnicities: African American, Mexican American, Chinese, Vietnamese, Native American, and various European ethnicities who primarily attended the "middle-class" school. Further, in New York, Los

Angeles, and Oakland the "lower-class" schools had students attending representing various immigrant generations—first, second, third, and beyond; while in the "middle-class" schools of Los Angeles and Oakland the students were primarily of individuals from second, third, and beyond generations.[23]

Having provided a general socioeconomic overview of the students who composed the current study, I now want to turn to a discussion regarding the procedures I followed. The method used to gather the data for all the studies involved in this book was participant observation, a method in which the researcher directly observes the behaviors of individuals while they are engaged in their everyday activities. This requires that the researcher has access to their subjects as they go about their everyday activities.[24] I gained access to the schools in this study using the research protocol required by my home institution's human subjects committee. I first made contact with school authorities, explained the nature of the study to them, and then explained it to school administrators, teachers, staffs, parents, students, and school police through formal presentations, public announcements, and written material disseminated throughout the broad school community. None of the studies involved formal interviewing, although I conversed with the various groups in my study. Gaining access to each school and community required that my study be made public so my position as a researcher was known to participants. In brief, the first two studies followed the standard protocol of protecting research subjects from any unintended physical, psychological, or legal harm. After receiving access from school authorities, I was able to interact freely in all the schools.[25]

While Study 1 and Study 2 were focused on slightly different subject matter, I did record observations of student interactions with administrators, faculty, staff, peers, and family members that directly related to the process of education and to the factors that increased or reduced students' ability to succeed. I first recorded data using the Gregg shorthand technique when directly observing behavior in the field and then transferred it each evening to a computer-assisted qualitative data program. For the first study, I used a first-generation computer-assisted qualitative data program called AskSam. For the second and following studies, I used the computer-assisted qualitative data program Folio Views. Both provided tools in the first stage for organizing, coding, and storing qualitative data, and in the second stage for analyzing the data for patterns.[26]

For the follow-up studies, access to the schools adhered to the same procedure as in the first two studies. Reintegrating myself into each school's social and academic environments was facilitated by the fact that I had already been a part of them, and there were administrators, teachers, and staff that already knew me. I proceeded in the same fashion as I had in the previous studies, informing all who were involved about the nature of the study, and observing students' physical behavior as well as their verbal expressions concerning goals, desires, values, and attitudes toward objects and objectives related to academic success and the transitioning to the next educational stage. As in my previous studies, the methodological process was to first record data during the day using Gregg shorthand and then transfer it in the evening with my developed coding scheme to the Folio Views qualitative data program.

Each follow-up study was comparative and involved the same number of schools as the two previous studies. Taking a comparative approach meant trading off in-depth time at one site for the ability to spend more time at multiple sites. The advantage of a comparative approach to participant observation is that it allows for determining continuities and divergences across populations, thereby increasing the ability to understand the factors causing certain outcomes.[27]

The data collected in all the studies were coded to make retrieval quick and efficient. My analysis involved establishing patterns of consistency as well as uncovering any idiosyncrasies. Patterns for physical behavior were considered to exist if a behavior either had been recorded at least fifty times throughout the studies or had been recorded at least twenty times but all in the same type of social situation. Patterns for verbal behavior were determined to be present when a verbal response with reference to a specific topic / object occurred at least fifty times during the years of study or occurred at least twenty times in the same type of situation.

In brief, the descriptive statements throughout this book are supported by patterns in the observational data. Thus, what is being reported in the text are patterns and not something that, while interesting, was observed or heard only once or twice. Finally, when a physical or verbal counterfactual or idiosyncratic observation is presented, it is identified as such and used for comparative purposes.

Before proceeding to the empirical chapters, it is important to clarify the nature of the data on which the results are based. As noted, the data come from studies over a twenty-three-year period. However, the study is not an analysis of change; rather it is a study to identify and explain persistent factors that remained salient across time and policy regimes. The findings presented in this book therefore represent patterns based in more than two decades of work to identify forces that proved both powerful in shaping student success and resistant to change. These are important additional forces that policy must address in order for schools to produce more equitable outcomes. Finally, and very importantly, I want to emphasize that all the names of individuals and schools that are used in presenting the data in this book are pseudonyms and not the real names of the persons or the institutions.

ORGANIZATION OF THIS BOOK

In the empirical chapters that follow, I demonstrate that youth from low-income backgrounds face obstacles that frequently inhibit their accumulation of knowledge and skills and can limit their progress in making educational transitions. The chapters are arranged to identify obstacles related to structural, cultural, and personal decision-making issues.

It is particularly important to point out that my analysis focuses on how issues related to social life can create problems for students and how this affects students' transitions throughout high school and beyond. There is no intent to argue that all youth from low-income families faced the same problems or that these problems had a uniform adverse effect on their schooling. The reader should understand that what follows in the empirical chapters of this book is a description of factors that created challenges for low-income students, what turned the challenges into academic problems for these students, and how these problems affected their ability to transition to the next stage of their education. Further, the data presented throughout this book uses pseudonyms for the high schools and all the individuals quoted or referred to in the text.

Finally, as was indicated earlier in this introduction, the analysis in this book focuses on the role that structure, culture, and agency play in creating challenges and problems which low-income students face in making transitions to the next stage of their education. Of these three factors, it is fair to say that assessing culture's role in creating problems for students has produced the most controversy. The general reason for this, as it applies to the academic problems that low-income students face, is that when the focus is placed on the role of culture in determining outcomes, it can appear as though school failures are being blamed on the students themselves, their families, and their peers—i.e., blaming the victim for their situation.

In the present study, however, I acknowledge that aspects of culture related to ethnicity and social class reflect collective adaptations to structural circumstances. Culture, which I define as shared understandings, motivations, and behaviors, had some influence on student transitions. This parallels a broad literature that connects culture to human action generally and education specifically.[28] While I show when and how culture shapes academic success for my subjects, it is important to note that I am not blaming anyone for a negative outcome. Rather, it is simply part of charting the full range of empirical factors influencing student behaviors that are connected to outcomes through a variety of mechanisms. It is often thought that social structures are inherited and dictate what behaviors an individual can assume, thereby according individuals little responsibility for the outcomes of their actions. However, it needs to be understood that like structures, cultures can have the very same impact because individuals do not choose the cultural context they inhabit and are exposed to through interactions with family, friends, and various authorities over their life course. Because of this, aspects of culture, such as norms, have an important impact on individual educational behaviors and outcomes, and to minimize the influence of cultural norms would miss an important piece of why some students have difficulty in the academic transition process.

Chapter 1 looks primarily at structural and cultural issues related to educational organization. It examines the politics associated with the goals established by society and education administrators for the modern American high school and its management. This chapter identifies how education has been influenced by political concerns and how those considerations affected the daily learning experience of low-income students.

Chapter 2 deals with both structural and cultural issues by identifying the elements directly associated with the interaction of the family and school in impacting the educational achievement and transition process for low-income youth.

Chapter 3 focuses on the ways that a school's internal operational design can affect the educational outcomes of students from low-income families. This chapter shows how the interaction of structure and culture within schools creates obstacles that can impede low-income students' transitions.

Chapter 4 examines the roles of social and cultural capital in educational transitions. Sociologists and education scholars have extolled social and cultural capital as factors in students' educational accomplishments, and this chapter examines how the type and dimension of accumulated social and cultural capital can create challenges for a low-income student.

Whereas chapters 3 and 4 address questions that have been at the center of education research, chapter 5 takes up an issue that is often neglected:

students' individual choices and the impact of these choices on their educational trajectory. Individuals make choices throughout life, but the decisions students make during high school can be pivotal. This chapter looks at certain choices and how they impacted students' educational behaviors, accomplishments, and futures.

The conclusion offers lessons to be drawn from the study concerning the obstacles low-income students face, as well as those faced by school professionals, and the implications of those obstacles on the role of education in the maintenance of American society. It will be argued that no single factor is responsible for underachievement among low-income youth. Rather, it is the interaction of factors and the sequence in which they are experienced that has the greatest impact. Thus, the conclusion lays out the challenges that educational institutions must confront in order to fulfill American society's promise that formal schooling can erase socioeconomic inequality and foster progress, and then offers some policy suggestions to address these challenges.

CHAPTER I

The Politics of Education Management

These schoolmasters, as Plato says of their cousins the Soph-
ists, are of all men those who promise to be the most useful to
men, and who, alone of all men, not only do not improve
what is committed to them, as does a carpenter or a mason, but
make it worse ...

MICHEL DE MONTAIGNE,
Of Pedantry, 1572–78

WHEN STUDENTS COME TO HIGH SCHOOL, a structure awaits them. Although it welcomes all students who walk through the school's doors, the content of this welcoming structure will be responsible both for student success and, as it turns out, for creating obstacles to that success. A considerable amount of research has found that the structure of schools has a significant influence on student achievement.[1]

For students from poor family backgrounds, there is evidence that school structures can have a profoundly negative impact on their education experience, particularly during high school.[2] Yet most research has not considered how politics influences this structure or, if it has, researchers have looked at the politics associated with funding, rationalizing that the decisions surrounding school funding show the extent to which divergent elements within the general body politic value schooling for all. There should be little argument that funding decisions have a good deal to tell us about priorities, but funding alone cannot tell us about how politics affects young people from low-income families while they attend high school.[3]

This chapter focuses on how politics directly associated with the education system affects both the system's management and classroom learning. This includes ethnic-racial politics because, like many other school districts in America, those included in this study were overwhelmingly attended by members of non-White ethnic groups and many political decisions involved issues related to these groups.

STRUCTURE AND CULTURE IN
EDUCATIONAL OPERATIONS

In an equitable world, individuals who become members of the school board would be civic-minded and interested in setting evidence-based educational goals for the community, hiring experts they felt could best lead the district in achieving these goals, and providing those experts with all the resources necessary to do their jobs effectively. However, an education system managed by people free of politics is rare in the United States. Many, if not most, top educational administrators are political appointees who answer directly to a political authority figure and / or are interested in maintaining the opportunity to move up the political ladder at some point in time. Both of these situations require them to be sensitive to the interests of those who control their prospects for maintaining their current position and gaining the subsequent position they may covet. Consequently, examining the political dynamics within the education community is necessary to more fully understand extant inequalities in educational opportunity.

Because there is often a multiplicity of interests in a large and diverse urban community, elected school board members as well as top district administrators must be capable of managing enough of those interests to maintain their positions of power. This is often done by board members providing favors to the various constituent interests such as in the choice of a superintendent and what that person represents for a particular constituency, as well as the allocation of contracts and funding for construction, supplies, hiring, or promotions. However, when a superintendent is appointed by the mayor, as in New York City, that person becomes a member of the mayor's executive staff and shares the responsibility for promoting the mayor's political platform. In this case, the superintendent must manage the challenges related to the mayor's political interests, as well as those directly related to education and the various constituencies within the educational world (such as unions for teachers and classified staff) and the greater community. In sum, the board of education and superintendent positions integrate professional and political interests at the highest level.

In order for educational politicians such as board of education members and superintendents to be considered effective, they must show their constituency that they can provide direction and manage the resources distributed under their authority. In the context of the local school systems of this study, their primary tasks were to create an environment where learning could occur, establish sound policies for teaching knowledge and skills, ensure test scores were at or above the national average, and manage resources efficiently and economically. These objectives were important to everyone at the administrative level, from the board of education to the local school principal, but they were seen by administrators as difficult, if not impossible, to achieve without creating and maintaining social order within the schools themselves. Thus, creating and maintaining social order also was a priority for the leaders of the Los Angeles, New York, and Oakland school districts that form the basis for the current study.

It is important to understand, however, that along with pursuing stability and the objectives just mentioned, leaders were fundamentally interested in gaining and keeping positions in the education bureaucracy. The pursuit of these individual interests contributed to the establishment of an administrative culture. What is more, this administrative culture will be shown to have pervaded local high schools, ultimately affecting everyday activities within classrooms and creating obstacles that high school students would confront.

The central administration of each district I studied consisted of a superintendent (although in New York the superintendent is called the "chancellor"), the superintendent's organizational team, and people in the bureaucracy charged with overseeing the district's education system. Above all else, the central administration was in charge of setting the philosophy and managing expenditures and functions of the system such as staffing, security, property construction, and maintenance. The central administration also developed a budget each year, submitted it to the board of education, and managed it. As in most organizations, the central administrators were concerned with either making sure things ran smoothly or that they had the appearance of doing so. The central administrators' *modus operandi* was that if something was wrong, it would eventually present itself publicly, and only then would it be addressed. The comment of Edward, a member of the central administration in Los Angeles Unified School District, was representative of this position:

> We're not going to address any of these issues under discussion immediately because they really have not presented themselves yet. Basically, we're going to work with problems that exist and have been made public. If they have not become public, then we won't address them as problems. We just have to remember that we can only respond to problems that have reached the public's attention because there is not enough money to do anything but respond to these.[4]

Of course, this district-level approach left administrators at the school level in a reactive rather than proactive mode, inhibiting their ability to confront everyday problems that students faced. Central administrators in each of the districts under study tended to use four data points to assess their own and their district's performance: (1) scores on standardized tests; (2) the share of students graduating; (3) the number of disciplinary incidents that either involved violence or caused a break in normal educational activities; and (4) the maintaining of expenditures within the prescribed budget. However, as will be detailed in subsequent chapters this evaluation schema would create periodic problems for how and what a student was taught and learned, which in turn impacted their experience in making a smooth transition to their next educational stage.

The people comprising the central administration in each of the school districts studied, who held positions highly valued for both their salaries and the future opportunities they opened, were selected through complex processes that balanced the political interests of various elites in the public sector. Importantly, the selection of a superintendent did not end political competition, however, because the factions that supported an alternative candidate, or simply not the current one, remained active and ready to seize the opportunity whenever the chosen superintendent and their immediate staff faltered.

This political underpinning required that the superintendent and their staff be continuously alert to ward off situations that could indicate they were incompetent, inefficient, or ineffective, because each of these would leave them politically vulnerable. The result was that these central administrations stressed the importance of a routine that did not reflect weakness in their leadership. Therefore, the appearance of business as usual throughout the system was important. This appearance may have had little to do with what was actually occurring educationally or behaviorally within schools, but it was important to keep negative images from surfacing publicly and being used by competitors to undermine the incumbent leadership's authority. The comments of a central administrator in the Los Angeles Unified School District were representative of those from administrators in all three districts:

> The big thing I have to be concerned with is seeing to it that the system is working smoothly, or at least that there are no obvious problems that have become public, because when there are public problems this creates problems for the [superintendent], and that creates problems in implementing our program for the district. I mean everyone who wants to have their program implemented uses any trouble to push their agenda, and that creates problems

for us and what we want to do. So, keep an eye on this, and report to me anything that indicates everything is not running smoothly.[5]

Superintendents in the districts studied had little hope of accomplishing anything if they could not stay ahead of the political maneuvers of opponents, who hoped for mistakes that could weaken the current administration's coalition of support. Because these superintendents were not in a position to control the everyday workings of the systems they had been charged with directing, and in schools serving students from low-income families where they had evidence the public was willing to acknowledge that educational excellence is difficult to achieve and fragile to maintain, the policy focus was first and foremost on social control. This precarious situation provided the various district administrators with the rationale that an orderly teaching environment was a prerequisite for learning, and it created a façade that made it difficult for anyone outside the system to observe shortcomings within the system. The comments of an administrator from New York were representative of this strategy:

> Well, the first thing that I focus on is making sure that each school is operating without any type of disturbance within them. That is the key to establishing the conditions in which learning is possible, and if that is not accomplished then the issue of governing the system is called into question and everyone from the chancellor to me is going to be subject to losing our jobs. I really don't have an issue with that because we need to prioritize social control.[6]

As in any political system, public education encompasses competing political interests. Central administrators in the districts of this study used promotions and transfers as their primary means to control, manage, and eliminate conflict. Promoting individuals who were tied to the political interests of the incumbent central administration was a time-honored and effective means of political influence. Often, this had an ethnic component that mapped onto the political organization of the neighborhoods more broadly. For example, issues associated with the politics of ethnic representation were handled by promoting individuals of certain ethnic groups to posts throughout the system. Generally, it was possible to discern what ethnic groups had garnered the most power from the number of members of that group who were promoted to positions of authority in the system. This strategy had the advantage of appeasing those who had an interest in seeing certain individuals promoted, while at the same time establishing a dependent relationship for the person who was promoted. In brief, a person who felt obligated to the central administration for a promotion generally worked to prove they were grateful.

When using this strategic approach, a practical advantage for the incumbent group was that conflict in the lower levels of the bureaucracy could be defused. Difficulties with students, parents, and neighborhood groups could similarly be massaged because representatives of their ethnic group would reassure them that their interests were being addressed by the mere presence of a member of their group. The fact that one of their group was a member of the decision-making clique would inhibit them from suggesting that their interests were not being addressed, either because they actually believed the administrator was working in their best interests or they wanted to avoid being seen as slighting a member of their ethnic group. Both the administration and the person who was promoted expected that, when a problematic situation emerged, the newly advanced person would absorb the brunt of the political attacks on the central administration and assume the role of mediator. The comments of an administrative educator in Los Angeles who recently had been promoted were indicative of this strategy:

> I told the community leaders last week that since I was now on board, I would see to it that the interests of the Latino students would be a priority, especially keeping the students safe from attack by African American students. I think they are confident that this will happen because they have stopped calling the district and complaining. So, on this issue I've at least earned the promotion the central command gave me. They thought I could be helpful, and I was.[7]

The central administrations of the school districts in this study used the satisfaction of group and individual interests to maintain consensus in the system. As mentioned above, they used promotions as a resource to reduce unrest among principals and teachers. In six of the subdistricts studied, there was a significant amount of unrest among the teaching corps, and the teachers' union supported teachers' efforts to make their complaints public. Some teacher and parent groups suggested that the changing demographics of the district that produced a new ethnic majority necessitated an administrator representing this new majority. In each case, there was an effort to promote a person of the new emerging ethnic presence to a position of authority in the district as a concession. This type of appointment was tied both to the new group's demographic strength and to the group's power in the broader political institutions of the union, political parties, and the city council. Such "concession" appointments strategically served to maintain the existing management regime; that is, the regime prior to the demographic shift.

A counterexample can emphasize this point. In Los Angeles, the Latino population (particularly Mexican) was expanding into traditionally African American neighborhoods.[8] This caused African American student enrollment to decline as a percentage of the total student population in some subdistricts where they had been dominant. However, despite this demographic shift African Americans dominated the higher levels of the administration in these subdistricts for a number of reasons. First, after a sustained effort over time, the African American population had gained some influence in the local Democratic Party, the teacher's union, and the school system's bureaucracy. This situation encouraged the African American community to continue to press for more representation.[9] Secondly, because Mexican Americans had organized later, and they moved into what had long been African American neighborhoods, there was some lag between when they reached a majority and when they could press for more representation within the area's leadership, including educational leadership. It was during this "political lag period" that tensions rose among students, faculty, and staff that affected education in the classroom.[10] More will be said about this effect later in the chapter, but it needs to be noted that the politics of administrative representation often caused professional educators to shift some of their attention to group political interests and away from education lest they lose power.[11]

SUBDISTRICT ADMINISTRATION POLITICS

Subdistrict administration politics emerge as a result of the political interplay of demography, the teachers' union, the networks within the central administration, and the various local political organizations that influence the decision-making process. Los Angeles provides the clearest example of the more general processing in all the neighborhood districts studied. At one particular research interval in Los Angeles, all but five people in one subdistrict administration were African American. Given that the area had a long history of being predominantly African American, this was not surprising, but the area had changed dramatically in the previous ten years, and the vast majority of residents now were Latino, primarily Mexican American. Likewise, the overwhelming majority of the students in the district's schools were Latino (Mexican and Central American), but there were very few Latinos in subdistrict administration and none in the top leadership positions. Thus, given there existed a significant number of Latinos in the overall education system with similar credentials, how was this disjuncture possible if school administrations are sensitive to changing demographic and political realities?

As mentioned earlier, the answer lay in the fact that African Americans had gained considerable political power in the area covered by the Los Angeles Unified School District—which includes the city of Los Angeles and many nearby communities but not all of Los Angeles County—even though they never reached 20 percent of the population. This process began with the civil rights movement of the 1960s, through which African Americans became integrated into the Democratic Party.[12] The combination of being the leading group pressing for minority rights throughout the nation and tying this initiative to the platform of the Democratic Party established African Americans as not only the most prominent minority in the country but also in many ways the "official and legitimate minority of the nation." Their voting numbers, activity in political demonstrations, and civil disorders transformed them into a political force and one that the Democratic Party viewed as a means for it to gain political power.[13] This power base helped establish African Americans as the most influential minority group in many communities where they had a presence, even when that presence did not constitute a numerical majority of the minority population, as in parts of Los Angeles and the Bronx, where the populations of Mexicans and Puerto Ricans were equal or larger.[14]

In the case of Los Angeles County, the population of Mexican Americans has historically been numerically larger than the African American population, but because of the timing of immigration and the segregation of housing in the city proper, there was a period where African Americans briefly outnumbered Latinos. During the present study, Latinos outnumbered African Americans in both the county and the city by a considerable margin.[15] What had significantly limited the potential political power of Mexican Americans in Los Angeles involved one or more of the following factors: a large number of Mexican residents were not US citizens, or they were citizens but not registered to vote, or they were registered voters but simply did not turn out to vote. Further, Mexican workers without legal permission to work in the United States remained outside of the control of local labor unions, whereas African American workers were heavily involved in unions, which helped to strengthen their power within the Democratic Party. Finally, African Americans have a long history of training to be teachers.[16] These factors combined to help African Americans establish themselves as the dominant minority within not only Los Angeles Unified but also Oakland Unified and New York's education system.[17] Over the last thirty years, most of the district administrative positions in Los Angeles were filled with African Americans, who as a result became the entrenched non-White minority within the school bureaucracy just as the Irish had become the entrenched White ethnic group in the Democratic Party machines of many eastern cities. Thus, many subdistricts in what had been traditional African American areas remained dominated by African American administrators even when the Latino population became the majority.[18]

The significance of subdistrict administrations being dominated by African Americans was that management patterns established when African Americans were the majority remained even after the schools became predominantly Latino. These patterns included: (1) a focus on the particular learning needs of African American students; (2) the support of principals who had been ineffective in increasing student exam scores and graduation rates but were a member of their group; and (3) the replacement of principals in these schools with other African Americans rather than with Latinos or a person from another ethnic background. In essence, "the politics of ethnicity" was a significant factor in school leadership, and that sometimes, though not always, hindered effective educational leadership because other competing groups would be constantly complaining about the educational quality this leadership was providing to their non–African American youth.

HIGH SCHOOL ADMINISTRATIONS

Exactly what impact does the politics surrounding school leadership have on education? The answer lies in how the school board and superintendent craft the strategy for their political decisions. Thus, it should be understood that the education bureaucracies in the present study functioned like any other bureaucracies in that priorities established at the top filtered down and made their way into the classroom. The first priority of each of the administrations in this study was social control in the classroom and common areas of each campus because this corresponded with the overall goal of providing students with the minimum necessary in the environment for learning.

To maintain control, most schools adopted a series of codes that were intended to motivate students toward self-regulation. These codes specified what was impermissible and which violations would lead to disciplinary action. At the school level, administrators determined which codes they strictly enforced and which they enforced periodically if at all. These decisions had important implications for the students attending each high school. For students not focused on learning, knowing which codes would be enforced and which would not helped them decide how to behave in the classroom, public hallways, and areas where nutritional snacks and lunch were provided. When students knew the administration would take a lax approach to codes that regulated social behavior, they were more likely to take liberties in the classroom, hallways, and common areas. Common areas do not directly affect students' ability to learn, but the atmosphere in classrooms and hallways does. Noise in hallways disrupted teachers in adjoining classrooms and the students who were trying to listen and understand what the teachers were presenting. Disruptions of this kind directly took time away from teaching and compromised the amount of material students were introduced to.

Administrators at all levels in this study wanted to control their campus environments, so it is reasonable to consider the political factors that affected administrators' decisions concerning disciplinary codes and their enforcement. The community that a school served had the potential to present problems for the school's administrators. For example, some school administrations were composed of individuals who were not members of the same ethnic group as the majority of students; or the school was composed of a number of ethnic groups, and the administration represented only some of them. In each of these cases, there was a reluctance to do anything that would irritate the community and spark public protest because there was a fear these protests would draw the attention of higher administrators, especially the superintendent's office, who were continually monitoring whether schools received negative public attention.

Probably the area that had the greatest potential to upset and mobilize parents was the perception that ethnic and racial prejudice affected the operations of the school their children attended. Thus, avoiding public complaints about this perception permeated most levels of the education administrations in this study. The comments of Willard, an administrator in one Los Angeles subdistrict superintendent's office, were representative of this attention:[19]

[He is talking to a principal of another school on the phone.] You have to do something about Latino students complaints that they are being harassed by Black students while they are in school. If this gets to their parents and the parents start with complaints to their leaders, then we have got a big problem, and that is something the superintendent does not want to have to deal with . . . . You do understand that we feel this should be your first priority? OK, as long as we're clear about this.[20]

Negative public attention at both the community and district levels was to be avoided because it created an impression that the superintendent was not capable of enforcing the standards required for quality education; therefore, any social disruption was cause for concern because it could lead to allegations of leadership ineffectiveness. Further, when there was public attention on some aspect of school operations, it forced the central administration to switch its attention away from its normal duties and toward controlling negative publicity.

Since school principals knew the importance of appearances for the superintendent and for themselves, they knew that conflict with the community must be averted, and they included ethnicity and politics among the factors in their choices of academic department heads, deans, and counselors. There was a consistent attempt to balance three competing interests. The first was the teachers' union, which represents both the interests of its membership overall and the interests of individual members when they have disputes with their administration. Thus, appointing individuals to positions of authority required school administrators to consider who among the prospective candidates had the most seniority, that being the union's time-honored principle for deciding who should have priority in getting a particular job.

The second interest that principals balanced in choosing their leadership team dealt with the ethnic composition of the community and school population, and the desire to reduce conflict and promote communication with all these groups. The third interest related to the ethnic group holding the most power positions in the community's, city's, and county's formal and informal political organizations. Often, the justification for the principal's selection would be that students would be better served with a diverse set of administrators who could keep communication open and aid all students equally. There was, of course, a kernel of truth to this argument, but the politics associated with the three interests mentioned above, particularly the politics of the formal organizations, played a significant role. The comments of a principal at one of the New York schools were representative of these political concerns:[21]

> Well, Mr. Adele and Ms. Barren are leaving the school, and I've decided to appoint Ms. Curry and [Ms.] Davis to the staff. They're both the same ethnic group [as Adele and Barren] and have seniority, which should meet the wishes of everybody who cares. They may need some assistance to begin with, but once they do, it will definitely hold problems down, especially the complaint type, and keep the school running the way we like.[22]

Thus, the attempt to satisfy as many political interests as possible was no less powerful a motive in choosing administrative staff than was the assessment of their potential educational effectiveness.

ADMINISTRATIVE POLITICS AND PROBLEMS IN ORGANIZATIONAL CHANGE

Over the past several decades there has been an understanding among politicians and policy professionals that the vast majority of America's inner-city schools are failing to provide students the skills necessary to compete for well-paying jobs in the current labor market. Acknowledgment of trouble in inner-city schools has led to a variety of presidential initiatives, such as President Bill Clinton's "Expanding Educational Opportunity," George W. Bush's "No Child Left Behind," and Barack Obama's "My Brother's Keeper." However, education system change efforts are not only made when a new presidential administration starts but also can become a regular outcome whenever a new principal is appointed to head a school that has had problems with its graduation rates and academic performances. Thus, one way in which politics affects schools and their students is in leadership choices, because it is leaders who provide both the policies to be followed and the strategies for doing so.

School principals who were newly appointed and wanted to change the way the school operated typically had three reasons for doing so. First, they may have been chosen by higher administrators within the superintendent or subdistrict superintendent's office for the precise purpose of changing the way the school carried out its daily duties in order to improve social control and / or academic performance, which in turn would help maintain the top administrators' job security. The comments of Gavin, the principal of a New York high school, were representative:[23]

You know that is why I was appointed. The assistant superintendent came right out and said it. He told me that there had been a long history of trying to keep the students under control at the school and that this had to change, because if it did not, then he and his boss would be the next to lose their jobs. I said I would do the best I could, and he told me that I would not have a lot of time to get things right for that reason. I told him I understood and appreciated the chance .... Yeah, I must have done something right 'cause we're all in the same jobs [there is laughter among the four people he is talking to].[24]

Secondly, some of the new principals were intent on furthering their careers as administrators and viewed the chance to make improvements at a school with poor academic performance as an opportunity for advancement. The comments of Horace, a principal in one of the Los Angeles high schools, were representative:[25]

Well, I took the job because if I can make some significant improvements in how well the students do on the SAT and the number going on to college, I'll be in line for an assistant superintendent's job, and if I get that then I'll be in line for a big cat job [superintendent] somewhere. That's what I am aiming for, but first things first.[26]

Finally, there were those who had been in the education system for a significant number of years and thought the schools needed to change in order to improve the chances of success for students from low-income families. They believed their experience taught them exactly what needed to be changed. The comments of Denise, who was being promoted to principal at one of the Los Angeles high schools in this study, are an example:[27]

I just got appointed to take over this high school. I am excited about it. I've been doing education so long and seen so many bozos come and go with no clues about how to change what is an awful school. I've been at this so long, I know what works and doesn't, and I'm pretty damn confident that I'll turn this school around in half the time they think it will take.[28]

In each of these cases new principals assumed their duties with a great deal of zeal, but they were not always successful for six main reasons. First, in their efforts to reorganize the school, they had underestimated the reaction of various constituents who saw it in their interest to maintain the status quo. The new principals generally were surprised that individuals within the school or associated with it, people who they thought would support change, were not only uncooperative but actively resisted their efforts to make the changes they saw as necessary. These constituents included teachers, members of the teachers' union, local community leaders, and some students.

Second, new principals were sometimes unsuccessful in making changes because academic performance was often dependent on faculty and other administrators who lacked the competence to execute their new programs. For example, some teachers did not have the academic background or experience necessary to improve instruction, and various assistant administrators lacked competence in organizing and implementing the policies in their area of responsibility.

Third, because sometimes a new principal lacked organizational and leadership expertise, there could be a mismatch between what the new principal wanted to do and their ability to engineer that change. In these cases, the principal had the support of faculty and assistant administrators but was unable either to present an effective plan for the changes they wanted or to provide guidance for those who needed to cooperate in executing the plan. When this occurred, the faculty and staff lost confidence in the principal and resorted to the way things had been done in the past because that was what they knew.

Fourth, evaluations by the school district's central administration played a major role. Although many times the superintendent's office was interested in creating change, there were other times when change was not a priority. For example, in situations where social control was not a significant problem, and a small percentage of students performed well academically and went on to college, the central administration tended to communicate less urgency in making changes to the incumbent principal. This position was adopted because change can require the transfer of human and material resources from one school to another, which could lead to the unwanted outcome of producing poor results in a school that had been doing well. This potential situation influenced the central administration to support a principal in maintaining the status quo. The comments of an assistant in New York's upper-level administrative office were representative:[29]

> I don't think that we should do anything radical at this time to alter the situation at [that] High School. I'm saying this because we don't have that many resources to pour into that situation. If we did decide to allocate more resources there, we would have to take some away from schools running very effectively, like [X] High School, and if things got bad at [X], we would not be any better off. Maybe we'd be worse off, so on the whole it's best to maintain what we've been doing and see if we can increase our resources in the next few years so that we can direct some additional ones to schools like [Y].[30]

Fifth, new principals often did not succeed with reforms when central administrations were confronted with strong negative reactions from teachers, the teachers' union, or local leaders who saw their interests threatened. In these situations, there were instances when the administration viewed the intended changes as creating a mass of new problems that would require more attention than the current problems and decided it was best to forgo or make minimal changes, as illustrated by the comments of an assistant in the upper-level administration of Los Angeles Unified School District:

> We just can't afford to go make wholesale changes at [Y] High School because we'll have teachers that'll say we've changed their contract, and the union will get involved. Once that happens, we've got two choices: change the contract, which will be a nightmare, or do nothing and keep what we got. Can't risk it now, so even though we need to make big changes, they are going to have to wait; that's all.[31]

Lastly, there existed among senior administrators the view that if any negative publicity emerged from their efforts to create change, it would jeopardize their authority and threaten their current employment. Thus, avoiding public controversy weighed heavily in what would appear to have been merely a professional judgment about increasing the effectiveness of the education system. The comments of an assistant in a Los Angeles subdistrict superintendent's office were representative of this concern:

> Look, I would agree that there needs to be a number of administrative changes in at least three schools, but unless we do it at all three, we'd be looked at as targeting one or the other. Plus, if we removed the principal at that high school, there would be such a reaction from the local community who loves him that the publicity would just make our lives a lot more difficult. We're just going to have to reluctantly stay the course with what we got for the time being.[32]

Here again the political cost and benefits of making changes in school administrations took precedence over professional educational assessments.

PRINCIPALS AND SCHOOL OPERATIONS

When principals wanted to change how their schools operated, either because they were appointed for that purpose or they saw a need for change, they would try to remove both members of the administrative staff and teachers whom they saw as resisting or challenging their efforts. Removing those who had shown an opposition to change was delicate because a "cause" must be documented, so the norm was to have them transferred out of the school. However, transfers must be based on an assessment that the school was administratively overstaffed or that the teacher had failed to execute their official duties appropriately, effectively, or legally. Thus, although transferring staff was preferred, principals who wanted to replace individuals sometimes chose between two additional options. One was to demote an individual from an administrative position and reassign them to the classroom. The other was to assign teachers who were resisting change to classes and duties that were considered more difficult and tedious, and then once they cooperated, to reinstate them to their previous positions. If they did not cooperate, the principal would keep them in the more difficult and tedious job until they became so frustrated they requested a transfer out of the school. Because teachers are represented by a union, the use of "punishment" tactics can be ineffective if a teacher files a formal grievance that must be adjudicated, so reassignments initiated by principals must strictly follow official procedures.

In contrast with principals who wanted to create social change within a school, or were appointed to do so, there were administrative appointees whose primary goal was to maintain the status quo because there were teachers and administrators in the school who were satisfied with the existing arrangements and considered their position more secure under these conditions. For example, there were times when some teachers in the schools run by these principals complained publicly that the school was not providing students with the education they needed to transition successfully to the next stage of their lives. These teachers posed a threat to the existing social order, and neutralizing their impact became a priority. This was generally done by reassigning them to more difficult teaching positions, not merely as a punishment but as a means to increase their workload and leave them less time for complaining. The comment of an assistant principal at one of the New York high schools was representative:

> We assigned Mrs. Albert to the beginning English classes, and that'll really up her workload. So, I doubt she's going to have the time to keep up her objections to what we're trying to do here.[33]

Further, assigning teachers to courses that had difficult subject matter or a history of uncooperative students had the strategic advantage of placing these teachers in the awkward position of either generating higher academic achievement among those they were working with or face criticism because their students were underachieving. An example involved Maxine, a 31-year-old English teacher at one of the Los Angeles high schools. She had complained at a faculty meeting that the school's administration was not providing guidance or trying hard enough to implement new requirements, and she happened to mention that if this got out to the media, the school would receive considerable negative publicity. Her message was heard as a threat by the principal, who no doubt took note of the negative publicity part, something every education bureaucracy in this study wanted to avoid at any cost. In a conversation two days later, an assistant principal said:

> Maxine was quite adamant about improving our academic approach. I was really unclear whether she was just warning us about making changes or threatening us that if we didn't make changes she'd go to the media. We'll have to see what can be done about this and then move forward.[34]

Three weeks later, Maxine was told she would be teaching the first- and third-year students the following year. These were the most difficult students to teach because the first-year students often had difficulty in reading and writing and the third-year students, who were required to take her course, generally were not intellectually interested in it so maintaining order and their focus was a constant challenge. Two weeks later, Casey, a dean at the school, said:

> Maxine was complaining today in the lounge about getting two of the hardest classes to teach next year, but I don't know what she expected, given what she was complaining about at the big staff meeting. I mean she sort of threatened them to do more or there'd be bad press. Everyone got it, so they gave her the hardest classes to see if she can make a difference, and if not, it's on her .... Hey, they [administrators] are just covering their asses. Nothing new about that, especially in this place.[35]

The upshot was that Maxine's classes did not show improvement, and she found the classes so taxing that at the end of the year she put in for a transfer to another school and left.

Principals intent on either creating social change or maintaining the status quo were vigilant about keeping track of anyone who might not want to cooperate and who potentially could expose them to removal. This included individuals in their own administration, such as assistant principals and deans who were involved with issues of social control and discipline. As with many inner-city schools having large numbers of students coming from low-income families, the schools of this study had problems creating and maintaining the social control necessary for education to occur at a maximum level. If one department had the power to affect a school's everyday operations, it was the department that administered school discipline. Therefore, principals first observed who was in charge of this area and how they administered their duties, and then decided whether they wanted to change the personnel or the manner in which they executed their duties or both. Generally, those who wanted to maintain the status quo would go with the prevailing pattern of disciplinary actions.

When there was conflict among administrators over discipline, it nearly always involved an individual dean or assistant principal who wanted to change the status quo and was attempting to institute new criteria and procedures for discipline. In such cases, the person initiating the changes was generally removed or their disciplinary duties reassigned by the principal intent on maintaining the status quo, even if the status quo was understood to be educationally wanting. This was a strategy invoked by those principals who believed that the best way to protect their own job was to maintain the status quo.

POLITICS AND STUDENT OBSTACLES

The actions discussed immediately above fit into an administrative culture that attempts to handle its problems internally so that external politics do not compromise the job security or opportunities of those currently occupying official positions at various levels of the education bureaucracy. A critical question is how these politics impact students by placing obstacles in their path. There were a number of ways these types of politics impacted the students from low-income families in the schools studied. These impacts were often not directly seen, or so blatant that students could pinpoint their origin, and students regularly experienced the impact of politics through the medium of the school's formal curriculum or the manner in which it was implemented. In all of the schools included in this study, instructional policy followed one of two general approaches that I describe as "discrete" and "continuous."

My application of the term "discrete approach" involved teachers developing lesson plans where material associated with a particular topic was given to students and, once they completed it, a new topic was introduced. In this approach, one informational unit was not pedagogically bridged to the next but treated as discrete. That is, all the material related to part of a subject like mathematics or language arts was covered in one unit, and a new set of material was covered in the next semester. In brief, the discrete approach lacked a strategy of development in learning.

My use of the term "continuous approach" involved a continuity schema, where each element of the curriculum was directly tied to the previous one and cognitive bridges were used to aid students in making transitions. Continuous approaches can be taken within a semester, between semesters, and between years to aid student advancement. For example, a continuous approach would show math students the relationship between what they learned or were learning in algebra with what they would learn in geometry, and then how geometry and algebra were related to what they were or would be doing in advanced algebra, trigonometry, or calculus. In language arts, a continuous approach would include concrete examples of how syntax relates to poetry and prose and to creative writing skills. The continuous approach requires coordination between teachers and material, whereas a discrete approach does not.

Principals who used a "discrete approach" were inclined to rationalize this decision by saying they were confident in teachers' professional skills in implementing the official curriculum. This allowed principals to avoid a reorganization in the execution of the official curriculum that could disrupt the social order integrating students' and teachers' everyday behavior, which in turn could lead to dissension, resistance, and efforts to challenge the principal's leadership. The comments of Nicolas, the principal at one of the Los Angeles high schools, illustrate this position:

> Well, yes, there are some at the central office and some here at this school that would like us to change the basic way we are teaching. There are new approaches circulating the district, but I'm really inclined to stick with the way we are currently doing things because the other approaches, especially the one that wants to utilize a team approach to emphasize continuity, are going to require I make wholesale changes, and this will create havoc at the school. There will be teachers who will hate it and complain all the way to the top. It is not worth all that. I'm going to trust they will do their jobs, and that will help me do mine.[36]

On the other hand, principals who were intent on creating change in their schools using a continuous approach needed not only to reorganize their staff but also to convince teachers of its merits and reorient them to the coordinated instructional strategy. This required more work from them, including meetings to settle on immediate goals and maintain constant communication as to what each was doing and had done in order for the other teachers to build on. Convincing teachers to switch to the "continuous approach" was very challenging for principals because it required additional instructional work for the teachers. Although the "continuous approach" had the potential to be more successful in maximizing student learning, it also was more challenging for principals to implement and maintain because they had to manage teacher activity by evaluating and monitoring in-class instruction and logistics among teaching staff, and making corrective interventions. Teachers often reacted by resisting even constructive criticism, accusing the principal of professional harassment, and asking the union to intervene, or by passively resisting and then asking for a transfer. All of this tended to undermine the effort to implement the "continuous approach."

Both approaches presented challenges to students. In the "discrete approach," students depended on the pedagogical talent of the teacher. The more talented teachers a school had, the more likely better students at the school mastered the material. When students met a teacher in the math sequence who was not particularly effective, the next teacher in the sequence, even if he or she were excellent, would need to reteach some material, which often limited the teacher's ability to cover all the designated curriculum, or cover it in an effective time frame.

In a "continuous approach," when teachers did not fully accept and execute their duties in a coordinated way, a similar problem emerged. Thus, principals who were trying to create instructional change could create a situation where parts of the old system worked simultaneously with parts of the new, and this presented students with disjointed instruction that impaired academic achievement. This occurred mostly when competent teachers resisted attempts to increase their workload through increased meetings with colleagues to coordinate instruction. They often viewed this as a challenge to their professionalism, and when they contacted the teachers' union for assistance, it became an issue of infringement on workers' rights, the creating of a contentious working environment, and an increase in employees' workloads. In addition, when principals tried to institute a "continuous approach," it inevitably introduced discomfort among the teaching staff and pushed some teachers to request a transfer. Regardless of the effectiveness of the teacher, turnover in teaching staff impeded coordination because new teachers needed to be assimilated into the school's approach and this took time for training and the mitigation of emergent difficulties. The result was that some early student cohorts were negatively impacted, not necessarily in terms of the information and skills they were offered but in terms of the amount of information that could have been offered.

TEACHERS

Teachers are professionals who instruct many succeeding generations of students, but they are subjected to, and engage in, politics as they practice their profession. This affects their everyday duties and, by extension, the education they provide. Politics for teachers in this study centered on issues of institutional management and normally came to prominence when a school district's central administration decided to change a school's principal or its practices.

Like the leaders of any organization, those running a school district must answer for the results of their policies, so a record of consistently negative academic outcomes makes them vulnerable to being replaced. Thus, district officials closely followed the progress of troubled schools and the principals who led them. Various criteria were used to evaluate principals, including retention and graduation rates, scores on standardized tests, the number of violent incidents on campus, and the number of formal complaints from parents and community leaders. A principal could be removed when the upper administration and the public determined that the evidence indicated they were ineffective in leading the school, but politics was a part of any decision to change personnel. So, although politics appeared to originate in the central administration, they quite often were initiated as a result of the politics occurring in the school.

It is important to understand the situation that teachers found themselves in when the central administration appointed a new principal to their school. If the appointment was the result of the central administration having to replace one bureaucrat with another, and the administration did not see problems with the way the school was operating, then the transition was relatively smooth. However, if the central administration was unhappy with the way the school was managed or it was trying to satisfy the political interests of board members or others, and it appointed a new principal for those reasons, there usually were problems.

To understand why changing a principal to satisfy political interests or remedy problems was in itself problematic, it is best to understand that this change in leadership was essentially an effort to replace one education regime with another. Education regimes are composed of professionals who identify and support a set of leaders, their philosophy, and the present practices. These regimes set the political tone for what behavior is appropriate and expected of faculty and staff inside and outside of the classroom. Therefore, teachers must support the new regime or face some form of administrative reaction that can only be understood as punishment. A representative example of this involved a social studies teacher at Tongva High School in Los Angeles. This teacher was not convinced the policies the new principal was initiating were the best for students.

This teacher especially did not like that instructional periods were being reduced to fifty-five minutes because she felt this was not enough time to present material and explain it to students. Her constant memos to the department head and the principal were seen as opposing their reforms. The principal responded by directing her to comply with the new policy and having her assess its impact after the semester ended, but she continued to write memos informing the principal of the difficulties the new policy presented to her and her students. As a result, in the subsequent semester she was given classes that had significant numbers of students with learning difficulties, who were also very disruptive. This was a message to her that if she wanted to criticize the new principal, there would be consequences, and the message was not lost. After the new semester, she stopped writing the memos or voicing her concerns at staff meetings and applied for a transfer.

Attempts to change the education regime of a school by appointing a new principal usually instigated an intense internal power struggle that involved three political factions among the teachers and staff who welcomed the change. One faction included teachers who were hopeful that new policies and their enforcement would produce better results for students they felt were poorly served by the previous administrators and teachers. The comments of Dana, a math teacher at Lanape High in the Bronx, were representative:

> No, I can't believe that we are finally going to get a new principal. The last two were so bad, and the kids suffered for it. They just had no desire to make changes, and since we were one of the lowest schools in terms of graduation

rates and test scores, you would've thought they would make changes, but no, they just wanted to get their salary and take it easy, I guess.... So I'm definitely looking forward to the changes this new [principal] said were going to happen. Don't you agree?[37]

A second faction was composed of teachers who believed the past administration and their faculty supporters penalized them because they disagreed with their policies and were hopeful they would fare better with a new supervisory group. A typical comment was that of Lara, a biology teacher at Knickerbocker High School in Brooklyn:

You don't know how bad it was for me at this school having to deal with that idiot principal. He would just dismiss any suggestions that I had to help the kids learn better and took offense that I would say that the way things were going made it impossible for students to learn what they needed to. He even gave me monitoring duties during lunch hours because he didn't like me.... He never said much to me, but every time I went to him with a request he told me that it couldn't get done, and then someone else would go and ask for something that was just about identical to what I had asked, and he would give it to them. So, I know that the new person can't be any worse, so I just hope they picked someone with a brain this time.[38]

A third faction included the teachers who were hired by the new administration. This group included people who were grateful for an opportunity to work in a new environment they hoped would be better, or who had been selected by the new administration for a position that constituted a promotion in pay and responsibility. These teaching staff members' first allegiance was to the new administration. Take the comments of Jeanie, a 31-year-old English teacher at Miwok High School in Oakland:

In my last school, I asked each of the last three principals to change some of the faculty around and have them teach certain courses.... I was diplomatic, I just said some were better at teaching some science courses than others, and we should use them for that. I didn't say they didn't know anything or couldn't teach, but it didn't matter because they just told me to do my job and let them deal with staffing the curriculum.... They even gave me a number of beginning courses that are harder because the students know less so I would stop with my constant suggestions.... So, I transferred to this school and I met with the new principal and shared my ideas. I think he is more agreeable with the suggestions and with him I'm going to be a department head, where in the past I didn't have a chance because they didn't like me. So, I'm definitely supporting this new principal one hundred percent![39]

Of course, change is rarely met with unanimous approval. In fact, many faculty and staff in those same three schools did not welcome a new administration. They had become comfortable with the way the previous administration ran the school, either because they had been granted favors or because they had been able to create a work environment that was much less demanding than it could have been or than the norm for the district. For those who were in this camp there was the sense that their lives would be made much more difficult or they were about to lose the personal benefits they had accrued while interacting with the previous principal and administration, or both. Thus, they began by getting to know the new principal and the intended change, then they assessed whether they could negotiate an arrangement that would maintain their personal interests, and finally they decided how to proceed to maximize their well-being. If the changes were considered extensive and there was a general recognition that there was no way for members of their group to avoid a net loss in benefits, then their only options were to accept the changes or to plan some form of resistance that would either maintain their benefits or precipitate the new principal's removal in the hope that a replacement would be more amenable to operations beneficial to them.

For those who opposed changes initiated by a new principal, the primary foci of their resistance had to do with time, space, responsibilities, and instruction. Each act of resistance would be passive-aggressive so it would not be obvious they were creating problems. This strategy was particularly effective because it could give the impression the problems that students were experiencing had more to do with the policies the new principal was trying to implement than with the actions of people intent on sabotaging the new policies.

The first examples of resistant behavior by teachers involved time and how to manage it to subvert the new program. When new policies were initiated to improve academic achievement, there was always more work for the faculty as they had to redraft some, or most, of their curricular objectives and develop some new methods of instructional presentation. This required a greater investment of their time, and those who opposed this effort would avoid or postpone expending the time required. The importance of this resistance was that the teachers simply did the minimum to prepare and present the academic material. This, first and foremost, negatively affected the information and skill levels of their students for varying periods of the academic year, but it also impeded the efforts of the new principal to initiate a new instructional program. Ultimately, this often negatively impacted the standardized test scores of some students.

In addition to the issue of professional time commitment, those opposed to change resisted new initiatives by restricting the space in which they interacted with students.[40] When faculty and staff limited their contact with students to their classroom and then retreated to the faculty conference and cafeteria rooms, this reduced students' exposure to new experiences and information. For example, students from all walks of life, but especially from low-income environments, need the opportunity to be taught about problem-solving from a variety of perspectives, and getting to know teachers who can tell them about their experiences and how they managed their problems is particularly important. This part of education is associated with the concept of role models, and teachers can be quite important for students from poverty backgrounds because so few people from their community can talk with them about what is involved in becoming successful educationally. Thus, when teachers resisting changes implemented by a new principal did not plan field trips or avoided interacting with students in social situations outside of the classroom, it reduced the possibilities that students would gain the additional knowledge about how things and people worked, and this in turn had the potential to impact a smooth transition to their next educational stage. In essence, greater teacher-student interactions outside the classroom had the potential to increase a student's cultural capital, a topic that will be discussed in detail in a later chapter of this book, and when such opportunities were reduced, it decreased the opportunities to acquire it. The comments of Lea, a 17-year-old student at Van Twiller High School in the Bronx, were representative:

> I just came from trying to see my English teacher, and he was busy again. Last year, he always had time for us to talk about college and the stuff we need to do to get in, but this year every time that me or Evelyn or anybody, I guess, wants to talk—you know, ask him something about college or stuff—he says he can't talk. . . . I don't know what is going on with him. Maybe he's got trouble at home or something. [He actually objected to the changes the new principal initiated and decided he would do less during his time at the school.][41]

Finally, the issue of professional responsibility was utilized by the "resisters" to thwart new policies. Generally, this began with a teacher refusing to act as an official agent of the school. In so doing, teachers defined their responsibilities solely in terms of classroom instruction, and they would refuse to monitor or supervise inappropriate, illegal, or code-violating behavior on campus. This meant they would not admonish students for inappropriate behavior such as littering and foul language. Nor would they stop or report students engaged in illegal behavior such as physical fights, weapons possession, placing graffiti on school property, stealing, or using or selling drugs. Neither would they stop or report school rule violators who were outside of the classroom without formal permission or were wearing officially banned clothing. The failure to assume this role allowed additional disruptions to school operations and undermined the authority of a new principal to establish the social order required for optimal instruction. A representative comment came from Darren, a 16-year-old student at Polk High School in Los Angeles:

> Hey, this school is out of control. Nobody cares what goes on here. People be smoking weed and stuff, or carrying some kind of knife in the open, and teachers don't do nothing. . . . Did you see [that English teacher] just walk by those two girls in that fight yesterday? She done nothing, not even called the [school police] officer! Some student went and told the officer . . . , but yeah, it's a mess here trying to learn shit.[42]

To protect themselves from being seen as uncooperative or being reprimanded for being obstructionists, faculty who resisted new policies would publicly define their professional responsibilities more in line with those of an hourly contract employee than those of a salaried professional. This allowed them to do the minimum and, if problems arose with school administrators, solicit their union representative to protect them. The comments of Lester, a math teacher at Lanape High School in New York, were representative:

> Well, the other day Mr. Jaden [an assistant principal] asked me to lead a remedial session for students having difficulty with the work. I told him that I didn't want a reduction of one instructional period, that if he did not have the funds to pay me overtime, I did not have the time to do that. He was miffed, real miffed. He said that Mr. Younger [the principal] had specifically made the request so that school performance on the SAT could improve, but I just said if he had problems with what I said, to take it up with the union. He left miffed but said that he'd check with Zelda [the union representative in the school].[43]

The resisting teachers also sought the support of four important constituencies in their efforts to thwart change. The first of these constituencies was students. Elements of the student body would support the changes being implemented, so teachers who resisted change sought out students who disliked the changes or simply had no opinion. The resisting teachers would tell these students that the activities they liked and wanted to participate in would cease to operate as they had in the past. They hoped this would be successful in galvanizing students to react hostilely toward the new principal's efforts. Further, these teachers would encourage students to have their parents contact the principal's and superintendent's offices to voice their objections to the new policies.

Disgruntled teachers also used neighborhood political leaders to resist change. They would contact local leaders and tell them the new principal was changing the school so much it was becoming worse and everyone at the school was unhappy. The local leaders who wanted to maintain their voters' support were sensitive to such accusations because they wanted to be seen as advocates for the interests of the community. Therefore, because local leaders generally had access to the school superintendent's office, their involvement in school politics and operations could be particularly disruptive in a principal's efforts to create change.

The third constituency used by the teachers who opposed change was the union, which was established to protect teachers' rights and interests. Any teacher was entitled to request the union to intervene when they believed their work environment changed in some fundamental way that negatively affected them. The union representative did not always agree with the teacher requesting assistance, but they always honored the request. The sequence in which unions were called upon generally followed a pattern that started with teachers identified as resisting the principal's change efforts being moved to positions of lesser authority, which resulted in them losing privileges. For example, dissident teachers who were department heads, part of the athletic program, or engaged in special school programs were removed from these positions. Once this happened, the union was contacted and became involved in attempting to protect those teachers from such actions. This nearly always impeded the principal's efforts to implement change.

The fourth constituency that dissident teachers used to disrupt change was the media. Usually, some teachers would contact the local newspapers or television stations with an accusation against the principal. Accusations that had the most power were those that involved impropriety on the part of the principal and his immediate staff such as mismanagement of funds, sexual misconduct, or racial prejudice. Because each of these accusations was grounds for removal, they had to be taken seriously by the districts' central administrations, particularly when they became public. The accusations may or may not have had merit, but they fed emotions that stimulated further rumors. However, their strategic importance was that they often promoted the initiation of an investigation, and while this was occurring, little was accomplished programmatically at the school because the principal had to spend extra time defending his or her professional reputation and policies.

An example of this occurred at Chester Himes High School in Los Angeles when a new principal attempted to change the school's instructional culture. Over the course of five months, changes had produced higher scores on standardized tests, but there was resistance to the new principal's policies. When the teachers who opposed the new policies failed to halt them, they went to the media with information about the management of textbooks. They accused the principal of being negligent in monitoring the number provided to the school and described a discrepancy between the official number of books that had been brought to the school and the number that actually were in use. Although this accusation was eventually found to be baseless, the publicity seemed to be effective as the superintendent's office transferred the new principal to another school the next year. This aborted the reforms she attempted to implement, and the school was assigned a new principal who ran it as it had been run when student achievement levels were their lowest and the number of students transitioning to college was small.

SOME FINISHING COMMENTS

Political scientist Harold Lasswell wrote that politics is the study of who gets what, when, and how.[44] This is certainly true in public education, where politics is a significant factor. Deciding who will manage the education system of a city and how it will be done is a process often infused with politics.

This chapter identified the areas where politics impacted the everyday learning environment of the high school students in the low-income neighborhoods of this study. Political decisions concerning personnel, the management of social order, as well as curricular implementation, were identified as particularly salient. How each of these played out presented students with instructional challenges to navigate.

In sum, this chapter presented evidence that the persistent problems school administrators face in educating students from low-income communities create an administrative political culture that permeates every aspect of the education bureaucracy. This culture works under the umbrella of providing every young person an equitable education, but its operative norms of protecting the professional positions and future opportunities of those working within this bureaucracy often overwhelm progress toward that goal. In the end, politics associated with this culture determines how school instruction will occur, how much of it there will be, and the quality of it. The upshot is that this culture creates obstacles for some students, which leaves them vulnerable in transitioning to their next educational stage. Thus, even though there seems to be consensus in proclaiming that no child is to be left behind, the politics associated with managing schools in fact leaves some students behind.

CHAPTER 2

———

The Interface of Family and School

I agree: then some will achieve more some less, but never find one who has not achieved something by his efforts. A parent who grasps this must devote the keenest possible care, from the moment he becomes a parent, to fostering the promise of the orator to be.

MARCUS FABIUS QUINTILIANUS,
The Orator's Education, 95 CE

Perhaps home is not a place but simply an irrevocable condition.

JAMES BALDWIN,
Giovanni's Room, 1956

THERE HAS BEEN CONSIDERABLE RESEARCH on the factors that support student success. One of the most important is the family. Researchers have consistently found that having an advantaged family background improves educational outcomes.[1] Less well documented is just what it is about the low-income family, if anything, that matters most for the lack of success. Is it the everyday interactions within a low-income family that impede formal learning in school? It has often been argued that the problems youth face in high school originate in childhood. Annette Lareau's book *Unequal Childhoods* advances the position that family resources are instrumental in children's futures. Her primary argument is that children from low- and moderate-income families have fewer opportunities to acquire the socially validated skills and modes of interacting with institutions that help create the skills and knowledge required for high educational achievement. She posits that this is a result of different levels of financial resources and concomitant child-rearing practices employed by parents from different socioeconomic backgrounds as they either seek to cultivate their children or allow them to develop naturally.[2] Other analyses of the family's role in children's educational achievement assess the various impacts that components of the family, such as the parents' education, income, and marriage status (two- or one-parent family), have on student grades, standardized test scores, and dropout rates.[3] These studies identify what factors improve the chances of a student being successful, but they do not tell us much about how those identified factors were produced.

The analysis in this chapter will focus on family-school interactions that impeded the educational transition process of some low-income students and how this unfolds over time. We will see that the school and the family take turns impacting each other, with the result being a constant state of interaction that produces obstacles for low-income students.

HOME AS AN EDUCATIONAL ASSET

The home is both a social space and a physical environment. Researchers have generally accounted for the effects of home life by looking at the parents' or guardians' education level and the human capital and cultural resources that the parents have available to aid their child's education.[4] The findings concerning parental background have consistently shown it to be a factor in children's educational achievement, but it is less clear how these factors produce their respective outcomes. To address this question, this chapter examines several key aspects of educational success and failure: homework, parental and home resources, cultural norms operating in the home, and patterns of behavior among family members.

Monitoring of Homework

Educational achievement is often associated with attending school and by applying the skills learned while school is in session to substantive exercises completed after instruction has formally finished. These exercises are generally referred to as "homework," and thus "home" becomes a particularly salient place in the educational process. As a result, home then needs to be understood as both a social and a physical space that can have an interaction effect on the educational outcomes of family members. On the social-space front, the home is a place that has fostered learning—particularly, though not exclusively, by having some of its members encourage other members to study and complete their homework. Thus, parents and siblings are agents in actively monitoring other family members' academic work, and where possible they serve as a resource to answer technical academic questions students may ask concerning their homework. If there was a persistent problem consistently highlighted by professional educators in each school of the present study, it was the quality of students' completed homework.

In the eleven schools of this study, teachers consistently over the twenty-three years identified the lack of parental involvement in monitoring homework as a problem that affected students' academic achievements in both their course and the broader high school experience. The comments of Victor and Sherry, twenty-one years apart, were representative of teachers identifying this as a recurring problem. Victor was an English teacher at Los Angeles's Chester Himes High School in 1992:

> You know, I got so many students that are just struggling to get through the material. They just don't seem to understand the stuff. Each of the last five years I've been teaching here, it's been the same way. I blame the parents for this because they just don't help the students with the homework the students don't understand. The students tell me all the time that they didn't hand something in because they didn't understand, and when I ask if they asked their parents for help they tell me their parents didn't look over their homework and didn't help them.[5]

Sherry was a history teacher at Van Twiller High School in the Bronx in 2013:

> ... yeah, one of the big problems the students have in getting their work completed satisfactorily has to do with them not ever having any parent involvement. The parents here are just not a consistent part of their children's academic lives, and as far as I can tell they never were. These kids need parents to monitor them and give them some help with homework when they need it, but the parents here just don't seem to be able to do it, and the kids have really suffered academically as a result.[6]

Evidence supports teachers' assertions that having someone monitor and, when necessary, help with a student's homework has a positive impact on the student's grade point average. Over the twenty-three years covered by the various studies included for the present book, there were a significant number of families that did not actively monitor their children's homework. I observed multiple causes for this. The first was related to the flow and timing of academic information that students provided to their parents.

To begin, students provided little or no information to their families about their homework and how well they were doing in their courses. One reason was that they were more interested in doing something else with their time that was more fun and did not want to have their parents interfere, so they made a deliberate effort to not mention homework. A second reason for not discussing homework with their parents was that they had little, if any, understanding of how to complete the assignment and did not want to expose their lack of knowledge to their parents. The comments of Emil and Stacie were representative. Emil was a 16-year-old junior at Brooklyn's Knickerbocker High School in 1992:

> Hell no! I ain't even starting this homework tonight. A bunch of us is meeting at the Dairy and from there we're going to J's house for a party in his backyard.... My cousin was asking if she could study with me tonight, and I just laughed and said, "Yeah," but it be over in two minutes because I ain't spending time doing any homework shit when fun is out there.... Yeah, my mom's going to ask if I got my homework done, but after I tell her, "Yeah," she'll leave it at that.[7]

Stacie was a 15-year-old sophomore at Oakland's Kaiser High School in 2003:

> I know I should've asked my older sister who's good at math how to do the math homework because I sure don't get it. But if I had asked her again she'd complain to my mom and dad that she had to help me again, and I'd look stupid—so I'm not doing that![8]

A third reason students were reluctant to tell parents about homework was that doing their homework would leave little to no time to complete the chores their parents were counting on them to help with. The comments of Lena, a 15-year-old sophomore at Los Angeles's Polk High School, were representative of these students:

> No, I didn't get the homework fully done last night either, but I just ran out of time. When I got home, my two sisters were starving and fighting with each other, and they made a mess in the kitchen. So after I got done cooking, I had to clean up their shit.... I didn't say anything to my mom when she got home from work. I mean, she did ask if I got my schoolwork done, but I didn't want to say anything 'cause she'd just feel bad for counting on me to help her.[9]

There was a significant gender difference when it came to responsibilities for house chores and more will be said about this later in this chapter. In all the homes that I observed, girls assumed more of these responsibilities than did boys and this did impact their ability to finish homework.

A fourth reason students did not discuss homework with their parents or guardians was that they had a strained relationship and simply did not want to share information with them, especially when it had to do with school. The strained relations had to do with feelings that either their parents were too punitive and the students wanted to avoid any conversation that would elicit a physical confrontation, or their parents were focused on their own problems and interests and not interested in their children's lives.

The second cause for unmonitored homework was directly related to parents. Some were too busy to effectively monitor homework. Three factors in the families observed inhibited parents from checking to see if their children's homework had been completed each night: they had a number of children to look after and did not have enough time to monitor everyone's homework; they were too burdened by household chores to make the time; they were simply too tired. Although I observed each while I was a guest in various family homes, the comments of Lucas, Raleigh, and Micah verbally illustrate these parental behaviors. Lucas was a 17-year-old senior at the Bronx's Lanape High School:

> No, man, I don't have any trouble with my folks about that [homework]. My dad and mom don't bother me about my homework 'cause they got all my brothers and sisters to think about, too. So, they just ask us if we got it done, and if we say yes, they just go to the next one. It's easy to skip it if I want, and usually I do.[10]

Raleigh was a 15-year-old sophomore at Oakland's Miwok High School:

> We're lucky; my dad and mom never check if we got our homework done because they're too busy running around at night trying to get all the cooking and cleaning done after they come home from work. To tell you the truth, I think they're glad that we don't ask for help.[11]

Micah was a 16-year-old sophomore at Los Angeles's Chester Himes High School:

> There ain't no way I won't be able to go to the game tonight because of homework. My mom is the only one who'd even ask about homework and she don't even get home from work 'til nine, and then she's way too tired to even ask most of the time. So I'll meet you at the store to go to the game.[12]

The third cause for parents not monitoring homework had to do with parents not being consistently informed by school authorities that their children had not been handing in their homework, or had been handing in work only partially completed. This occurred in part because, within the educational institution, it was the responsibility of teachers to monitor whether homework assignments had been handed in, and when that did not occur it was for two reasons. The first stemmed from the understanding of some teachers that one of their obligations was to foster a sense of personal responsibility in students and that was best done by assuming a position that each student would complete their homework without close monitoring. The comments of Benjamin, a science teacher, as he is talking to a new teacher at Lanape High School in the Bronx, were representative of this position:

> I know you just started at this school, but one of the things that you need to learn is that there are multiple things that are being taught at the same time. When you give homework you can, if you want, check to see that they did the homework or even keep reminding them that they need to get it in on time like in elementary school. But that's not going to help these students in the long run. They're going to need to develop the self-discipline to finish their homework every night, and really the best way to do that is to treat them like adults and just let them know that you are going to assume they will finish. Obviously, there'll be some that will not follow through, but this approach is the only one that will help them throughout their lives.[13]

As a result of this position by teachers, they would allow a significant amount of time to elapse before they would intervene when homework wasn't completed or was poorly executed, and this generally placed the student behind the expected educational performance level for the course.

The second reason for teachers not monitoring homework had to do with feeling overwhelmed by all the responsibilities associated with their job. In such cases, teachers often felt burdened by the number of students in their classes, so they either did not have the time to contact each student's parents when they found issues with homework, or, when their first effort to contact parents was not successful, they did not have the time to continue trying to alert them that their children were in jeopardy of falling behind. The comments of Linda, a language arts teacher at Oakland's Kaiser High School, were representative:

> I'll be honest with you. I just really don't have the time or even the inclination to check on student homework. Don't get me wrong, I think checking homework can be a good thing, but finding the time to do it and then reaching parents who don't give a damn or are too busy themselves to keep checking is just too taxing. So, I just occasionally do it and just with some of the students.[14]

Children inhabit the home environment established by their parents or guardians. This home environment is composed of various components that have a direct impact on academic learning. The first of these components consists of physical space. Youth from low-income families often live in apartments or homes that are spatially limited. What is more, their families are generally large, putting a premium on private space for any individual and making it something to struggle over.[15] When space is limited in terms of square footage, there is a premium on establishing a place where reading, thinking, and writing are easily done because interactions involving parents, siblings, and neighbors create varying levels of noise.

If there was a consistent challenge to students in this study completing homework and studying for exams, it was interruptions by family members. Some of these interruptions would be from noise of others watching television or listening to the radio, while some would be from family members talking loudly or screaming for something. Students living with younger siblings would inevitably have to deal with them crying, screaming, arguing, running in and out of rooms, or asking for help or attention.

Any of these episodes would break the students' concentration, making homework more difficult. Figure 2.1 presents the observational data I recorded concerning the impact of home disruptions on homework over the twenty-three years covered by the studies I have included in the present analysis. An "interruption" in figure 2.1 was defined as "a stoppage in performing an act directly related to a designated school assignment." Although the data is limited to the students who I observed, it clearly indicates that the number of interruptions can impact the time to complete homework or whether it was completed at all.

What figure 2.1 does not show is the quality of the completed homework. Over the entire time period of the present study, it was common for teachers to complain about the quality of their students' homework. The comments of Mr. Stevens and Ms. Randal were typical of teacher views concerning this problem. Mr. Stevens was a math teacher at the Brooklyn's Knickerbocker High School:

> I just got done with my fifth- and sixth-period algebra classes' homework for this week, and it was really bad. I had four students that got the right answer and proof, and the rest either got the right answer and the proof was wrong, or they got both wrong. When I tell them in class that they need to do better

FIGURE 2.1. Interruptions and hours needed to complete homework.

FIGURE 2.1. Interruptions and hours needed to complete homework.

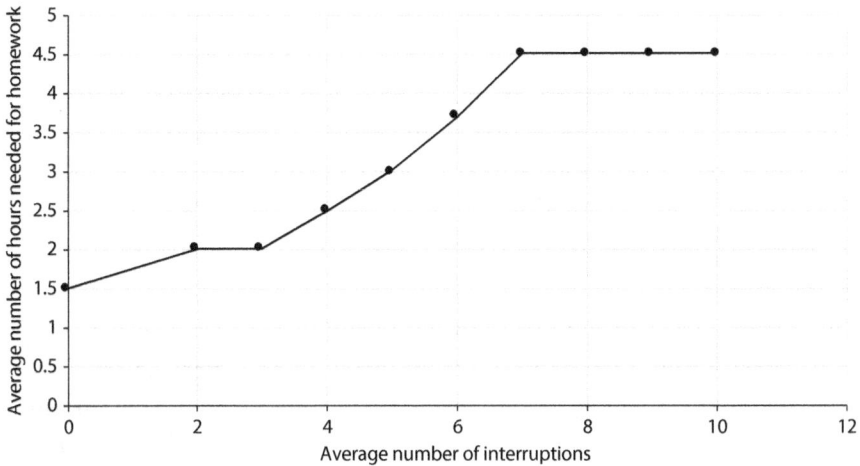

Note: The data comes from the observational notes of the two main studies and the six follow-up studies. Obviously these data do not represent all students only those directly observed.

with their homework, they will say, "I finished it and handed it in on time." All I can say to them is to be careful and complete all the homework correctly, but so far that does not happen for a good number of them.[16]

Ms. Randal was an English teacher at the Bronx's Van Twiller High School:

I gave my third-hour class the assignment to read and then asked them to give me a one-paragraph review of the book we are reading in class. All but two of them handed in the assignment, but let me tell you I really can't figure out whether they did not read that section of the book, didn't understand it, or just have real difficulty expressing what they did read. I do know that after reading all their synopses I wondered if they and I read the same book [the other two teachers chuckle].[17]

Of course, Ms. Randal's comment about the quality of students' homework does not point directly to the issue of disruptions at home as being a singular cause. It is possible that disruptions had an impact, but there could have been other reasons such as the students simply wanting to complete the homework quickly and not taking care in what they were doing. What figure 2.1 points out is that disruptions could have an impact on the completion rate and quality of the work, and these disruptions were an issue students had to manage.

From the student's perspective, the ability to create private space would vary, producing difficulties in completing all their assigned homework or completing it at a high level. This is often underappreciated as a hurdle in learning. The comments of Donna, a 17-year-old senior at Brooklyn's Knickerbocker High School, were representative:

> I had to tell Mr. Kenny [her calculus teacher] that I did not get my last night's homework done. Shit, first it was the fucking neighbor in the next apartment practicing his drums and then after he stopped someone over there was having some fight about something and just kept screaming and yelling until I just said, "Fuck it. Who can think with that shit going on?!"[18]

Besides shortages of space and quiet, students had to deal with insufficient lighting, due to broken fixtures, improper bulb wattage, or service having been suspended for nonpayment. Students with poor lighting generally became fatigued reading for sustained periods. Steven, a 15-year-old student at Lanape High School in the Bronx, would always use the kitchen table, which was lit with a fluorescent lamp that was halfway between the table and the stove. Another light directly over the table had been broken by his younger brother and, after having been repaired by a custodian, worked only intermittently due to faulty wiring. As a result, there were shadows over whatever Steven was reading, causing him to constantly move papers around to capture the light necessary to study. He would work this way for about ninety minutes and then put everything away and complain to his mother that he would have to get up early in the morning and finish his homework.[19] This continued, and his report card included a number of C grades, which upset him immensely. He would complain to his mother that the reason he did not get higher grades was that he could not finish his homework due to the bad lighting in the kitchen. Finally, his mother bought a small desk lamp and extension cord to supplement the ceiling lighting. As a result, he completed his homework before class, and all of his grades improved over the next semester to high Bs.

Likewise, there were families that could not control their housing unit's temperature, resulting in periods when the dwellings were either extremely hot or extremely cold. There were other cases where the heating and cooling appliances in a student's living quarters were in good working order, but their parents found them too expensive to use full-time and this made the housing unit periodically uncomfortable. Both of these situations impacted students' stamina and concentration while they were trying to complete their homework. Sheila, a 16-year-old junior at the Bronx's Van Twiller High School, was an example of this:

I know tonight is going to be a long night doing homework, because I got so much work from Mr. Dorn [her English teacher], and it just takes me so long to get everything done. I start OK, but it is so cold in our apartment that I am always getting up to move around so I can feel warmer. It's awful, but when my dad comes by and says, "What's wrong with you?" and I say, "It's too cold in here," he just says, "We got to watch our expenses, so just go get your coat!"[20]

In sum, homes that had limited quiet space, inadequate lighting, or insufficient climate control created obstacles for students to concentrate and influenced them either to finish their homework quickly in order to seek a more comfortable space or to work more slowly to complete the assignments competently. In cases where students spent a lot of time completing their homework, they generally were more fatigued the following day during school. This made concentrating on the new material that the teachers presented difficult as well. While physical discomfort did not cause students to fail their coursework, it was a factor that contributed to them doing less well than they might have without such challenges.

HOME AND LEARNING

One important aspect of the home involves students obtaining the support they need to execute each day's activities to their full capacity.[21] This includes optimal nutrition and physical comfort. Research has suggested that there is a strong relationship between nutrition and student concentration and performance, so I made a concerted effort to directly observe consumption patterns of students and their subsequent behavior in class throughout the day.[22]

Students whose family income qualified them for free or reduced-price meals often went to school without having had any food. Nearly all of the students in this category that I observed over the twenty-three years would become involved in disruptive and / or inattentive behavior in their classes until they could consume some amount of food that furnished them with energy to concentrate and become engaged in course discussions and activities.[23]

Lack of sleep was also a substantial issue in academic performance. There were times during the research projects when the parents of students had invited me to stay in their residences for the night, and while I was there I took the opportunity, after gaining permission from the parents, to take notes on the behavior of household members. I observed a consistent pattern: youth who went to bed and were awakened with less than seven hours of sleep would often close their eyes and stop concentrating on the material being presented by the teacher during their first two morning classes the next day. In addition, if they were challenged by either their fellow students or the teacher to focus on the material being presented, they reacted with some form of verbal belligerence with the teacher or physical aggressiveness with fellow students.[24] Depending on the severity of this reaction, the interruption would generally be brief, followed by the student reverting to being quiet and resuming their resting mode. However, there were times when the student aggressively reacted, and when that occurred it led to a break in teaching for the instructor and in learning for the other students. This caused additional work for the other students because the teacher was not able to complete the planned material and generally added it to the homework assignment for that evening.[25]

Resources that homes could provide also included computers, and their location in the home was critical. Some homes lacked a computer, had one that students had to share with many others, or lacked reliable internet connection for financial or technical reasons or both. The upshot was that many students found it difficult to complete some of their homework assignments because they did not have access to information they needed or to teaching aids available for their courses.[26] The comments of Dida and Taylor, two 16-year-old juniors at Chester Hines High School in Los Angeles, were instructive on this point. These comments begin after Taylor handed in his homework at the beginning of class.

TAYLOR: I couldn't figure out the fourth and fifth problem for geometry last night. Did you get them?

DIDA: Yeah I did get them, but I had to do some extra work to get 'em done. I Googled the problem and found a site that explained it. I really wouldn't have been able to complete them without that help.

TAYLOR: Oh fuck, we don't have internet now 'cause we couldn't pay, but we'll get it back next month. Fuck it, I don't have access and I didn't get the homework done![27]

The absence of a computer creates a learning impediment for students because many assignments require, or assume, that a student has a computer at home and has free access to it, and that the computer is connected to the internet. It was common in all the schools included in this study for teachers to suggest students use the internet to get information for a paper they were writing. Thus, having access to the internet was an unofficial necessity and the lack of internet access was an obstacle to overcome.[28]

HOME AS A SOCIALIZATION AGENT

The low-income parents from the various studies for which I had field notes overwhelmingly expressed awareness of the significance of education for their children, the importance for their children to dream of an economically successful future, and the need for their children to develop the skills necessary to achieve their dreams. To these parents, their responsibility was to encourage their children to set goals and to instill in them the discipline necessary for success. Further, over the twenty-three years covered in this study there existed a constant conversation among parents centered around the frustration they experienced getting their children to set goals for themselves and to maintain the discipline to complete their assigned homework and study for each course throughout the school year.

There is little debate among educators that maintaining consistent effort is a key to educational success, and families play a central role in this aspect of the education process. Therefore, this section will focus on the strategies parents employed to create and maintain educational discipline in their children. I used two aspects of educational discipline for the analysis: (1) a person's focus and fortitude to maintain a work ethic leading toward consistent educational success; and (2) punishment for the lack of a focus and the fortitude to maintain it. It is necessary to be cognizant of both to understand some of the difficulties experienced by the low-income students in this study.

Understanding the challenges low-income families faced in inculcating educational discipline requires attention to three general interactive processes. The first of these involved parents' and school officials' efforts to create disciplined behavior in students' study habits in order to increase the probability of them maximizing their potential. Parents attempted to instill discipline in multiple ways. One of these was the use of incentives to get their children to complete their homework every night or study the material they were learning and required to master. This could take the form of either an allowance or a promise to buy something their child wanted if they consistently studied and received good grades. Of course, there was constant negotiation as to what constituted good grades, and how much money would be involved, but agreements would be reached, and they would be honored within a time frame that parents with limited financial resources needed. A typical example involved the conversation between Bernice, a 15-year-old student at Tongva High School in Los Angeles, and her mother:

MOTHER: I told you, you get good grades and you can get that new phone you been talking about. But you got to do better than what's been happening!

BERNICE: I been doing better.

MOTHER: I know, but you got to get 'em up to Bs, and then you can get the phone.

BERNICE: OK, but don't keep changing the deal—we're at Bs and nothing more, OK?

MOTHER: Alright, I'll agree to that.[29]

Sometimes a student's request for clothing forced the parent to use the layaway plan at a store or, if they could, a credit card. Other times, if the student wanted to attend an event, such as a concert, it forced the parent to forgo a need in the house, including those related to another child. The comments of Doris, a 40-year-old mother of three living in the Bronx, illustrate this dilemma:

JoLeen has got her heart set on them clothes, but I just don't have the money right now for her to get them. I did promise her that she could get them if she got good grades, and she got all As and Bs. So she done well. I got to get them for her, but it's going to be hard. I guess what I'll do is just not get the couch I was planning for the living room—at least for about three months, until I can get back the money I need for it. I guess I could stop paying for Junior to go to his football program for a month. He won't like it, but it'll only be for a month.[30]

Another incentive parents used was to allow their child to participate in an extracurricular activity if they did well. This usually involved sports that the school supported or a cultural or academic program the school sponsored. Sports included teams at the freshman, junior varsity, and varsity levels for both male and female students, such as football, volleyball, swimming, basketball, wrestling, baseball, softball, soccer, cross country, and track. Examples of cultural and academic activities included chess club, the debate team, language clubs, cultural dance clubs, cheerleading, and performing arts. Each school studied did not offer all of these activities, but all the activities mentioned existed among the collection of schools in the study. So, there were parents who used participation in these extracurricular activities as a carrot to encourage their children to remain focused on doing well in school. The interactions of Courtney and her mother were representative:

COURTNEY: Mom, you said that if I got Bs I could be in the dance club, and I have been doing that. So, can I go to the organizing meeting tonight?

MOTHER: I think it is going to take a lot of your time, but you can do it as long as you don't go down in your grades. Now, I ain't sure about cheerleading, but if you keep up with the grades maybe you can go out for cheerleading too. But before that, we just got to see how you doing.

COURTNEY: OK. Great![31]

A common strategy used by parents, particularly those who had recently immigrated, was to emphasize the rationality of doing well and completing school by pointing out that most people who did well financially had applied themselves at school.[32] Parents who used this straightforward approach felt there was no additional incentive necessary. Their thinking was that children had seen this so much on television and in the movies that there was no real need to say anything more. Examples of this approach can be seen in the comments of Homer, a 30-year-old Salvadoran living in Los Angeles, and Anita, a 29-year-old Barbadian living in Brooklyn.

HOMER: My goodness, if my son and daughter want to have a good life, they need to study in school and do well. I tell them that it is no secret what it takes to get ahead. So, I just remind them if they ever forget that they need to do well in school, just turn on television and see who has a good life and who doesn't.[33]

ANITA: I be telling all my children, and I got all five in school right now, that they got to do their homework and do well in school 'cause everybody knows that's the only way to get a decent job and have good things in life. I don't feel I need to say too much about it because they see it all the time on TV and they could hardly not get it. They'd have to be daffy not to see that, and I know they ain't that.[34]

Parents and guardians also encouraged self-discipline in their children using a strategy that combined positive reinforcement with various forms of guilt. The positive reinforcement side would include accentuated praise for academic practice (studying) and performance (grades). On the negative side, there was the use of two types of guilt. The first was related to the parents or guardians informing the youth that they have sacrificed a great deal for their youth's success in school. The sacrifices mentioned most were working an additional job, or working at a job that taxed them physically or mentally. Some parents also would mention they were paying for additional support in the form of tutors or specialists for educational disabilities so their child could achieve academically, which in turn would lead to more opportunities and socioeconomic mobility when they became adults. The comments of Chet, a 40-year-old father of three, including two boys attending Brooklyn's Knickerbocker High School, were representative:

> I was like you and tried to use the stick on them [his kids] to get good grades and all, but it just never helped that much. I finally told them that I was work-ing at this job that I hated because the boss was on me all the time so they could get the education I never had, and that kind of made them feel guilty, I guess, and they did work harder. So now I just use that to get them to keep working hard, but you can't use it all the time. You got to pick and choose when it's best.[35]

An additional calculated strategy parents used was to communicate that they very much wanted their children to work hard and receive the education that the parents wished they had gotten but did not because they made bad decisions themselves. Many times, this strategy was included with the mes-sage that the child's educational success would be a validation of the parents' lives. When parents used this strategy, they would tell their children that if they were successful in school it would make up for the regret the parents felt about their own lack of success.

The case of Elvi, a 42-year-old mother of five children, two of whom attended Los Angeles's Chester Himes High School, was representative. Elvi would tell each of her children she was a good student when she went to school in Alabama, and that she got all As during high school but that she met a young man and became involved in an intimate relationship and got pregnant. She would say that her mother had warned her to stay away from boys until she finished college but that she had not listened, and the result was that she never attended college because she had to work to help her par-ents support her and her new baby. Elvi would go on to tell different versions but always ended the story with her hope that all her children would go on to college so "that I would know my life made a difference for you." This nearly always had a positive impact on the older children, and it did get them to work harder at finishing their homework. At the end of the research project, two of her five children were attending college, and the two youngest children were both enrolled in high school and doing well academically. Her middle child ran into academic difficulty resulting from a number of issues discussed in this book. After barely graduating from high school, he enlisted in the US Army and was intending to make a career of it.[36]

Another ploy parents used to elicit educational discipline was to warn their children that if they did not pay attention to their studies, they would not only fail to attain their dreams but probably work in the same occupations as their parents. The comments of Elena, a 31-year-old parent of two students who attended Los Angeles's Chumash High School, were representative:

> My daughter is giving me such problems at school. Her grades are low, and she hasn't been doing any work at home. So, I just told her that if she keeps this up that's her business, but she needs to see that she will have the same job as me [working in a canning factory]. I said, if you want to do this, then OK, but you know what our life is like. . . . Well, you know, that talk seemed to scare her, and she has started to do her homework and get good grades.[37]

In addition to guilt, parents used a second form of negative reinforcement— physical force. Some parents with children in the schools I studied used force as a means either to get what they wanted or to inflict pain in response to a feeling that they were unjustly denigrated by the actions of the child.[38] There were many reasons for these parents hitting their children, but they fundamentally revolved around the lower-class cultural idea that physical force was a legitimate resource for obtaining a personal goal.[39] This cultural idea comes from the world that these parents have experienced, a world that is primarily physical, where getting someone to do what you want just requires being stronger or more adept at using a weapon.

A representative example of how parents in this study used physical force involved the interaction between Suzanne and her mother. Suzanne had been removed from class multiple times for getting into verbal arguments with her classmates and continuing to talk when the teacher ordered her to cease. Suzanne was sent to the assistant principal's office for detention multiple times in response to this behavior and was officially suspended from school. Her mother was required to pick her up, and when they got home her mother yelled at her for not behaving and paying attention in class. Suzanne retorted that she was not going to be told what to do by anyone—her classmates, a teacher, the principal, no one. Her mother told her she had better start behaving because her mother could not get off work to come pick her up from another suspension, but Suzanne said she didn't care. At this, her mother turned, got a broom, and started hitting Suzanne very hard all over her body. Suzanne tried to fight back, but the mother kept up the attack. Suzanne finally started to cry and ran to her room. The mother ran after her and told her she had better start acting right in school and not "bring her defiant attitude home because it was not going to be tolerated." Suzanne had two additional detentions at school for her behavior and was physically punished each time at home. Eventually Suzanne started to behave in class, but it is difficult to determine whether that was because of the force her mother was using at home, or because her boyfriend liked school and if she got any more suspensions she would be expelled and unable to see him as often.[40] It was likely a combination of both.

A clear result of her suspensions was that teachers thought of Suzanne as a troublemaker and did not provide aid to her even when it was obvious that she was struggling academically in their courses. When she did turn her behavior around and was studying, she found herself behind and not fully capable of making up for the time she had not studied or been out of class for disciplinary reasons. This limited what she was able to achieve, and she received mostly Cs and a few Bs in her courses for the year. This also made her transition to the next grade more arduous, but she continued her progress in the first reporting period the following year, receiving four Bs and just two Cs. In sum, Suzanne's attitude toward her schoolwork had changed, but I was not able to determine whether that was solely predicated on a new appreciation for education or was simply the result of wanting to avoid the negative sanctions she would receive in the form of punishment from her mother and expulsion from school. I recorded thirty-two cases in which negative reinforcements produced behavior changes that improved academic students' achievement.

Before leaving the subject of negative reinforcements, it is important to report that they, like positive reinforcements, did not always have the desired effect of producing an improvement in a family member's academic performance. I recorded twelve cases where negative reinforcement from parents produced no change in attitude or behavior. An example involved Ricardo, a 16-year-old attending Lanape High School in the Bronx. He had received poor grades and been disruptive in a number of classes, and the principal had called his parents and warned them that if Ricardo continued this behavior he would be suspended. After arriving home from the meeting with the principal, Ricardo's father told him he had been to the school for this same reason two previous times and could not continue to take off from work or his boss would dock him his pay for the time he missed. Ricardo said the principal was wrong and was just picking on him. His father then erupted and started swinging his fists at Ricardo, telling him that he was lying and it better not happen again. After he was hit numerous times, Ricardo retreated to his room. Ricardo later told his friends what had happened and said, "That's just the way my father is, but when it's over, it's over," indicating the negative reinforcement was ineffective.

After this altercation, I observed Ricardo continuing to neglect his academic work and acting the same way in class. It was clear that Ricardo understood the physical punishment from his father as the penalty he paid for not behaving the way the school required and for inconveniencing his father. It was also clear that once the penalty was delivered, it was over until the next time he was caught doing something wrong. Instead of changing his behavior at school, Ricardo focused on simply not getting caught.[41]

YOUTH REACTIONS TO PARENTAL INTERVENTION

All of these parental maneuverings generally met with some resistance from students. In one form of resistance, the students agreed that they needed to become disciplined in studying and handing in homework, but did not commit to the amount of time their parents wanted or thought necessary. A second form of resistance was to simply reject the premise that discipline in schoolwork was necessary for success in their present or future lives. The students who rejected their parents' calls for better study habits often did so based on the belief that their parents were simply repeating the values of contemporary society, which they considered illegitimate both because they conflicted with those of their peer group[42] and because adopting them, which involved isolating themselves while studying, inhibited them from expanding the experiences they thought they needed to forge a unique personal identity that was not associated with their parents.[43]

A third form of resisting their parents' insistence on self-discipline related to the youths' general fear of failure. Many wanted to do what their parents and society more generally wanted of them, namely to be conscientious in their studies, but they also felt doing so included the possibility their work would be inadequate and they would receive a low grade. These thoughts left them more vulnerable to feelings of inadequacy than if they simply did not make their best effort and blamed their inadequacy on laziness or some other indulgence. Anxiety about failing, and the use of the tactic of resisting studying so as to have an excuse for not doing well, was a defensive response that had origins in previous transition periods.[44] For example, students' fears of failing were most often associated with an incident where it was suggested that they lacked the intelligence to meet the standard requirements as compared to the "average student" for their grade level. This produced a patterned response that began immediately after it was suggested they were intellectually challenged. This response started with anger over the insult that such a designation carried, followed by doubt about their abilities, which continued to the next stage, where the individual tried to hide the implied flaw from others who they feared would form a prejudicial opinion about their social and intellectual worth. Ultimately, these individuals generally gave up trying very hard in school because to try and fail would only heighten the sense of inadequacy and bring further embarrassment and shame. Cynthia and Carlos were representative of this dynamic. Cynthia was a 16-year-old student at Brooklyn's Knickerbocker High:

> My mother said that, according to my teacher Mr. Cox, I didn't participate enough in class so he had to mark me down because he was not sure I had done my homework the night before. That's not right, 'cause I did do my homework and went over the stuff he assigned, but I don't like to talk in class because my last-year teacher, Mrs. Duncan, said that I may never be able to get math completely 'cause it is too hard for me to understand. So, I'm not going to raise my hand and get it wrong because they'll just say, "See, she's too stupid to get the right answer!" So screw Mr. Cox, I don't care if I get a bad grade from him.[45]

Carlos, a 16-year-old tenth-grader who was attending Los Angeles's Polk High School, was asked in a biology class I was observing to answer a question that he had difficulty with. Carlos proceeded in giving an incorrect answer, and the teacher mentioned it "might be beyond him."[46] A number of students in the class laughed, and Carlos was silent. When the teacher then asked another student the same question, she answered it correctly. Subsequently, when the teacher initiated a "question and answer exercise," Carlos would often play around in class and be asked to leave the class for being disruptive. Since he only did this during this type of exercise, it was a clear tactic to avoid being asked a technical question on the subject material.

In fact, a year after the interaction that I just described, Carlos was talking with a couple of friends during lunch hour and said the following:

CARLOS: My dad is like hassling me about doing my homework and stuff. He's even been saying that I got to get better grades to have him get me a car, but you know sometimes if you do everything the teachers ask, you could just be set up to be laughed at if it don't work out right.

DUANE: What you mean by 'don't work out right'?

CARLOS: You know, like you get something wrong even though you studied.

DUANE: Yeah, I know, sometimes I just don't do stuff so there ain't nothing bad they [teachers] can say.

CARLOS: Exactly, that's what I mean, I know I ain't dumb. I don't care what they think, but I ain't setting myself up to be laughed at either.

DUANE: I get it, I'm the same way. . . . Them assholes in class [who laugh at wrong answers] is just assholes. Fuck 'em![47]

Carlos and Duane both had problems reading, which impacted all of their coursework. Both passed their math courses with B and A grades. They listened intently in class and could follow the teacher's explanations. They also could answer questions in class correctly. This made it apparent for anyone paying attention that they were intellectually capable of completing their schooling and doing work above average, but their reading skills were so underdeveloped that they would resist giving a maximum effort in classes where reading was a dominant feature because they were afraid of looking like a failure.[48]

In addition to negative interactions with teachers, the reluctance to commit oneself also resulted from negative interactions with peers and family members. For example, during intrafamilial competition, family members might say things that indicated to the student that they were "stupid." This normally drew an angry response because it implied a genetic incompetence that was so stigmatizing it had the power to place social, academic, and economic opportunities off-limits for the person so labeled.[49] Being stigmatized also could create self-doubt, particularly over time. It is important to point out that being labeled "stupid" or "intellectually challenged" has been used far more extensively on individuals from impoverished ethnic minorities than those from White, middle- and upper-income backgrounds.[50]

Another source of self-doubt among students I observed was the schoolwork itself. Many could not read at grade level, and this affected their work in all their courses because reading is one of the most fundamental skills in formal education. Given that it is taught early in elementary school, the idea that a student does not read well by the time they get to high school often suggests to both professionals and laypeople that there could be something cognitively wrong with them. The so-called "normal group" generally asks themselves why a person who was not intellectually disabled and did not have a learning disability like dyslexia would still have difficulty reading in high school. The categories of "cognitive disability" and "learning disability" producing "underdeveloped reading skills" share a capacity to stigmatize, but the "learning disability" category is somewhat less stigmatizing because the prevailing view is that it can be overcome with the proper interventions, whereas "cognitive disability" is seen more as irremediable.

The experiences of students in this study who were stigmatized as "academically challenged" were very similar, and the damage to their sense of self was significant.[51] It is here that parents became instrumental. Parents who intervened with school officials and advocated for additional assistance for their children obtained remedial services and improved their children's chances for academic success. However, officials at each of the schools in this study reported that only a small percentage of parents at their schools advocated for additional academic assistance for their children. The primary reasons for this were that parents were often too busy with work or personal problems to intervene with school officials, they felt powerless to get school officials to do anything, or they simply did not know that remedial intervention was even possible.[52]

Students who had not been advocated for and had not received interventions were often observed engaging in sports or socially deviant activities in an effort to reclaim self-worth. A representative example involves Damian, a tenth-grader at Van Twiller High School in the Bronx. Damian had been reading at seventh-grade level and was struggling in all of his tenth-grade courses. In his history class, when his teacher asked him a question prefaced with "this may be beyond you, but try" and Damian did not answer the question correctly, the teacher used a sensitive response. However, it was clear that everyone in the class thought Damian had limited ability to answer questions appropriate for his grade level. When the teacher later told a colleague the story of Damian during lunch, she was asked why she mentioned aloud that the question might be beyond Damian to answer, and she answered that she knew his scores on standardized tests indicated he was several grades below where he should have been and it was not clear whether he had a "learning disability or was intellectually challenged," and she was simply "trying to make him feel comfortable" in attempting to answer the question.

There was no question Damian knew he was not performing at grade level in each of his classes, or that he was unsure what the problem was, because in conversations with his parents he would occasionally say, "I'm not as smart as everyone else." The upshot was that Damian slowly gravitated to other individuals who were seen by their teachers and peers as "intellectually marginal," and he was later arrested with two peers for armed robbery and sent to a juvenile detention facility, where he continued his education and received a high school degree. Ironically, while in juvenile detention, he received remedial help in reading that must have increased his confidence and skill, because when I reconnected with him in 2016 he had just received a bachelor's degree from a state university.[53]

HOME AS A RESOURCE CENTER

It has generally been thought that to become successful, one must have aspirations to succeed and that this value begins at home, where families provide the vision and expectations associated with education's role in improving socioeconomic mobility. A good number of professional educators and commentators talk about the lack of desire and commitment that many youths from low-income families exhibit during high school.[54] In many cases, these comments emerge from direct and indirect observations that the young lower-class individuals who one would think should want to do everything possible to get an education and live a better life than their parents are not studying as hard as necessary to be successful. As a result, these observers have become frustrated.[55] In their view, low-income students can be divided into categories separating those who would benefit from additional attention and resources to improve their performance and those upon whom such additional attention and resources would essentially be wasted.[56] In short, what upsets these observers is their belief that when low-income youths do not commit themselves to studying hard every day, they are not taking full advantage of the educational opportunities that are being provided to them. Despite obvious issues related to the content of the opportunities being provided to low-income students, which are discussed in other chapters, these commentators and many members of the public ask why low-income youth choose not to study hard, given the evidence indicating a clear and consistent economic return on education attainment.[57]

Self-discipline is only one factor in academic achievement, but the concern among some educators focuses on the apparent lack of discipline exhibited by low-income youth in school. A primary resource for youth developing self-discipline is their family, and having examples of family members engaged in disciplined behavior can be very important. The examples of disciplined behavior do not need to be directly related to formal educational activities. Low-income parents can provide important examples when they go to work every day at a job that is considered by them and society to be difficult, thankless, dirty, and low in status. Students who were influenced by this kind of example often said it showed them that life required a person to do things that they did not like in order to support themselves and their families. However, there were low-income parents who failed to provide this example. One reason was that they simply went about their everyday lives without emphasizing the difficulties they managed, thereby making everything seem "normal," which hid the very discipline they were exercising. A second reason had to do with parents living without discipline themselves and thus lacking the means or motivation to teach their children the discipline that could be beneficial for schooling.

Parents who tried to emphasize discipline in their children completing homework faced a number of problems that often undermined their efforts. Many parents came home physically and mentally tired from work and simply too exhausted to monitor their children's homework in a timely manner. Often when parents did find the time and energy to help their children, it was later than when their child had asked for assistance and this often caused the youth frustration and resentment over the fact that they did not get the attention of the parent when they had asked for it. When this situation occurred, there were some individual students who assumed a rebellious disposition by not finishing their assignment and telling their parents that they had figured out the problem themselves; and there were others who tried to finish it without parental help but failed because they lost interest. In both instances, the effort to instill self-discipline was undermined. Two representative examples of problems associated with giving and receiving educational aid at home involved Jeanne and Tamara. Jeanne was a 39-year-old parent whose son attended Van Twiller High School and daughter attended Cross Intermediate School, both of which were in the Bronx:[58]

Last night, I got home from work [as a house cleaner in Manhattan] and Ronnie wanted me to help him with his English. All he wanted me to do was read what he'd written, but I just could not for the life of me concentrate—I was so tired that I told him that I would need to do it a little later, but after I got done cooking and doing the dishes I fell asleep and when I woke up he had already left for school. I tell you, I felt so bad about it, but then again, I was so, so tired. I hope he did OK, and I'll just try to do better next time.[59]

Tamara was a 16-year-old junior at Miwok High School in Oakland:

I was asking my mom about something in math because she got good grades in math in high school, but she was busy with Luis and Laura [her brother and sister] and she kept saying, "Wait 'til I'm done, and I'll help you." By the time she was done and came to help, I was trying to talk to you [her friend] and didn't want her help. So, I just told her I already got the answer because by then I was over her helping![60]

In addition to aiding their children becoming self-disciplined, parents were often called upon to provide educational assistance. However, there was often, though not always, a lack of parental assistance in completing homework assignments for the simple reason that the parents lacked the academic knowledge and skills required to do so. Many parents had not finished high school, or they finished but had not mastered the skills required to aid their children. In many of the low-income homes in the present study, parents often could not read well enough to help their children understand homework assignments or lacked the skills required to explain the solution to a math or science problem their children were having difficulty with. Thus, students from these families were forced to either figure out how to do a particular exercise themselves or call a friend from their class for help. When they did reach out to a friend for assistance, the friend often would simply give them the correct answer with no explanation of how it was derived because the friend was primarily interested in socializing and not teaching. Since the person wanting the help did not want to seem like they were intellectually deficient, they would not press for an explanation. As a result, they either completed their homework with the correct answer they were given or did not complete it at all. Either way, they were left not knowing how to solve the problem themselves, and this ultimately made them vulnerable to a low grade on an exam.

Given the general lack of skills to aid their children, low-income parents tended to defer to the high school's education professionals for their children's learning needs. They felt they did not have any recourse but to accept whatever instruction was provided their child during normal school time, and to accept the evaluation of their child's academic progress provided by school personnel. The comments of Emmett, a 40-year-old father of three children, one who attended Kaiser High School in Oakland, were representative:

> My daughter Erika asked me about something in history last night, and I said wait till I'm done eating and I'll help. When I got to her, she was doing something else and said she [had] asked a friend and got the answer. . . . I was kinda glad she did because the last four times I helped her at things, she said the teacher told her that she got the wrong answer. I just don't think I can help her anymore. I got to leave it to the school people. [All four people he is talking to nod that they too find themselves in that situation.][61]

Even when parents found the money to hire a tutor to help their children, there were cases when their child would not fully cooperate because they viewed it as adding more schooling to their day. The comments of David, a 15-year-old student at Chumash High School in Los Angeles, were representative:

> Can you believe my mom and dad went out and paid for me to go to a geometry tutor? I definitely ain't going to do that at all! They're fucking crazy if they think I'm going to do that! I hate geometry, [and] I ain't going to spend even more time after school doing it![62]

In addition to the issues just discussed, home could be a source that negatively affected students' academic achievement in other ways. Home was a place where youth learned about responsibility, and in many low-income families the reality of having limited financial resources had the impact of merging the idea of responsibility with a set of family obligations. Some students assumed certain responsibilities that cut into the time that could have been devoted to their homework or study time. These responsibilities were in two general areas. The first was related to sibling care when parents were not at home, including the making and serving of meals, seeing to it that their younger siblings had started their homework, and finally making sure that younger members of the family had gone to bed at the time the parent specified. Here there was a general gender bias because usually, though not always, this responsibility was assumed by the oldest girl in the family. Even when there was an older boy or the father was at home, it was often expected that the oldest daughter would assume this role unless she was substantially younger than the son and then the older boy would assume the parental role.

An example of this can be seen in the case of Ana-Luz, a 16-year-old student at Polk High School in Los Angeles. Ana-Luz's mother worked from 3 p.m. to 11 p.m. at a local hospital as a nurse's aide, so Ana-Luz was given the responsibility of coming home from school and cooking for the family even though she had a brother living in the house who was 17. Her two sisters and a younger brother were also in school, and their father, a construction worker, came home at 7:30 every night. Ana-Luz cooked for her siblings and father and then saw to it that the younger kids took a bath. Her father helped out by doing the dishes, but Ana-Luz had to help the other children with their homework because she was more fluent in English than her father. She could not start her own homework until 9 p.m. and usually did not finish before 11 p.m. Some evenings, if her siblings had been particularly difficult to control, she couldn't finish her homework before falling asleep. When this occurred, it often resulted in her being tired for her first two classes the next day and vulnerable to not fully grasping all the concepts and facts presented in those courses. She generally earned C grades in all her subjects, but her teachers thought she could do better because they were aware that she had consistently scored very high on standardized tests. In addition, she sometimes received an A for an assignment or test, and this always occurred when the assignment or test was scheduled for a Monday and her mother was home to feed and bathe the younger children during the weekend, leaving Ana-Luz with an extended opportunity to study.[63]

A final area of home life with the potential to interrupt learning had to do with family relationships. This started with the relationships between parents, and whether there was a constant stream of anger and conflict. Parental conflict raised the anxiety level for children, and then it took time after any conflict before calm was restored. For youth in the home, the aftermath of parental conflict involved rehashing what happened, why it happened, and wondering if it was going to get worse. Further, the youth pondered the moral calculus of who was at fault and how to deal with their own disappointment, anger, or rage concerning the parent judged to be accountable for the conflict. Such thoughts remained with students well into the subsequent day's classes and reduced their focus on educational material. An example involved Gene, a 16-year-old student at Lanape High School in the Bronx, whose parents often fought physically. Each time this occurred, he would have difficulty focusing the next day. His teachers would ask whether everything was okay and then encourage him to finish his work.[64]

Parents with some form of addiction also generally had a negative impact on their children's academic life as the challenges of addiction compounded all of the issues mentioned above. During adolescence, youth are refining their morals and ethics and are quite sensitive to what they think are immoral or unethical behaviors on anyone's part.[65] They are especially sensitive to their parents' behavior because children normally look to parents for guidance in these matters. What is more, children's own identity is to some degree associated with their peers' assessments of their parents. A parent's addiction to drugs or alcohol is embarrassing to a student who feels vulnerable about having their identity linked with their parent's weaknesses.

A representative example involved Sara, a senior at Polk High School in Los Angeles. Her father was an alcoholic who worked at a furniture factory six days a week. Every day after work he became completely inebriated, and he drank all day on Sundays, talking loudly and constantly using profanity. His addiction and behavior embarrassed Sara and other members of the family. Sara would not invite her friends over and never told her father about school events, particularly those where teachers were scheduled to talk to parents about their child's progress or problems. This hindered her education because she missed out on the teacher communicating to her parents what she needed to work on for college. In addition, when she was picked to participate in a program that would allow her to attend classes at a nearby university, she was so fearful that her father would come to the required meetings drunk that she opted not to participate rather than risk being embarrassed.[66]

Before finishing this section, it is important to mention that there is no specific discussion of issues related to single-parent families. However, two of the key issues faced by single parents in trying to aid their children's education—not having enough time to provide assistance to all who may need it and being too tired from the work they had done during the day—were discussed earlier in the chapter.

STUDENT PHYSICALITY IN THE EDUCATIONAL ENVIRONMENT

During a teacher preparation period in the faculty lounge at Los Angeles's Chester Himes High School in 2013, a new English teacher asked two of her colleagues, "The students from these backgrounds are very aggressive; where does that come from?" The other two teachers just shrugged.[67] It is a question that often was on the minds of many of the teachers, particularly those who came from middle-class backgrounds, who would see aggressive behavior and try to locate its origins. Aggressive behavior did exist among youth in the low-income schools of the present study and much of this behavior emanated from the cultural norms of the lower-class segment of society. Outside of these schools, it was common to observe among families and community members the belief that physical power was an important resource in protecting oneself bodily and emotionally, and some youth brought this belief and its underlying value orientation to school where they viewed it as something normal. This directly derives from the world that lower-class individuals inhabit. It is primarily physical, as opposed to intellectually abstracted and aestheticized.[68] Work, leisure, and status are all based in physical activity. In this regard, they are not asked to use their intellect to complete their work, but to simply physically execute an order. Thus, adults have learned to prioritize and focus on the physical in their lifeworld, and they socialize their children toward this adaptive orientation.[69]

Within this lower-class cultural orientation, being aware of things associated with the body was common among the youth in these schools and they were constantly making reference to objects and issues that involved bodily functions. Strength, beauty, sex, bodily functions, altered states of mind, and their opposites were topics of everyday conversation and often discussed in the classroom. This focus reflected the centrality of the body as a resource, locus of experience, and status symbol in poor communities where other forms of capital are scarce.[70] The upshot was that physical movement was valued, and this encouraged students to prioritize movement over being sedentary, which in turn could influence their study habits. Once these ideas about the importance of physicality were internalized, physical aggression was seen as "normal."[71] An example can be seen in the comments of Horton, a 16-year-old junior at Oakland's Miwok High School:

> I don't understand what the fuck Mr. Stupid [his teacher] is sending me to the counselor for! All I did was fucking hit Dewey and Shane a little, nothing like heavy or anything. Who doesn't do that? He [the teacher] is just fucked up, man, he's just fucking stupid! What's the problem, they had some paper, I asked them for it, they weren't getting it to me, so I just took some and let them know not to play around like that—and now I got to go to the assistant principal's office? That's fucking insane![72]

Obviously, Horton does not see anything wrong with his behavior, but officials in his school as well as in each of the other schools of this study viewed this belief—that being physical with classmates was normal—as deviant or an impediment to them executing their professional duties.

Another aspect of physicality centered on students being restless and not concentrating on what the teacher was presenting, or not executing the drills the teacher directed in class to refine their skills. Sitting is usually required to do this, but most professionals I observed assumed that sitting was to be taken for granted. This was a big mistake. Sitting still for an extended period of time could not be taken for granted and was not experienced the same way by all individuals. Therefore, it should have been considered a skill and been taught, like any other skill. In brief, children from low-income families frequently lived with parents and siblings who had difficulty sitting because few had been trained to do it.

Professionals at the schools studied needed a better understanding that the skill of sitting was integrally linked to the personal discipline required to concentrate and complete educational tasks that a student might find difficult or uninteresting. Even when a student had an assignment that required them to read a significant number of pages on a topic they were interested in, they might still find it difficult to complete the assignment because they didn't have the skill to sit as long as necessary.[73] The case of Jackson, a 16-year-old at Los Angeles's Chester Himes High School, was representative. Jackson wanted to do well, but had difficulty with his courses mainly because he could not sit for long periods and concentrate without doing something else or talking to someone. At home or in the library, Jackson would read for about ten minutes and then get up, talk to someone, or fiddle around with an object like a pen, a ruler, or a set of keys. He would rarely finish his homework at one physical place. His regular pattern was to finish each course's homework in a separate location over the course of an evening.

Teachers generally considered his work "uneven," meaning that some of it was good and other parts were disconnected or wrong. What teachers did not observe was that, outside their classroom, as Jackson moved from one location to another, there was a disruption in his train of thought and he found it difficult to reconnect with his previous thoughts in order to finish his homework. When they expressed their observation of his unevenness to Jackson, he responded by pretending to be someone interested in girls and drugs but not school. He was not really interested in either drugs or girls, however, and on numerous occasions voiced his desire to attend college, but his inability to settle down and concentrate led him to maintain self-respect by taking on the identity of someone not interested in school.

Jackson graduated with a C grade average and joined the US Army. He became a medic and did one tour in Iraq and another in Afghanistan. After leaving the service, he attended college and graduate school. Near the end of my research, I visited Jackson at his workplace; he had become a nurse practitioner in a large health clinic.[74] Some readers might ask if this example is an extreme case involving a student who was atypically smart and motivated, but that would miss the point. The point is that Jackson was smart but lacked a skill that is usually taken for granted and, as a result, was denied the assisted training in sitting he needed during high school to transition immediately to college.

The professionals at Jackson's high school were not able to accumulate the evidence to diagnose his issues and create a plan to help him build this skill. In sum, Jackson's road to becoming a professional required the additional disciplined training of the military for the skills required for him to transition to college and postgraduate instruction, but much of this discipline might have been provided while he was in high school if his problem of sitting for sustained periods had been addressed promptly.[75] For example, schools could have provided remedial reading courses in which techniques to sit and concentrate for extended periods were an integral part, and / or provided parents with techniques to develop this skill while the student was at home.

Another factor that influenced restlessness among youth from low-income families was the high schools' formal schedules, which produced feelings of confinement in some students and a desire to move without restriction. At the beginning of the school day, most students did not exhibit signs of feeling trapped, but as the day progressed their feelings of confinement grew, and students looked for opportunities to ease them. This usually took the form of physical movement in class, talking in class, physical play in the halls between classes, and occasional verbal sparring or physical jostling during lunch or homeroom periods.

The anxiety that grew out of being sequestered at school for hours was often transferred to their time at home and resulted in parents finding it difficult to motivate their children to complete their homework. A typical example involved Joan, a 15-year-old at Van Twiller High School in the Bronx. Joan would come home from school and tell her mother she needed to study later because she had an exam the next day. Her mother would cook her dinner and then wait for her to finish and start studying, but Joan would never study more than fifteen minutes before getting up and watching television. Her mother would get frustrated and tell her to get back and finish studying. Joan would get so irritated with her mother that she would simply yell back, saying, "I'm told what to do all day at school, so leave me alone when I'm home!"[76]

One final aspect of students' physicality confronting school authorities and parents had to do with the "excessive activity" some youth displayed while at school. Usually, this was considered a problem for everyone concerned. The problem for teachers was how to handle youth who presented excessive physical activity during instruction and whether to treat the resulting disruptions as a disciplinary situation. In most cases, school personnel were likely to be sympathetic and treat it more as a personal physical abnormality than a disciplinary problem. What generally followed was an official meeting with parents, where it would be suggested that their child could be suffering from attention deficit disorder (ADD) or attention deficit hyperactivity disorder (ADHD) and that it was advisable for the parents to consult a doctor.

These disorders are associated with having a difficult time concentrating on one subject for any length of time. Often these youths would jump from one topic to another, constantly losing track of their place in books they were reading, or they would unexpectedly get up and walk around the classroom. They also exhibited a tendency to be very unorganized or have difficulty handing in homework because they failed to correctly record assignments or lost their completed assignments at home. However, determining whether a student's excessive physicality was an expression of activity normally seen among low-income youth or the result of ADD was difficult for parents and teachers.

The situation was challenging for all concerned. For teachers and school administrators, a student with ADHD who presented all the symptoms just mentioned and moved around and talked excessively generally disrupted the class and exasperated everyone. That often led to a sequence of interactions culminating in the student heading to a counselor or detention. However, the youth suffering from this disorder nearly always expressed a complete lack of understanding as to why they were asked to leave the classroom. Simply stated, they could not determine what they had done wrong, as illustrated by Miguel, a 15-year-old sophomore, as he spoke with a dean at Oakland's Miwok High School about his behavior:

I don't know what Mrs. Evans is talking about. She always says that I'm say-ing things that disrupt the class, but it's just in her mind. I mean I say things in class, but it's always when she is asking the class questions and I join in. I mean, I ain't different from anybody else in the class. I just don't think she likes me, that's all.[77]

Shortly after this incident, Miguel was diagnosed by a doctor at Children's Hospital in Oakland as suffering from ADHD and was prescribed the drug Adderall to reduce his activity and improve his concentration at school.

ADD and ADHD are conditions where neurotransmitters operate differ-ently from those in the brains of students who do not have the disorder. There was no evidence that ADD or ADHD limited the intellectual capacity of affected youths. So, parents were often told that one option to increase their child's ability to focus on academic material was to medicate them before they went to school with one of two primary drugs: Adderall (amphetamine and dextroamphetamine) or Ritalin (methylphenidate). The parents who were in contact with school authorities said the drugs allowed their child to calm down, and teachers reported that they observed these students concentrating better, although they reported that the maximum impact came during the first three class periods of each day and that increased activity would gradually reappear as the day proceeded. This meant that when it came to doing home-work the youth would express the full range of symptoms and usually could not complete it. In addition, these drugs had the side effect of significantly diminishing the youths' appetites. Thus, the medical intervention did not fully solve the educational problems confronted by the ADD / ADHD-induced physicality of these youths and sometimes added new physical problems.

An additional problem facing low-income parents was trying to deter-mine whether the diagnosis of ADD or ADHD in their child was accurate, or whether the excessive physical behavior was simply the result of the physi-cality valued among lower-income populations and did not require pharma-cological intervention. When I observed these parents and heard their con-cerns, they demonstrated a worry about making a mistake that would undermine the quality of their children's education. For example, how should they evaluate the professional authorities' assessment that their child had a learning disability that did not require a chemical drug intervention such as dyslexia or an auditory processing problem against the possibility that they had ADD or ADHD and did need medication? Or the possibility that their child was simply very active because of a social or dietary stimulant against the possibility they were merely a normally active child?

Parents were troubled about how to solicit cooperation from their child in addressing the problem when they knew stigma was associated with special programs designed to attend to these identified problems. It should be remembered that because adolescence is a developmental period when individual differences are normally avoided, students tended to want to avoid being identified as having any disability for fear of being stigmatized as different from their peers.[78] Thus, youth nearly always resisted any identification of them as either "odd" or requiring a special program separate from their peers, and sympathetic parents responded by refraining from forcing their children to participate in special programs or put off making a decision on the issue.

The upshot for students who had been identified as hyperactive often was that teachers treated them as uncooperative and disruptive and, if the behavior continued, recommended placing the students in a special education program or suspending them. These discriminating assessments presented challenges to these youths' sense of self-worth, and as the teachers exchanged information about specific students these assessments prejudiced students' relationships with subsequent teachers and administrators. This in turn affected these students' abilities to manage the other challenges they would confront in trying to transition within and from high school.[79]

SOME FINISHING COMMENTS

The data presented in this chapter should not be understood to suggest that low-income families were responsible for the educational difficulties experienced by their student-members, but that they could contribute to these difficulties, either by presenting additional obstacles or by being unable to remediate the difficulties that their children experienced. In sum, the amount of time diverted from knowledge and skill acquisition affected the ability of low-income youth to learn and smoothly transition to the next stage of their formal education. There was never a time when all was lost or all gained, but a youth's ability to progress often was affected by hitches and bumps associated with both internal family interactions and their parents' relations with educational officials.

The data indicate that in general most parents and school officials wanted students to achieve academic excellence, but in the process of trying to maximize excellence, both parents and school officials passed along to one another the problems they experienced in realizing this goal. It should be clear from the evidence presented in this chapter that when one analyzes how elements associated with the family impact students' educational progress, it produces a picture of two institutions in constant interaction. Therefore, if we are concerned, as we are in this book, with what factors impede successful educational transitions, it is important to understand that no one element in the family or school produced success or failure. Rather, their constant interactions produced challenges that most often fell on students to confront and solve.

CHAPTER 3

School Organization and Its Challenges

The authority of those who teach is often an obstacle to those who want to learn.

MARCUS TILLIUS CICERO,
On the Nature of the Gods, 45 BC

WHEN IT COMES TO PROBLEMS that students from low-income families face in the United States, a great deal of scrutiny and criticism has focused on school structure. The most common argument of studies of inequality in education is that the structure of most schools serving low-income students significantly decreases the probability of a successful transition from high school to the next level of education—college or technical school. There is a long history of research that connects structural flaws in the schools serving low-income families with low achievement by students who attend them.[1] At the same time, research has shown that the structure of schools serving middle- and upper-income communities is a positive resource for students that parents in those communities appreciate and want to maintain.[2] Since school districts across the United States operate under a specific structural design, it is reasonable to ask how school structure creates obstacles for low-income students. Generally, when structure has been used to account for inequalities in education, it has been conceived as an overarching unit having a total impact on students. More accurately, however, the structure of a school includes a variety of elements that have both partial and diverse impacts on students. As will be seen in this chapter, each of the elements of a school's structure can have an impact on a student's educational experience. I will identify some of the important structural components that present challenges for students from low-income families and show how these work to create hurdles for students in the transition process.

EDUCATIONAL ARCHITECTURE AND
THE PROBLEMS IT CAUSES

Historically, schools in America have been responsible for educating a diverse population of students, and most educators have recognized these students as possessing a variety of intellectual capacities, skills, and knowledge levels. Though this is rarely explicitly articulated, this diverse group of students has been assumed to be distributed in the shape of a statistical bell curve, where the mean would represent the intellectual capacity, skill, and knowledge of the "average student." In this model, students who found their levels to the left of the mean were categorized as needing varying amounts of remedial help, and those who found their levels to the right of the mean were categorized as more cognitively developed, or gifted, and in need of constant intellectual challenge. To provide the appropriate educational experience for all students, school districts have generally developed a multilevel instructional approach. This approach informs each school's structure and, although the structure is intended to maximize the educational competency of every student, in practice it presents differential challenges that students from low-income backgrounds struggle to overcome.

Curricular Regimens

The goal of most education systems is to create an environment to accommodate students with divergent educational interests (e.g., academic, vocational, or artistic) and varying knowledge, skills, and cognitive competence. This often involves dividing students into homogeneous groups based on their assessed cognitive competence, skills, knowledge, and interests. "Tracking" is the historical name for the system of grouping students into curricular regimens. Much has been written about the inequity of tracking because a disproportionate number of low-income students and students of color land in vocational and lower academic tracks, but less is known about how this system can impact an individual student in making a successful transition to the next stage of their education.[3]

Most school districts abandoned the pure tracking systems that one found operating in the 1960s through the 1980s, but they went on to adopt some of the past systems' elements of separating students by assessed levels of ability and interest.[4] Some of the schools in the present study utilized a system designed to focus on students' interests or a particular subject they were interested in, and this system generally required students to apply for admittance. This was often called the "school-within-a-school approach." Other school districts maintained general classes that were completely integrated in terms of differences in student abilities, along with classes that were designed to accommodate students identified as being advanced, often called "advanced placement" or "honors" courses. Finally, most school districts offered a high school curriculum associated with "vocational education," in which students who wanted to transition immediately after high school to the labor market, or were deemed unprepared to complete the academic curriculum, could participate.[5]

The rationale for these designs was based on addressing the demands of parents to maximize educational opportunities for their children, on one hand, while managing the varying levels of student interest and competence with different subject matter, on the other. In essence, by offering them separate programs these systems attempted to minimize the possibility that those with less ability or preparation would inhibit the progress of those who were more advanced, or that those who were more advanced would impede the progress of those needing more assistance. Thus, the quasi-tracking systems found in the schools of the present study were attempts to facilitate the success of students who wanted to attend college, those who were not sure, and those who wanted to enter the labor market after finishing high school.

Separating educational regimens in the way just described seems both rational and reasonable, and many students in the schools of this study said it helped them make transitions. The comments of Deidre, Francisco, Darcy, and Alejandra were representative of students who found value in separate courses for students with different goals. Deidre was a senior at Brooklyn's Knickerbocker High School:

> Being in honors courses has made all the difference in the world for me getting a terrific education. If I were in the general education courses there would be people who didn't want to do the work or couldn't do it, and then all of us would have to wait until the teacher dealt with them before we got taught anything. I was in that type of system at my last school, and it didn't work because we didn't learn what we needed to get into a good college. Here, the teachers push us with difficult assignments in the honors classes and, because we are all at the same level, we all learn faster. No question, I wouldn't have gotten into Yale without this system.[6]

Francisco was a senior at Los Angeles's Polk High School:

> Did you hear the conversation today at lunch? Some people were saying they didn't like the system we got here at Polk, but I think it was good for me to be in the honors program because I got more advanced stuff than the other students in general education. I don't think I'd be going to UCLA next year without being in the honors courses.[7]

Alejandra was a senior at Oakland's Miwok High School:

> I'm excited about college. For me, I was fortunate to get assigned to the general educational group because when that happened, I really didn't read too well and being with others that were just average helped me to get it together. The teachers had programs to help me, and after some time I just got better and better, and that's really how I got into [the University of California at] Santa Cruz.[8]

Darcy was a senior at Los Angeles's Chester Himes High School:

> What are you doing after graduation? [he is asking another student] . . . [then he answers when asked by that student] Me? I'm going to work for this furnace and plumbing company putting them in places. It's a really good job because the pay is really good, and I like doing that stuff. . . . Well, I was different than you. I didn't want college shit. I wanted to do this kind of stuff and vo-ed [vocational education] really taught me the stuff I needed. That other school shit was useless to me.[9]

Despite the rationale for separating students by ability and goals, these systems were not always rationally executed, and some of their structural components created significant obstacles for students from low-income family backgrounds.

Managing Placement in Separate Curricular Regimens

In order to better understand where, when, and how these quasi-tracking systems affected students, we will focus on the early actions of those charged with executing them. Usually the structure associated with the creation of more or less homogeneous groupings of students with like or similar interests and capabilities centered on organizing students around the idea of an "aptitude" for particular subject matter. What was understood as "aptitude" often came from an assessment of what the student did well, in relation to what they did not do so well. Such a determination was made by evaluating the student's standardized test scores, their grades, and their interest in various academic subject matter. Students' academic interest was evaluated by focusing on the effort they made in completing homework, engaging in class discussions, and seeking contact with teachers during free time to continue an intellectual conversation. The results of these evaluations, some of which were clearly subjective, not only characterized a student's aptitudes but formed the basis for assigning students to instructional regimens.

The comments of two assistant principals were representative of administrators who supported a differentiated curricular system. Ms. Yancy was an assistant principal at Los Angeles's Chester Himes High School:

> The system that we have installed here at [Himes] is an effective educational structure, and one that I believe is also fair. By fair, I mean that the overwhelming majority of students are evaluated without prejudice as to their current achievement level, and this has allowed us to determine which students have an aptitude for success in specific subjects, and those who are competent, but do not necessarily have the capabilities of handling extremely complex material. The decision of where to place the student includes the grades they have achieved, their scores on standardized tests, and the assessment of previous teachers. I know that everyone involved in the process takes this seriously and wants what is best for each student. The result allows us to present to students the appropriate material for their capability levels so that they can be successful.[10]

Mr. Mack was an assistant principal at the Bronx's Lanape High School:

> You'll find that there is such a range in student capabilities here at [Lanape]. Some of the students just have an aptitude for various subjects and they will succeed in mastering material with little effort, others have to struggle to pass the course because they either lack the skills necessary to successfully complete the requirements or are simply not interested in school. So, separating individuals by their skill levels allows everyone to progress at their own speed, and since each individual is evaluated by teachers, counselors, and an administrator we generally place individuals in the appropriate curriculum.[11]

If it was determined that a student had aptitude for "advanced" intellectual subject matter, that student was placed in the "honors" or "advanced placement" curriculum. Students who were assessed to have aptitude for transitioning to college, but not "advanced" skills, were placed in the general educational curricular regimen. Finally, students determined to have aptitude for nonintellectual subject matter were placed in vocational curricular regimens. Often, the concepts of aptitude and interest merged, which was problematic because they are different and quite often separate within an individual.

Hector, a student at Van Twiller High School in the Bronx, for example, was said to have both "aptitude" for and "interest" in fixing cars, but in talking to Hector it became clear that, while he could fix cars, he was actually interested in becoming a doctor. When he was assigned to vocational education courses his sophomore year, he told his friends and a teacher that he wanted to be a doctor. His math teacher intervened and talked to a counselor about Hector's ability in math and suggested that they provide him more college preparatory classes, particularly in math and science. They did, and the next semester he was placed in an advanced math course. He struggled at first and told friends that because his previous class had not gotten to the material that classmates in his advanced course had, he needed to catch up. He asked for, and received, after-school tutoring and passed the course with a B+. Hector ultimately graduated from high school and college and was in the second year of medical school the last time I had contact with him.[12]

The example of Hector suggests several observations: First, mistakes could be, and were, made in assigning individuals to curricular regimens.[13] Second, mistakes could be reversed, but students had to persistently advocate for themselves. Third, students had to find someone in the bureaucracy who would advocate for them. Fourth, when mistakes were made and rectification sought, success was determined by personal persistence and some luck. The issue of luck as a factor in student achievement will be discussed in more detail later in the analysis.

In a situation similar to Hector's, Janice, a student at Chester Himes High School in Los Angeles, was thought to have both an aptitude for and interest in science because she performed well on standardized tests, but she really was interested in becoming a graphic artist. Assigned to advanced placement courses in math and science, she received C grades in her first two years of high school. She often expressed doubt about her ability to learn and told a teacher during her junior year that she did not know what she would do after graduation. In this case, assigning a student to advanced placement courses created self-doubt and impeded both her educational development and her transition. Two years after graduating from high school, Janice enrolled in a community college, where she did well enough in all of her courses to transfer to a four-year university, and eventually earned a bachelor's degree in graphic design.[14]

These two examples highlight the problem with using the concept of aptitude in deciding placement. The concept of "aptitude for a particular subject" matter carried the connotation that the student's brain was designed to excel at that subject—a predisposition or innate ability—when in reality it emerged from a time-specific assessment that could change as the student undertook further training and formed new interests. So, the idea of having an aptitude for particular subjects created an intellectual foundation for school officials to place a student in one of the divergent instructional regimens, even though it often was an inexact procedure.[15]

In the current study, differentiated instructional groupings required that each student cope with their respective placement and work to excel within the standards established for it. If for any reason a student or their parents did not feel they had been accurately placed, they had to navigate significant obstacles to move to another regimen, the most important being a new formal reassessment using some or all of the same criteria utilized initially. This logistical problem was not easily solved within a semester. As a consequence, changes were usually made after the semester was completed, and this inevitably caused the student to spend a semester in an inappropriate regimen. The difficulty that emerged was in trying to assess the extent of harm such a situation had created. If there was any harm, the system was structured in such a way that it was the student who bore the responsibility to make up for difficulties that resulted from being inappropriately placed.

The experience of April, a 15-year-old student at Oakland's Kaiser High School, was typical. She was in the general curriculum math course but felt she should be in the advanced placement course. She talked to her mother, and her mother went to the school and discussed the situation with the assistant principal and a counselor. Even though April had received A grades for all her math courses, the counselor and current math teacher were not convinced she was capable of doing well in advanced placement calculus, so the principal decided they would retest her during a break and make an assessment based on those results.

April's new scores qualified her to join AP calculus. She joined the class at the start of the second semester and found the course work difficult. She told her mother her previous class had not gotten to the same material so she was behind. Her first grades were Cs, and she told her teacher she was struggling, but there was no systematic way to get additional support. The teacher did provide April with materials from the prior semester and offered to meet with her after class to answer questions, but it was April who had to put in extra work to learn the material that she had missed the first semester. As it turned out, her first formal grade in the course was a C. The following grading period she received a B−, and at the end of the second semester she earned a B. It became clear that she was capable of doing quality work in the advanced placement course, but the system made it difficult for her to progress unencumbered.[16]

One of the most significant problems associated with grouping students according to their abilities involved the impact it had on the student's identity formation.[17] Compared with performance and choice, the issue of personal identity has not received much attention in educational transition research.[18] However, during high school adolescents are in a key phase of the personal identity formation process, a phase when they choose and experiment with various potential identities. Some students try a new identity they have created to see how their peers respond and, in turn, whether they like that response. Others must face a new identity that has been given to them by their peers or adults they have interacted with. Significantly, the process of identity formation can combine a variety of identities or partial identities, with each carrying potential opportunities and limitations related to a student's goals.[19]

Among students in the high schools studied, the academic regimen to which they were assigned created a "labeled identity" for them, a social identity they believed they had only limited ability to shape but would have to manage.[20] As Calvin, a 15-year-old freshman at New York's Knickerbocker High School, said, "Shit, I'm in this honors curriculum, and I ain't even applied for it. Now I got to act smart and shit like that and ain't nobody going to like me! I'm fucking an outsider to my friends and I ain't done nothing to deserve it!"[21] This ascribed social identity was predicated on their assessed capability or their achievement, and it limited the types of public personas they could plausibly pursue. Therefore, the initial placement in a curricular regimen became problematic for some students as they tried to establish their own sense of self-worth, instead of one that corresponded with their institutionally ascribed identity.

When this was a problem for students, it was because their social identity depended on how their existing peer group judged the placement category and the subjective status it assigned to people placed there. For example, both students who were exceptionally accomplished and those who had severe problems with academics often were labeled by peers as "nerds" or "stupid" and placed in the lower rungs of a school's social hierarchy.[22] Of course, the content of these and other categories can change over time, but the fundamental divisions and strata do not. Among students in the schools studied, it was the "average" students, those with average academic standing, who were the most influential in placing individuals in the various rungs of their school's social status hierarchy. Thus, it was not merely the official curricular regimen system students confronted, but the unofficial peer-status system as well.[23]

The burden of labels was immense for both psychological and educational reasons.[24] First, many students were generally trying to simply fit in with their peers, as can be seen in the representative comments of Travis and Dianna. Travis was a freshman at Oakland's Miwok High School:

> Oh, man, the other day, Jay told me I said something stupid. I hope I didn't, because the group's going to think I'm some "retard," and that would do it for me hangin' with them, you know?[25]

Dianna was a freshman at Los Angeles's Tongva High School:

> I hope what I'm doing in class doesn't make people think I'm smarter than they are because I'm in the honors classes. That'll be it for me; I won't get any dates. Let me know if you hear anything about what people think about me, OK?[26]

Student Responses to Curricular Placement

There were five general responses by students to their curricular placement. First, those placed in the upper academic regimen expressed feelings of pride and insecurity. The insecurity was associated with the view that they must constantly prove they belonged in this regimen while trying to find acceptance and inclusion among the students in other regimens, who by absolute numbers formed the core of the school's social world. A typical example of this involved Kenny, a 15-year-old freshman at Van Twiller High School in the Bronx:

> I hate being in honors classes because I have to be around all these people I don't know and don't have anything in common with. I hardly ever get to see my old friends during the day and then at night I'm so busy with homework I can't hang with them at all. . . . I could not study so much and call them up,

but then if I didn't do well they'd take me out of honors, and everyone would think I was just pretending to be smart but was really stupid. All I know is that I'm not having that much fun here at school.[27]

The second response was to accept the placement in the higher academic curriculum, think of oneself as exceptional in academic issues, focus on building status within this grouping of students, and deliberately retreat from interacting with members of the other curricular regimens. The comments of Connor, a 16-year-old sophomore at Los Angeles's Chumash High School, were representative:

I don't have much if anything to do with Gabe and the rest of those other guys I used to be friends with in middle school because they're in the other [curriculum] and I don't see them much. Tell you the truth, since I'm in the classes for "exceptional students," I don't care what people in the other groups are about.[28]

The third response was associated with those who were placed in the general curricular regimens. It centered around students' doubts about their intellectual capability. The self-doubt response often resulted in a tendency to minimally apply themselves in the academics of their curriculum regimen. Most of these students were likely to seek their identity in activities outside the academic context and insert these identities into the school's social environment. Examples included being a superb athlete, primary actor in organizing parties and other social events, class clown, stylish dresser, good singer, bodybuilder, internet wizard, etc.

The fourth response from students placed in a general academic regimen was to simply accept their placement, consider themselves normal high school students, and focus on establishing an identity and performing well within the regimen. Because the largest number of students in the schools of this study were assigned to this regimen, there was no particular stigma attached to it and, as a result, it tended to play a significant role in establishing and maintaining the school's social hierarchy because it was the dominant middle.

The fifth response from students to their placement was associated with those placed in either the general academic and vocational regimens. This response focused on rejecting the basis of their curricular placement and aggressively labeling students in regimens considered higher as "clones of the outside world." Students who joined gangs, drinking-drug-oriented social groups, or became identified with an anti-establishment subculture exhibited this response.[29]

The experience of Maria-Luz, a freshman at Los Angeles's Chumash High School, is an example of the fifth type of response to placements. When she arrived at the school, she was placed in the general curriculum because her test scores had indicated her math and reading were at the seventh- and eighth-grade levels, respectively. In middle school, she had been in the top 10 percent of her school and her friends were also considered good students, so it caused considerable strain on her sense of self when she was placed in the general curriculum and her friends were placed in the honors curriculum. Maria-Luz felt inferior to her previous friends, shied away from them, and developed friendships in her new curricular cohort. Since she and her previous friends did not consider her to be in the school's elite, she rarely participated in school activities and she developed an anti-establishment presentation of herself, which included an anti–student establishment persona.

Maria-Luz dressed Goth and associated with other students who did the same. As part of this identity, like the other nineteen students in the various schools studied whom I recorded as identifying as Goth, Maria-Luz would cut herself. On one occasion, members of her group were questioned by police as to whether they had been part of a group of Goth students who had killed a chicken and used its blood to write "devil worship" phrases on the school's walls.[30] What is most telling about Maria-Luz's story is that at the end of her sophomore year, she was diagnosed as having dyslexia and provided learning support. After that, her grades improved, her math and reading scores rose to above grade level, she was moved to the honors regimen, and she stopped wearing Goth clothing, became active in the Spanish and debate clubs, and reconnected with her previous friends.[31]

In sum, once students were placed in a particular academic regimen, they established an identity related to that subgroup. After that identity was established, they strategically projected it when interacting with students in the other regimens and reduced their social and educational interactions with students in the other groups. The outcome in every school was the establishment of a stratified system of socio-educational groups.[32] More will be said about this in chapter 5, which focuses on the impact of peer groups within the transition process. However, it is important to point out that a school's academic placement system contributed to two identities—one in the academy, the other in the social realm—and both identities presented experiential challenges that affected the process of moving from one grade to the next and ultimately from high school to college.

Teacher Responses to Curricular Regimens

Teachers in each of the schools studied were informed about the school district's curricular requirements and about their school's specific goals for the current year. These requirements and goals were elements of each institution's educational architecture and provided the foundation for learning services students received. They also presented structural constraints on both teachers and students because they established the parameters within which learning occurred and was assessed.

The first of these foundational elements were the curricular regimens discussed earlier, which had associated with them a set of expectations emanating from the school's formal standardized assessment of each student. The curricular material used in each regimen varied, as did the approach to teaching it. In the courses offered in the honors and advanced placement regimens, the assigned books required a more advanced level of language skills and abstract thinking than was required in the other regimens. Each of the school districts studied had taken steps to determine the appropriate level of cognitive and skill development for students at a particular age and grade level; that is, they had developed curricular regimens corresponding to a constructed mean distribution based on required skills for each grade level.

The materials students were presented could be part of a general textbook on the subject, with students assigned sections determined to be appropriate for their assessed cognitive and skill level, or they could be completely different texts for each regimen. Thus, the teachers for each track were provided the material deemed appropriate for the "average student" assigned to it, but administrators did not prescribe a specific approach in presenting the information and developing the necessary skills to master it. The result was that students were confronted with a variety of teaching approaches within each regimen. It should be pointed out that despite the overall curricular approach for each regimen, and whether the principal as mentioned in chapter 1 wanted that executed using an "continuous" or "discrete" operational approach, when the individual teacher entered the classroom and shut the door, they were the curriculum and students received whatever they offered. In that regard, within each of the schools I studied over the twenty-three years, I identified three approaches taken by teachers as they interacted with their classes. I categorized these approaches as "Educational," "Instructional," and "Holding Action."

All of the students in the advanced placement courses and some, depending on the teacher, in the general curricular regimen received an approach that I will label "Educational." Within this framework, there was an emphasis on developing a full range of intellectual skills. This would be accomplished by using texts that were more abstract in the areas of math, science, and language arts, making assignments that encouraged creative writing, science projects that included the opportunity to design and execute an experiment, and advanced procedures for solving a particular mathematical problem. This made the material challenging, but there was a clear and often-repeated understanding that family members and fellow students could provide assistance. In brief, these students were presented material, and learning was done by the student themselves with support from individuals outside of the classroom.

Interestingly, teachers in the advanced placement courses were not the only instructors to use an "Educational" framework. Those who taught in what has traditionally been referred to as "vocational education" often used this approach, although they taught a specific set of skills related to a particular trade like auto mechanics, electrical circuitry, cooking, or carpentry. These teachers gave students readings that identified key elements associated with the specific trade they were learning, explained how they were associated with each other, and showed how these elements operated to produce a particular mechanical object or system of operation. Students in this regimen were generally interested in the substance of these courses, and because there was a combination of reading and practical activities in what could be considered a quasi-laboratory situation, most saw themselves as both being taught and having to teach one another to solve problems as they completed projects.

Most of the teachers I observed in the general curricular regimens provided students with knowledge and skills utilizing what I will refer to as an "Instructional" approach.[33] This approach is best described as the teacher making commands, prioritizing the use of repetitive drills with a focus on sharpening students' ability to memorize and recite material rather than developing their understanding or techniques (i.e., skills) to solve similar or new intellectual problems. In general, teachers using the "Instructional" approach adopted the role of a trainer, in contrast with teachers in the honors and advanced placement regimens, whose approach was closer to that of classical educators who took it upon themselves to present material and have students work out how it was to be applied to intellectual and practical problems.[34]

Students encountered a number of challenges when their teachers took the "Instructional" approach. The first was finding ways to supplement the fact that they received less information than was presented in more advanced curricular regimens. This was particularly important for students who wanted to move into a more advanced regimen. A typical example involved Dyson, a 16-year-old sophomore at Los Angeles's Chumash High School, who studied with two girls that were in advanced placement classes and lived next to him in public housing. He usually completed his homework in an hour and then talked to the girls. He would ask if he could see what they were doing in an effort to determine if he could do it. After a couple of weeks, one of the girls said to him, "Why are you doing our homework after yours? Aren't you tired of homework?" He answered, "I don't like it that much, but I hate being in my classes. So, if I want to get out and into AP courses I got to show the counselors that I can do what you do. So, I'm trying to practice what you guys do." After a year in the general education regimen, Dyson asked to be reevaluated and was placed in advanced placement math, science, and literature courses. After graduation, Dyson went into the Army, and after serving his contractual time, attended one of the University of California institutions, where he was majoring in economics.[35]

The case of Casey led in the opposite direction. Casey was a 15-year-old sophomore at New York's Lanape High School. She was in the general education curriculum and always wanted to go to college. She studied every day, but her instructors did not or could not present her classes with all the information required for entrance to college. She studied and did well in her courses but did not develop the skills required for success in college. After graduating from high school, she applied and was accepted to a four-year college, but she was forced to drop out because of poor grades. What is important to note here is that, while in high school, she had done all that was asked of her and at a level that her teachers assessed worthy of A and B grades.

As one might expect, Casey was very upset by her failure to graduate from college. Her problem was that her teachers had assumed an "Instructional" approach that approximated a training course, rather than developing the intellectual skills she needed to be a creative and independent problem-solver. After leaving the four-year college, she worked at a clothing store and took night classes at a junior college, where she worked on her intellectual skills and competence. After receiving an associate degree from the junior college, she was accepted to Rutgers University. When I last communicated with her, she was in the last semester of her senior year at Rutgers and majoring in political science.[36]

The second challenge for students who experienced the "Instructional" teaching approach was to find a way to overcome the boredom of the repetition endemic to this approach so they could focus on understanding the material the teacher thought was important. In classes where the teacher asked the students to complete an assignment before the period ended, it was common to see them looking up and asking another student a question, taking a long stretching motion before returning to their work, getting up and sharpening a pencil, or asking the teacher for permission to go to the bathroom. Each of these was the result of boredom, and by simply breaking the routine helped them to refocus on the material. The conversation of Lydia and Salvador, both 16-year-old juniors at Los Angeles's Tongva High School, was representative:

SALVADOR: Mr. Owen is so, so boring and I really have a hard time trying to find out what's important and what's not. Don't you?

LYDIA: Yeah, I have to do something so I don't just drift off and do nothing in class. Usually, I just get up and ask to go to the bathroom and that helps me to concentrate again. If that doesn't work, I lean over and ask Juana about hanging out after school. . . . If I do that, Mr. Owen tells us to stop talking, and we laugh and go back to work.

SALVADOR: I'm like you, I just stand and stretch, and Mr. Owen looks at me and says, "Something wrong?" I just say, "I'm just stretching." If he gives me trouble, it helps me because after I deal with him it's easier to do the work he wants us to hand in.

LYDIA: I always laugh when you and Mr. Owen get into it. I couldn't do that, but you seem OK with it.[37]

The challenge of overcoming the cognitive strain and fatigue associated with disciplining oneself to accomplish repetitive tasks was significant. As indicated above, interrupting the repetition with jokes, throwing paper or some small object at another person, or making noise that elicited a response from the teacher were functional, as well as entertaining. When asked by one of her counselors during a detention session why she always interrupted class by throwing things at her friends, Adelita, a 16-year-old junior at Oakland's Kaiser High School, said, "I don't know, it just breaks things up for me and then I can start studying again."[38]

The third challenge students faced in the "Instructional" approach was mediating their resentment that their intellectual capacity was constantly being insulted. The comments of Paul, a 15-year-old student at the Bronx's Lanape High School, were representative:

> You know, I hate these classes [in the general curricular regimen]. The stuff they give us is so simple and dumb. They think we're stupid or something. That's fucked up! So, I just have to think about them being stupid to calm down so I can get the schoolwork done.[39]

The third teaching approach in the general regimen I will label the "Holding Action." This approach was designed to occupy students for a class period without disruptive behavior or the appearance of it, so as to reduce teacher stress and disruptions of activities in adjacent classrooms. In this approach, teachers either presented a movie about the subject the class was covering or required students to complete an assignment (answer questions or outline the textbook chapter) to be handed in at the end of the period.[40] Of course, these activities were not devoid of educational value, but it was strikingly clear that, as in the "Educational" approach, the primary agents of instruction were the students themselves and not the teacher. The big difference was that in the "Holding Action" approach, much of the activity the teacher required students to do was copying material verbatim from a book, which did not require the development of critical thinking associated with the ability to independently and skillfully analyze a problem for the purpose of arriving at a conclusion or solution—a skill, it should be emphasized, that teachers using the "Educational" approach worked diligently to develop in their students.[41]

As I just mentioned, teachers lacking the pedagogical tactics to make the subject matter interesting employed the "Holding Action" strategy to reduce their own stress associated with trying to teach using an interactive approach. The exact reason a teacher was unable to spark students' interest in the subject matter did not necessarily have to do with not wanting students to be interested. Rather, it was an inability to connect the material with students' lives or interests. Often despite a teacher's effort to reduce stress using the "Holding Action" approach, students either drifted off or began to talk and carry on when they were free to conduct themselves as they wished, and this created the appearance of a classroom in which the teacher had lost control. When this ensued, and there were classrooms where it occurred daily, the teachers experiencing it would become more stressed, prompting them to panic and create tasks that simply occupied the students' time. The comments of Hugh, who taught history at Los Angeles's Chester Himes High School, were representative of teachers using the "Holding Action" approach:

I'm so frustrated with my second- and fifth-hour classes. They are just so disruptive, and it really doesn't matter what I try to do to get their attention. They just go off and do whatever they want to do—and let me tell you, they aren't doing school-related stuff. . . . I've tried a lot of stuff to get them interested, but whatever I tried hasn't worked, so I now just give them an assignment to complete by the end of class, and this holds their disruptiveness down. It also holds my stress down.[42]

Students who experienced this teaching approach faced several academic consequences. The primary problem was that they quickly recognized that when these teachers did present material verbally, it would be nearly a direct recitation of the book or other material so most students stopped reading the assigned material. This impeded their general reading ability, particularly their pace and comprehension in other subject matter. A typical example involved Susan, a 15-year-old freshman at the Bronx's Van Twiller High School.

When Susan was in ninth grade, she had two teachers who gave lectures on the material they assigned students to read. During her classes, I observed that Susan would busily take notes on what the teacher was presenting. She rarely, if ever, asked questions, but she would concentrate on what the teacher was discussing. During free time at school, I heard Susan on three occasions tell her friends that she would not bother to read her history or English homework because the teachers in both of those classes would tell them what was in it. Instead, she said that at night she would concentrate on completing her math and science homework. However, when Susan was in the second semester of her sophomore year, she complained that her teacher did not tell them what was in the book they were using and she could not keep up with the reading and was afraid she would fail the course:

I just hate this class I'm taking because it is so much reading and no matter how hard I try, I just can't read what Ms. Alonso is assigning. I'm really worried that I could fail this course because I'm not able to keep up. . . . Ms. Alonso is not like most of my other English teachers. She doesn't go over the reading in class. She just gives us additional information about it, and that's not like what I got before. I guess I'm out of reading practice, but I hope it doesn't mean I fail English.[43]

A second impact of teachers resorting to the "Holding Action" approach when they lacked pedagogical skills—even though they possessed the knowledge to be effective—was exemplified by Ms. Gables, a tenth-grade math teacher at Los Angeles's Chumash High School. She was teaching a geometry lesson on acute angles and began by asking the students to refer to the assigned reading in the textbook, whereupon a student asked a question that related to two of the fundamental properties of the math principle being presented. Ms. Gables responded by telling the class that those principles directly related to the ones she was presenting that day. When many of the students indicated through frowns, smirks, and shrugs that they either did not understand that material or could not see the connection, she tried to explain but had difficulty translating the abstract concepts. The students incrementally began to disengage and turned either to rereading the previous chapter's material or to talking quietly.

Even though Ms. Gables could see the inattention, she continued presenting while allowing the students to do whatever they wanted. She ended the class by telling them to complete the review questions at the end of the textbook chapter and hand them in the next day, and she reminded them that exam questions would come from the review questions. This type of interaction, where Ms. Gables found it difficult or impossible to explain geometry principles, recurred throughout the semester, and she did not once tell students who were obviously not paying attention to refocus on what she was teaching. In typical "Holding Action" fashion she instead allowed them to disengage and tried to compensate by telling them to read the chapter and complete the review questions. Because she weighted the homework assignments higher than the exams, most of her students passed the course, but it was clear that many did not master geometry. They generally said they liked Ms. Gables, but they also said they could not understand her. The comments of Melissa, a 15-year-old sophomore who received a B grade in the course, were representative:

> Ms. Gables is such a nice person, and she tries to explain things, but she really does a terrible job. I really don't have any idea about geometry, but she lets us do the review questions to pass the course so I just want to get out of this course and get to algebra again.[44]

The third reason that teachers used a "Holding Action" approach was that they were physically or mentally tired of teaching, and it provided the relief they needed to get through the day and remain employed. Generally, these teachers were in the middle to latter part of their careers and the fatigue they felt was related to the years of effort that they had applied to teaching. Many were quite vocal in their support of students and students' need for additional help, but in the classroom their tendency was to require little if any work from the students or themselves.

The example of Mr. Tayes was representative. He had been teaching for twenty-five years and was the instructor of a required history course at Los Angeles's Polk High School. Many students expressed interest in the material but said their interest would vary depending on the topic. Students in Mr. Tayes's third- through fifth-period classes were coming from their required math course, so they appeared to be looking to "de-stress" in Mr. Tayes's history course. They took time to settle down and stop talking at the beginning of class. During that time, Mr. Tayes would take roll and have them write down the two questions he had written on the board. Then he instructed them that the answers to the questions were in the current chapter of their textbook, and that they would have to find those answers, write them down, and hand them in by the end of the period. Mr. Tayes would tell them that if they finished this assignment before the end of the period, they could have "soft-voice discussions" in class. The comments of Mr. Tayes reflected those of other teachers who adopted this approach to teaching:

> I'm into avoiding problems until I retire in five years. So, I just give them a couple of questions that come from the readings and tell them to answer them by the end of the period; and after they do answer them they can do work for their other courses or talk in a low voice if they want to. I used to do it differently, but it was much more work and quite tiring because you got more problems keeping them from acting up. This way, I keep everything calm, which is what I want after teaching this long.[45]

Resentment toward students provided the fourth reason that some teachers took a "Holding Action" approach. Teachers who resented students were found to have developed this resentment early in their careers when they had come to teaching with the expectation that students from lower-income families only needed teachers with substantive and pedagogical skills and a commitment to teaching. They thought of themselves as this type of teacher, they prepared lesson plans, and they enthusiastically attempted to present the material in an interesting manner, but they were met with what they interpreted as indifference or rejection by students.

Some students did reject these teachers' efforts, but the vast majority either were preoccupied with nonacademic issues impinging on their lives or lacked the skills required to perform at the level these teachers expected. The upshot was that the teachers felt their efforts were for naught and reacted by suspending their commitment to present material in an interactive and interesting manner. In most cases, they would disengage and substitute their effort with an approach that left students with the task of completing assignments during class time and, in essence, with the primary responsibility for teaching themselves. The comments of Ms. Vernon, who was in her second year of teaching at Los Angeles's Chumash High School, revealed the interplay between dashed expectations, frustration, and resentment that led to the adoption of this teaching approach:

> These students just seem hopeless to me. You try to teach them, and all you get is attitude from them. So, if they don't want me to teach them I'm just going to give them the textbook, tell them to read it, and if they don't do it or don't get it, they'll just become unemployed! I've tried, God knows I've tried, so it's on them.[46]

What is particularly important about the teachers who had developed a resentment toward their students is that once this resentment emerged, it affected how those teachers regarded students from that time forward, believing that they simply were not interested in education. The comments of Mr. Manning were an example:

> I've been teaching in this school for nearly fourteen years, and before this at [Evergreen] which is just like this one, and the students attending both are just really not that interested in learning. They're interested in other things, and feel this is a waste of their time. There is just little, if anything, that you can teach these students. It's frustrating, but it's just the way it is.[47]

Since the schools in the present study were dominated by non-White students, it is difficult to determine whether this prejudice was based on race, class, or a little of both. Teachers having this prejudice were aware of the demographic composition of the school and unlikely to make prejudicial statements that included a reference to ethnicity or race. In all the years of research I recorded ethnicity or race used in a prejudicial way fourteen times, but there were 103 occasions when social class was mentioned. The comments of Ms. Banks were an example:

> I would not be too upset with your class because it is not you, it is just these students do not really care about education. They are from poor families and just haven't developed any interest in academics. It really won't matter how much time you prepare, they'll just go through the motions and not do much of any studying. So, don't drive yourself crazy because I been here nine years

and you are going to see that this is the type of student you're going to get every year.[48]

The fifth reason for teachers taking a "Holding Action" approach was when they had been granted a transfer to another school for the following academic year and wanted to put in the minimal effort to teach their current students. This usually occurred in the second semester of the school year, because in the first semester they would not yet have been officially notified that their transfer request had been approved, so they conducted themselves in ways that would be understood as "professional" to preserve the transfer option. A representative example involved Mr. Kaliki, who had been teaching for six years at the Bronx's Lanape High School:

> Hey, I'm not killing myself with these students any more. They need so much help that I'm just not running myself down to do it. Plus, I'm off to another high school next year and I just don't want to put all this time in and go home with a headache each day until the end of the year.[49]

When teachers took the "Holding Action" approach in the general curricular regimen, where students had fewer skills than in the honors and advanced placement regimens, it increased the academic risks for these students. I observed two student behavioral responses to the "Holding Action" approach. The first response, such as during a movie, was either to comply by watching the movie or to completely disengage and when there was some implicit agreement with the teacher, to put their heads down on their desks and rest while the movie was playing.

The second response was associated with classes where the teacher gave work to be completed in class. Most of the homework that was assigned by the teachers using the "Holding Action" approach simply required that the students find the material directly related to the study questions in the textbook and copy it word for word on a sheet of paper. This did not involve memorizing the material or developing any type of analytic skills that could and would be required in some of their subsequent classes or for success in their future standardized test scores. Thus, the important impact of this approach is that it established non-obvious learning impediments, which the students subjected to them would be required to overcome in their pursuit of reaching grade-level competency or else lag behind.

In sum, students were confronted with challenges associated with each of these three pedagogical approaches, and how well they managed these challenges affected whether they would be successful in transitioning to the next stage of their education.

STUDENT DILEMMAS AND DIVERGENT CURRICULAR REGIMENS

Students' placement in a curricular regimen forced them to acknowledge, either through acceptance or challenge, the placement and to assess their ability to reach their goals within it. For students in the advanced placement and honors regimens, who were thought to be either gifted or sufficiently prepared to meet the expectations of the program designed for gifted students, there was the constant challenge to master each new set of material. When the materials presented were either unclear to them because the teacher's presentation lacked clarity, was presented too quickly for full comprehension, or too advanced for the individual's present skill level, students became anxious. This anxiety was related to the general expectation that everyone selected for this regimen would understand the material, and thus it would be embarrassing if individuals placed in it would need to ask for help. The comments of Elvia, a 14-year-old freshman in the advanced placement regimen at Los Angeles's Tongva High School, were representative:

> I have not gotten what Mr. Driver [her math teacher] has been teaching the last week and a half. I just don't see the connection, and when he moves fast you need to know the parts before. I just can't stop worrying about this section because I'm not getting it, and the next section will assume I do. . . . I did not ask questions in class because we're supposed to be smart enough to get it, and I don't want to look like I don't belong [in the class].[50]

The two main strategies adopted by students confronting this problem were either to stay quiet and hide that they did not fully understand or to try to get help from another student after class. Most students claimed that these strategies worked because they understood enough to make it appear that they had understood it all, but that it eventually came back to haunt them when they needed a firm grasp of the material in order to answer another set of problems in future exercises and exams. Thus, even among students labeled gifted or exceptional, the interaction of a student with their teacher could create obstacles to a successful transition later if they were too shy or insecure to ask for help from the teacher.

Turning to the general curricular regimen, it should be remembered that students were assigned to this track as a result of a general procedure that involved some combination of scores on general knowledge tests, course grades, and teacher evaluations that indicated they were capable of completing material that would prepare them for college. What separated students in this group from those allowed to take advanced placement courses was the degree of assessed capability and skills. Teachers assigned to the general curricular regimen often acknowledged in conversations among themselves the enormous variation in knowledge and skills among their students. In part, they attributed this variation to the large number of students attending the school and the administration's goal to maximize the number of students in this regimen who were college-eligible. The comments of Emmet, an English teacher at Chumash High School in Los Angeles, were representative:

> I like teaching the students I've had in the school's general group, but it's a lot of work because we have so many students in this group, and they really have different levels of skill. I really think that because we have so many in this category and they vary so much, it puts too much pressure on us [teachers] to get them all where they need to be to get into college. . . . yeah, you're right, it is difficult for the students too because some will have a hard time catching up to where the rest of the class is.[51]

The impact of this situation for students in this curricular group was related to the "everyday curriculum" teachers chose. The demand to meet every student's needs, or some part of them, pressed teachers to concentrate their approach toward what they determined to be the average knowledge and skill level of a particular year's class.[52] At the extremes, this made some students in the schools I studied feel bored while others felt the same material was too difficult. Thus, for students at both extremes, this pedagogical approach had the effects of limiting them and making it more difficult to transition to the next education level. A representative case involved Emilio, a 16-year-old junior at the Bronx's Lanape High School. He was in Mr. Zim's advanced placement algebra course and having difficulty keeping up. In an effort to help Emilio, Mr. Zim spent time after school addressing his questions and what he needed to understand to improve. After one of these sessions, a colleague asked Mr. Zim why Emilio had been placed in the advanced math class if he was having problems. Here was Mr. Zim's response:

Emilio is quite smart and capable of doing well in this class, but he did not get all the background material he needed to do well at this point. It's my fault because I was his math teacher last year [in the general math course], and he was a straight A student, but I did not get to some of the foundations he needs for this advanced placement course because I had students who had real trouble with math and I had to teach them at a level they could understand. I always feel bad about students who get shortchanged, but in general algebra courses you've got to teach at a level that everyone will be able to understand; and that means somewhere between students who can understand complex math and those who have real trouble with abstract things.[53]

In brief, the largest problem facing students in both the general and vocational curricular regimens was that they were often being taught what was necessary for them to be successful in their present regimen, but not what they needed to be able to move to an advanced regimen. In terms of mobility, this created structural obstacles related to their academic preparation, the bureaucratic issue of having to be retested, and encountering teachers who would advocate for them to be placed in an advanced curricular regimen. In schools where both students and parents were reluctant to advocate for themselves or their children, these obstacles were significant.

One more issue at play for students in the general or vocational regimen had to do with their identification with a primary peer group and the pull of the feeling of belonging to it. In order to change direction and pursue an advanced curriculum, a student had to be dedicated toward that goal, which required leaving many of their closest friends, and the cultural pull of remaining with friends was strong.[54] Thus, in such situations, when a student was able to overcome their attachment to their friends and then confronted problems from the school's bureaucracy in making a change, they were inclined to abandon the effort and revert to their current regimen. In this way, primary peer-group identification and attachment made students' attempts at curricular mobility more challenging.[55] The comments of Nancy, a 16-year-old sophomore at LA's Polk High School, were representative:

Yeah, I'm in the math honors class, but I ain't staying. . . . Well, the work's really hard, and plus I'm in a class with assholes I don't even like, so I want to go back to the classes I had before, but it ain't easy to switch around. . . . Yeah, so I been thinking if I keep getting bad grades like I been trying to get, I bet they'll switch me, and that'll be great to me.[56]

A problem associated with teachers in the general curricular regimen who employed a "Holding Action" approach was that students in their classes did not receive adequate knowledge and skill development to move from one track to another. Teachers using that approach did not do much instruction, so teaching fell largely on students, which was a problem for lower-income students because they lacked financial and educational resources at home to compensate. Thus, the chances for a student in a general curriculum class who wanted to move into the advanced placement or honors regimen were structurally limited.[57] The comments that Georgia, a 16-year-old sophomore at Los Angeles's Chumash High School, made to the dean of her class highlight this problem:

> I don't want to be in Mr. Landry's classes. We don't learn anything. We just watch films or do stupid work of answering questions from the textbook. How am I supposed to get into college if I ain't learning the stuff colleges want? Please, get me out of his classes 'cause I want to learn just like the students in the honors classes, and we ain't. I want to get into one of them classes and I ain't never going to if I stay in his classes.[58]

As a result of their meeting, Georgia was assigned to a different class and teacher, and she did improve to the point that she was admitted to the honors history and English classes the following year. Despite Georgia's success, the structural problem created by teachers like Mr. Landry employing a "Holding Action" approach remained in all the schools of this study.

Turning to students in vocational regimens, the issues were somewhat different from those that students faced in other regimens. Most of the students that I observed in vocational regimens were quite interested in the skills being taught. They were generally focused, and each day worked diligently at their assigned tasks. The teachers were also quite competent in the skills they were teaching and in communicating how to successfully complete specific tasks. What became a problem for some students had to do with the types of vocations they were being trained in, not the training itself. Most of the vocations were traditional trades like auto mechanics, carpentry, electric circuitry, drafting, and elementary computer technology, which created three issues for students. First, the high schools seemed unaware when the trades they were teaching were highly competitive and students would find few openings. Second, technological advances in many trades would require students to undergo further training after graduation in order to be employable. Third, the vocations that schools taught were often not the newly emerging ones but those that were fading. The result was that many students were disappointed. The comments of Cynthia and Roberto were representative.

Cynthia was an 18-year-old senior in her last two weeks at the Bronx's Van Twiller High School:

> I was taking courses in computers, but it wasn't detailed or anything and so I wish I had gone maybe to one of those specialized schools in computers because I didn't get enough to give me a chance at a job when I get out. I didn't think so at the time, but it's kind of a waste of time for me taking these vo-ed courses because I ain't going to get a job from what I learned. . . . Now I'm going to have to go to trade school when I get out to learn what I didn't learn here.[59]

Roberto was an 18-year-old senior at Los Angeles's Chumash High School:

> This fucking course that I took from Mr. Innis is really stupid because I thought I'd be able to get a good job after taking it, but he didn't know enough about the new computer stuff that regulates the engines of a lot of cars now. If I don't know that shit, no regular auto shop is going to hire me. I'd have to get a job at a dealership where they'd send me to their school to learn, but getting a job at a dealership out of high school is a long shot 'cause everyone wants to get with them. I definitely should've taken something else.[60]

In sum, both the structure of the curriculum and its implementation created obstacles for students at these high schools, and they also made it difficult for students to change curricular regimens. When this occurred, it impacted the subsequent transition process for students.

THE COUNSELING OF STUDENTS

One organizational unit that has not received appropriate attention from sociologists studying education transitions is the school counseling department.[61] It is not clear why, but there is a perception that students have so few interactions with counseling staff that these interactions probably are not significant to the success of students' transitions. Nonetheless, my observations of student interactions with counselors—and of students who had no such interactions—show how that experience or its absence could influence a student's ability to advance.[62]

Each school in this study had a counseling staff of five to ten members with formal training specific to counseling, and some had teaching experience as well. The exact number of counselors at a school could vary depending on whether a school had been granted a special program(s) that included

TABLE 3.1 Five General Student Situations Faced by Counselors

Situation 1: Students indicated at the time of interaction with a counselor that they wanted to go on to college, but they demonstrated through grades and test scores that they had not achieved the level of competence in all required subject matter to be admitted.

Situation 2: Students indicated at the time of interaction that they were not sure if they wanted to go on to college, but they demonstrated through grades and test scores that they had achieved the level of competence in the required subject matter to be admitted.

Situation 3: Students indicated at the time of interaction that they were not sure if they wanted to go on to college, but they demonstrated periodically that they had the ability to achieve the level of competence in the required subject matter to be admitted.

Situation 4: Students indicated at the time of interaction that they did not want to go on to college, but they demonstrated consistently or periodically that they had the ability to achieve the level of competence required to graduate from high school.

Situation 5: Students indicated at the time of interaction that they did not want to go on to college and demonstrated that they had not achieved the level of competence required to graduate from high school.

counselors as a component. Each counseling staff confronted five general student situations, which are presented in table 3.1. It should be remembered that the five situations presented in table 3.1 are static, and students experiencing them could change their thinking about them and could increase the skills and knowledge they would use to address them over the time they were in high school; and when this occurred, it necessitated an adjustment on the part of counselors.

The five student situations presented in table 3.1 were followed by eight general responses by the counselors. For the first situation in table 3.1, counselors would either discourage or moderately encourage the student by pointing out their academic shortcomings at that point in time, emphasizing that greater effort and care was required to achieve the grades for college eligibility. Examples of moderate encouragement or discouragement can be seen in the interactions of counselors at Los Angeles's Polk High School and the Bronx's Lanape High School with students Darcy and Casandra, respectively. Darcy began his conversation with the counselor by saying, "I'd like to go to college, I'm really looking forward to going and becoming a lawyer." The counselor responded by saying, "That's good, but if you really want to do that, it is not going to be easy, and you will need to start working much harder at getting better grades because you will not be able to get into college with the grades you're currently receiving." Darcy responded, "Yeah, I know, but up 'til now I really didn't know what I wanted, and now I do."[63]

In the case of Casandra, the counselor began the session by saying, "Casandra, if you really want to become a nurse practitioner, you just have to make up your mind that you have got to take all the science courses and do very well in them. I can see you going to college and entering nursing, but if you don't make a bigger commitment, or you find the science part too difficult, then you shouldn't get too focused on that because you'll just become very disappointed and there are certainly many more occupations that you can be successful at." Cassandra answered, "I understand that. I been not applying myself because I hadn't known what I wanted to do before."[64]

For the second situation in table 3.1, counselors encouraged the students to maintain their excellence, reviewed whether they had taken all the courses required to that point, and established a schedule for the remaining semesters that would satisfy the requirements for graduation and admission to college.[65]

In the third situation in table 3.1, the counselors assumed one of two strategies. Some mildly encouraged students by asking them to continue to think about college, highlighting that their grades had indicated they were capable of doing well enough to become college-eligible and stressing what courses they would need in order to meet the entrance requirements. The other strategy was to take a more neutral stance, review what was required to complete high school, and make sure the students' schedules were appropriate to meet these requirements. The comments of Mr. Dennis, a counselor at Los Angeles's Chester Himes High School, captures both strategies employed by counselors at the schools studied when they confronted students who weren't sure they wanted to attend college but periodically demonstrated the capability of completing the requirements:

> Rudy is a good kid that just hasn't made up his mind yet about whether he wants to go to college or not. His grades and scores indicate that if he wants to go he is capable of being successful, but here again, until the kid makes up his mind you can't think that he will eventually come around to deciding to go or not because I have had countless numbers of kids over fifteen years at this school that have not decided one way or the other by the time they leave. My colleague [a counselor at another school] usually counsels this type of kid by telling them what they would need to do if they decide to go to college, but I would rather focus on telling them what is required to graduate from high school if they keep following their current path and emphasize that this will allow them to successfully get into college.[66]

The fourth situation in table 3.1 found counselors actively discouraging students from thinking about becoming college-eligible and concentrating on having them graduate from high school. Most of the students when asked would voice ambivalence about attending college, and a significant number were having difficulty passing their academic courses. Many of these students were reading below grade level, and the counselors focused on finding a solution so they could graduate from high school. An example of this can be seen in the comments of a counselor at Brooklyn's Knickerbocker High School:

> Yes, Jerry, I know you're not sure about college, but right now I think that you just need to try and do better with your grades in your core courses. If you do that you can at least get your high school diploma and then, if you decide that you want to go to college, then you can see what the college counselors tell you is going to be needed for getting in. You know, if they tell you that you need a course that you didn't have here, you can always take it at adult night school. But right now let's just have you pass all the courses needed for getting your diploma, OK?[67]

The fifth situation in table 3.1 involved students who said they did not want to go on to college. These students could be divided between those focused on getting out of high school and starting work and those who did not care if they graduated or not. For students who indicated they did not want to go to college but wanted to graduate, the general response from counselors was to mildly encourage them to continue passing all of their courses so they could graduate on time. The comments of Ms. Conti, who was at Los Angeles's Tongva High School, were an example:

> I told Jada what she needs to do over the next two years to graduate with the rest of her class. I used to try to help her improve her grade point average, but I found that it is better to counsel students like her as to what they need to graduate on time.[68]

The second group of students in the fifth situation of table 3.1 included students who said they were not interested in any formal type of education in the future and did not care whether they graduated from high school. These students tended to shy away from participating in educational activities and regularly handed in incomplete homework. They also presented themselves as simply biding their time in high school, and often expressed this to peers, teachers, and staff. When discussing students in the faculty lounge, teachers would sometimes ask each other why a certain student bothered to come to school since they showed no interest in what was being taught.

These teachers were frustrated, but these students were also frustrated and, if asked by teachers and counselors why they came to school if they were not interested in receiving an education, they were generally brutally honest in saying it was either required by law or their friends were there. A typical example involved the response of Terrence, an eleventh-grader at Oakland's Miwok High School, to this question from his math teacher, who was frustrated because Terrence was talking and not paying attention: "I come to school to see and hang out with friends. So, if I want to hang with them and have fun, I got to come here."[69]

Counselors at all the schools in this study would generally assume a neutral approach toward these students. They were generally friendly with the goal of keeping these students from dropping out. Thus, they would consistently remind these students what they needed to do to graduate and on occasion warn them that they might be asked to leave the school for disciplinary reasons, if they did not modify their behavior.

Counselor Actions That Create Student Problems

There were a number of motives for the actions taken by counselors. Motives are a delicate issue to research as they cannot be directly observed, in contrast with concrete behaviors and outcomes. I have taken great care to identify only motives that I observed through a person's speech and confirmed with three additional independent people who said they observed the counselor expressing this motive in at least two other contexts. Finally, to document the motive's impact, and this is key, I would connect a person stating a motive for a particular action or actions with that person's observed behavior to see if there was consistency or inconsistency with the stated motive. In cases where all matched, I have used it as evidence of not only the motive but its impact on a student's behavior.

Counselors had the responsibility of advising students on how to advance to their next educational destination. In that endeavor, they reviewed students' academic status and evaluated their performance in the courses they had taken, their progress toward stated long-term educational goals, and the curricular units they needed to move from one grade to another. On the basis of this review, they provided a plan for the student to achieve success. Thus, a counselor's job ideally involved encouraging a successful transition to further education or the job markets. However, in the process of executing these duties, counselors could inadvertently impact students in a variety of negative ways.

The first condition under which counselors could have a negative impact on students was when there was an error in the evaluation process. While reviewing a student's academic record in their current curricular regimen, counselors could incorrectly assess the student's academic skills, knowledge, and capabilities. In some cases, a mistake occurred because a teacher had made an error of judgment in evaluating the student's performance and was either overly generous or overly punitive. In other cases, counselors were victims of their own prejudices concerning the student based on the curriculum regimen to which the student had been assigned, and they accepted that placement as the result of an accurate evaluation and advised the student based on what was known in general about students in that regimen.

The result for students whose academic capabilities were higher than typical for their curricular regimen was that the counselor guided them toward courses that presented less material or material that was less challenging than they were capable of handling. Thus, even when the student received high grades, the counselor was less likely to advocate for them to transfer to a higher curricular regimen. The comments of Tina and Murray were representative. Tina was a counselor at Los Angeles's Chumash High School who had reevaluated how she executed her duties:

> I am definitely going to advocate for Jaime to be moved to advanced placement courses. In the past, I would never do this because I was sure that a student's current placement was based on solid criteria, but I don't believe that anymore because there are so many students and we make mistakes, and then the students change and get better and that is not incorporated enough into our counseling. Over the last six years, I am afraid to think how many students whose chances to go to college I hurt because I just went with their entry-level assessment and did not advocate strongly for them to be moved up when they demonstrated they could. I was so foolish, and I am haunted to this day by what I failed to do. So, tomorrow there are eight students that I'm strongly advocating to be placed in advanced placement courses.[70]

Murray was a counselor at Brooklyn's Knickerbocker High School:

> You know, in the past I would rarely get too involved in trying to move a student from one set of courses to a more advanced set. I am embarrassed to say that most of it was that I just believed that students were placed where they were for a reason, and that even if they were very successful, they needed to stay in it and remain successful. Plus, honestly, and I'm not proud of this, believe me, if you were going to try to get the student moved, you had to do a lot of preparation work to make the case, and any extra work I tried to avoid.

I am so mad at myself for not doing more in the past because a lot of students showed they could do more advanced work and I did not try to get them moved. Now, I can't tell you how all of my colleagues in counseling do their jobs, but I can tell you that I've changed and do what I should have done over the previous ten years.[71]

The second condition under which counselors had a negative impact on low-income students had to do with the large number of students each counselor was required to serve. This created a situation where the counselor was overburdened, which led them to pay more attention to helping a student complete the requirements for graduating from their current curricular regimen and less to providing counseling on what would be most useful for them in gaining entrance to a more advanced regimen.[72] The comments of Laura, a counselor at Los Angeles's Chester Himes High School, were an example:

I have so many students to see that it is all I can do to get the information I need to counsel them on getting through with their current curriculum, let alone figuring out what they need to switch curriculums, except to tell them to study harder and get better grades. For me to do a better job, I'd have to have time to go over a number of things and, given our workload, time is not something we have.[73]

In addition to the structural conditions associated with tests used to assess academic capabilities and counselor-student ratios that influenced counselors' motivation for how they helped students, a number of other issues impacted students that had to do with counselors' subjective judgment or personality. For example, there were times when a counselor would deliberately sabotage a student who had stated a goal of moving to a more advanced curriculum because they believed that they were acting in the best interest of the student whom they had assessed as incapable of being successful in a more advanced curriculum and who needed to be protected from a situation that would expose their weaknesses and create psychological stress. The comments of Jordan, a counselor at Chester Himes High School in Los Angeles, were representative of the counselors who did this and their rationale for doing it:

I was just talking to a student about their future here at the school and tried to get them to lower their goals a bit because their goals were just out of proportion to where they were academically. The problem is that he was getting Bs in his current courses, and I'm afraid that if he did move up he would find it too difficult and his confidence would be shaken. So, I've been trying to get him to stay where he's at and improve his grades from Bs to As.[74]

Another reason for counselors to undermine students was that they were at some level resentful that the students were receiving more opportunities than the counselor believed they were entitled to.[75] The comments of Carol, a counselor at Los Angeles's James K. Polk High School, were representative:

> Do you know Darnel? Well, he's a junior and has been given so much help since coming to this school. The kid thinks he's really smart and some faculty tell him that too. The thing is, he's an average student, nowhere near what he or some faculty think. Hell, I would have been valedictorian at my school and gone to Harvard if I had got the attention he did. . . . [S]o when I meet with him, I try to bring him back to reality by suggesting a more modest approach to courses he should take.[76]

Of course, the present research is not a survey. I have made no attempt to determine how many counselors had the motives discussed here or the number of students who were affected by these motives. The point is that I was able to identify these sets of motives, and when these motives were active in counselors' interactions with students, the students faced added obstacles. In these cases, students had to see how they could get around the counselor and pursue their goal. A typical example of this involved Ada, a second-semester junior at the Bronx's Lanape High School:

> Mr. Kallin [her counselor] tells me every time we meet that I need to keep getting good grades and go on to Hunter College, but I told him that I want to go to Yale or Swarthmore and have been in touch with them. I know he doesn't seem to like that because he never says anything about them. You know, he just avoids talking about them. I think he doesn't want me to go to Yale or Swarthmore, and I'm not sure exactly why, but I just got to figure out how to move forward without him messing me up.[77]

In sum, besides being a "positive gatekeeper" by ensuring that students get access to needed courses, counselors can have an important negative impact on students' expectations for not only their current semester and year but for subsequent ones as well. Depending on how they interact with students, counselors can increase expectations, reinforce and strengthen existing ones, or reduce the expectations a student holds.[78] Particularly salient for the present study was a dynamic where expectations had a direct positive or negative influence on performance, and the level of performance then fed back to influence expectations, which in turn fed back to influence performance.[79] This dynamic impacted some students' ability to make a smooth transition to the next stage of their education because they had fewer sources of information that could aid them in making the best choices for themselves.

SOME FINISHING COMMENTS

This chapter identified a number of problems students faced in the curricular structure that organized their instruction (i.e., a continuous or discrete approach discussed in chapter 1 and the various quasi-tracking designs), how the teachers chose to implement the curriculum (i.e., whether they chose the "Educational," "Instructional," or "Holding Action" approach), and the manners in which counselors who provided course and career guidance in the schools under study performed their tasks. As with the preceding chapters, an effort was made to avoid suggesting that all students experienced each of these problems, or that any one problem prohibited students from achieving academic excellence or competence. What can be confidently concluded is that each challenge had the potential to create an obstacle that was particularly significant for low-income students to manage. How successful students from low-income backgrounds were in overcoming these obstacles varied depending on their own skills and motives and the amount of assistance they received from various human resources they had access to at school and at home.

Obviously, school structure matters in terms of the quantity and quality of information students receive and the academic skills they develop. A student's placement in this structure will present them with opportunities for growth, but these opportunities are fraught with challenges, particularly for students in non-honors curricular regimens because they have to find a way to master the material and skills established for their regimen and, if they desired to transition to college, find ways to gain access to material presented in curricular regimens higher than the one they were in. Without extracurricular aid, their goals to move up among curricular regimens were difficult to realize; and without this mobility, their chance of being competitive in obtaining entrance to higher-status universities was more tenuous.

Now, let us turn to the issue of counseling. This book is about the obstacles that students face in making transitions to the next stages of their lives, so the focus has been on how these obstacles arise and the challenges they present. Most students, not all, have goals for their future. It is this basic part of the human condition that school counselors had to work with. It forced them to expand, reinforce, or reduce a student's horizon. The approach counselors chose was determined by the student's goals, their record of academic achievement, and whatever additional information they had to suggest that the record does not reflect the student's true capabilities. Further, the counseling staff could be an important organizational resource, though not necessarily the most important, facilitating transitions from one curricular regimen to another or from one grade to the next. However, the counseling staffs in each of the high schools studied had on average a ratio of one counselor to 100–150 students, and thus were too small to adequately address every student's needs, forcing students to assume much of this responsibility themselves—and creating additional obstacles in their transition process.

CHAPTER 4

The Impact of Cultural and Social Capital

... we should treat language like money marked with the public
stamp.

MARCUS FABIUS QUINTILIANUS,
An Orator's Education, 95 CE

Do we need friends more in good fortune or in bad? ... Friendship, then, is more necessary in bad fortune, and so it is useful
friends that one wants in this case.

ARISTOTLE,
Nicomachean Ethics, 350 BC(?)

THIS STUDY IS CONCERNED WITH THE CHALLENGES faced by low-
income youth in obtaining what scholars call human capital,[1] but there are
other forms of capital that can aid in the accumulation of employment and
workplace skills or supplement them.[2] The topics of cultural capital and social
capital have occupied many sociologists interested in accounting for inequality
in education. Researchers typically consider "cultural capital" to be the acquisition of language and social skills associated with what is currently valued in a
society, such as ways of presenting oneself and interacting with people and institutions.[3] "Social capital" is most often considered the human network one
accumulates that can aid in the pursuit of interests, although some researchers
include elements like organizational memberships and trust.[4]

Most researchers would acknowledge that social skills, knowledge, and
networks can vary over one's life, but those established during high school
often prove particularly significant because the high school years are a strategic point in a person's transition to adult life.[5] Renowned sociologist Pierre
Bourdieu argued that structural disparities in how people accumulate social
and cultural capital explain how contemporary European society reproduces
its inequalities. Many American sociologists also consider both social and
cultural capital—and structural disparities that underlie them—relevant in
explaining inequality in education.[6]

It would be fair to say that there is less supply of social and cultural capital for low-income students than their middle-class counterparts. That is the nature of these capitals, and their connection to material wealth. Middle-class students inherit a good deal of both social and cultural capital from their parents and the community they are part of. However, though in shorter supply, social and cultural capital do exist in low-income communities and schools. This chapter focuses on the cultural and social resources that might be used as capital in securing academic success, and on the difficulties students from low-income families face in their efforts to develop these resources into capital for themselves. Before proceeding, a clarification of the concepts of social and cultural capital is in order. At the root of these two concepts is the idea of "capital," and "capital" is a concept of something that can be used for gainful activity.[7] In that regard, it can be applied to the exchanging of one asset (an object or service) for another, or purchasing a desired asset. Or it can be used to produce something that can then be sold or exchanged.

Sociologists have used the concepts of social and cultural capital in a number of ways. I will use them in a manner that captures those aspects of capital mentioned above because they aid in understanding the difficulties encountered by low-income students as they pursue their high school education. As the findings discussed in this chapter indicate, the cultural and social capital accumulated by the students of this study had two time horizons: (1) the short term, where their "use values" had a specific purpose for a relatively brief period; and (2) the long term, where their "use values" were available over an extended period and in different arenas.

CULTURAL CAPITAL

It has often been theorized that cultural capital complements social and human capital among the assets—that is, the resources—that individuals need to advance socioeconomically. It plays a significant role in selecting or rejecting things and people, and in promoting or preventing an individual's pursuit of their goals.[8] The prevailing view is that lacking cultural capital during high school inhibits students' transitions within and outside of their educational institutions, particularly if they come from low-income families.[9] There have been critiques of the concept and its use in analyzing education outcomes, but I have found the concept—with my alterations described earlier in the chapter—useful in understanding the difficulties that many low-income students face in their educational transitions.[10]

What is most often taken to constitute cultural capital are the values and styles associated with the dominant culture. In the United States, these include the value of socioeconomic mobility as a perpetual goal; the intrinsic worth of working hard, saving, and investing in the future; the knowledge of middle-class etiquette in social interactions; proficiency in vocabulary, syntax, and pronunciation of English as used by middle-class society; and cultural skills to navigate societal institutions for success.[11] Now let us see how these aspects of culture can be subverted, aborted, or arrested to create educational transition problems for students from low-income families.

Two dominant expressions of cultural capital for the low-income youth in this study were language usage and social etiquette. Ultimately, the judgment of others as to what constituted a sufficient quantity and quality shaped the advantages or disadvantages students obtained. The schools in this study generally used and taught a middle-class English that they would consider "standard" because it was assumed to be an appropriate middle ground between upper- and lower-class dialects in accent and idiom.[12]

Students who recognized that they spoke a dialect of English, and that teachers expected them to speak middle-class English in order to succeed, faced a difficult choice and challenge. The choice was between using what was likely to help them become successful in school and the dialect or vernacular valued in their community or peer group.[13] There was no reason a student could not be competent in both, but that was not easy to accomplish, and the strategy to achieve competence required students to devote extra time to developing the skills of each language and being flexible enough to switch at the appropriate social times.[14] The challenge involved mastering the language skills expected in the school, which required an investment in instructional and practice time. In addition, for students who were committed to perfecting their language skills and willing to invest the time, it was important to have peers and family members who were proficient in the normative vernacular. Thus, as in learning a foreign language, students had to be instructed in grammar and given the opportunity to practice speaking the language.

Likewise, having people around who would correct errors in usage or pronunciation, or who pointed out when a phrase was structured incorrectly or used in an inappropriate context, was beneficial. Adelia, a freshman at Los Angeles's Polk High School, offered a good example of this challenge playing out. She often said, in English, "In two days more, I will be going to Ms. E's class." One day a friend told her she was using Spanish syntax and it was more correct to say, "In two more days, I will be going to Ms. E's class." She giggled and said, "Of course, I'll definitely remember that." It was much easier for students whose first language was not English to accept criticism, however, than it was for native speakers who used an English dialect and often interpreted a correction as a suggestion that they were "stupid." For these students, issues of language competency and preference dogged them throughout high school.[15]

Gilberto Conchas has highlighted the importance of teachers' beliefs and behaviors in creating success for low-income, non-White urban students.[16] Given that most of the students had few (though not zero) peers, community adults, and family members who were willing and able to speak the "standard" English vernacular, in most of the high schools I studied, teachers were responsible for providing examples of correct syntax and for correcting students' mistakes in pronunciation and usage, or letting them know if their phrasing was correct. In the present study, however, non-language arts teachers (i.e., non-English teachers) rarely if ever made reference to "a correct" way to speak, even when a student's speech or writing required a correction to meet society's generally accepted standard. Teachers most frequently corrected an imprecise pronunciation but left incorrect syntax to the language arts teachers.

When a student used incorrect syntax, there often were a number of reasons a teacher did not address it. One reason had to do with teachers trying to connect socially with students, to get the students to think of them as friends. These teachers reasoned that if the students liked them, they were more likely to try to please them by doing what they were asked. A representative example comes from Ms. Evans, an English teacher at Oakland's Miwok High School:

> I don't really try to correct the students when they say something incorrectly mainly because I'm trying to get them to like me, and that just doesn't help. Remember, if they like you, they will try to please you because at this age they don't really do things for themselves but for other people, and that means they'll complete more of their homework than if they don't like you. So, you get more classroom success from doing things this way.[17]

A second reason teachers did not correct usage and grammar was to avoid alienating students, in the hope they would be cooperative in class and not create trouble while instruction was occurring. These teachers reasoned that being critical of the way their students spoke would be interpreted as being disrespectful and cause those who felt disrespected to disrupt instruction. The comments of Mr. Raines, a math teacher at the Bronx's Lanape High School, serve as an example:

> I never try to correct the lousy English these students usually use because this is only going to cause the ones you correct to act out and interrupt the class so that nothing gets done for the entire hour. It's a lose-lose situation, nobody learns anything, and I get a headache, so I just let them say things the way they want, and usually it's the most awful phrasing you ever heard. But, hey, I teach numbers and it doesn't really affect that.[18]

A third reason was that some teachers thought it was more strategic to work through students' natural language usage to reach the course content. The comments of Ms. Lawrence, a social studies teacher at Los Angeles's Chester Himes High School, were an example:

> The best way is to concentrate on getting the students to know the content of the material, to just let them express themselves the way they feel best and not get bogged down with whether they are expressing themselves correctly. When they feel comfortable using their everyday language, they are more capable of grasping the content, and it's the content that is the most important part of learning.[19]

A fourth reason that non-language arts teachers did not correct students was that some teachers themselves used incorrect pronunciations or improper syntax. These were teachers who had come from lower-income or immigrant families and had not fully incorporated standard English pronunciation and syntax into their own speech, and this carried over to the classroom. In fact, I often observed teachers who were not aware of their own weaknesses in these areas and did not recognize the errors that students made. Those who were aware of their own inadequacies often refused to hold the students to a standard they themselves could not meet. Mr. Thompson, a science teacher at Los Angeles's Polk High School, commented:

> I'm not going to correct a student who is killing the English language. I'm no English teacher. I teach science. Hell, I also make mistakes so if I corrected them they'd just look at me and say, "You're correcting us, and you don't speak right yourself." So, I just let things like that go because otherwise I'd be telling them to 'do what I say and not what I do' sort of thing.[20]

As low-income students progressed, their chances for successful transitions depended on their use of what school officials reinforced as standard English.

It is significant to highlight that once they demonstrated language competency, they created a reputation for themselves, which formed an important
part of their cultural capital during high school and a resource to secure
future advantages. Demonstrating to teachers and administrators the ability
to speak without an accent and to use erudite expressions created a reputation
of language competence and, more importantly, of academic potential. As a
result, such students were often provided opportunities and advantages. The
comments of three teachers were representative of this occurring.

Mr. Larsen was a social studies teacher at Brooklyn's Knickerbocker High
School:

> Stacey did not do well on the last three quizzes I gave in class, but she is so
> good at articulating her positions during discussions that I have no doubt she
> will go on to be a very successful student. Of course, there were others in the
> class that did better than her in these quizzes, but she is just so far ahead of
> the others in the class in terms of her vocabulary and speaking that all she has
> to do is memorize to get an A in everything. . . . I just know that she'll get a
> great grade in this class, but if she has a hiccup along the way I'm not going to
> penalize her with a bad grade.[21]

Ms. Fitzgerald was an English teacher at Los Angeles's Polk High School:

> I have had Lucinda in class for just a short time, but she is not very good at
> expressing herself clearly. She gets the material and has done OK on the first
> exam, but I doubt that she will get anything above a C in the course. Students
> who talk street stuff are just treading water, no matter how smart they seem
> or really may be. I just know she's not going to explain the material properly
> and this will cost her not just in my class, but all of her classes to come.[22]

Ms. Jardeen was an assistant principal at Oakland's Kaiser High School:

> Eric, I've known you for a year and I have seen just how articulate you are in
> your classes, but you have been brought here today because this is the third
> time in a week and a half that you have been caught in the halls during class
> without a pass. You're a sophomore and know this is a violation of our rules.
> I'm not going to suspend you today and send a request home to your parents
> to return with you to school, but you have to start honoring the rules. It is
> clear to me that you are very articulate and have a very bright future, but you
> need to follow the rules.[23]

Although language was an important element of cultural capital, knowing
the conventional standards of social etiquette and when to demonstrate them

was an equally important cultural resource.[24] Such etiquette involved clothing, jewelry, body art, hairstyle, and verbal and physical behavior in social interactions. School districts often imposed restrictions on clothing, jewelry, and hairstyle in an effort to minimize interruptions attributable to student reactions to various presentations of individualism or religious affiliation.[25] By imposing these restrictions, school authorities became involved in building cultural capital related to the dominant society for those who abided by rules. That is, following rules allowed students to build cultural capital that was valued and thereby could be expended in the dominant society.

Alongside this official cultural capital, a set of social tastes emerged from peers and local adults, providing a parallel reserve of cultural capital whose value and expendability lay in low-income communities. Separating, or knowing when to separate, the local from the official society-at-large cultural capital proved challenging for students from lower-income families.[26] The comments of Dennis, Sharlene, and Ms. Calison were representative.

Dennis was a 15-year-old attending the Bronx's Lanape High School:

> I got in trouble in science class today 'cause the teacher says after I answered her question, "Talk right," and I say, "You talk right," and the class laughed. So, then she says I got the answer wrong, and I say, "No, I don't," and she says, "Well, maybe you're right, but I can't understand what you're saying," and I say, "I can't understand you either." Then, she fucking sends me to the office for disrupting class. That's fucked up! Who wants to talk like her anyway? Nobody, and if she be talking her way on the street, she get fucked up! [The student he was talking to laughed and nodded in agreement.][27]

Sharlene was a 16-year-old at Los Angeles's Chester Himes High School:

> That Mr. Legett is just trying to be White. Every time any of us [African Americans] talk, he's always saying, "Don't talk that ghetto stuff," and all of us just think, "Just because he ain't proud to be Black don't mean we have to be that way." Ain't nothing wrong with the way we talk. Who's to say he talks right? Who's to say White people talk right? I ain't changing to just impress them bigoted folks, so he can fail me if he wants.[28]

Ms. Calison taught English at Oakland's Kaiser High School:

> I will tell you that the students here are so difficult to teach language skills to because they're surrounded by people who don't speak correctly and think it's just not that important to speak correct English. It is so frustrating because when you correct them they just look at you like, "Whatever!" and then go on talking the way they want. I know that when I get them later down the

line in another language course, they'll just be talking the same way and since I know they know the difference, I just say to myself, "OK, if you want to be crude, it's your future you're ruining, not mine."[29]

For individual students who had acquired positive reputations, there was a tendency to see this as affirmation that they had made the correct choice in accepting the dominant customs. In fact, the accumulation of cultural capital from the dominant society more often than not produced a positive reward, even if it was not technically earned.[30] The comments of Ms. Leary and Mr. Daniels were representative.

Ms. Leary was a math teacher at Los Angeles's Chumash High School:

I have this student, Darin, who just failed his second quiz in calculus, but I had him two years ago in algebra 1, and he did wonderfully well. He was a serious student then and competent, and you can tell [from] how he dresses, talks, and comes prepared to class that he is still a student that wants to do well. So, I didn't count this grade for him because I know that he wants to learn. You can't do that for every student because they can be up and down, but there are others you can tell are good.[31]

Mr. Daniels taught English at Lanape High School in the Bronx:

J'Anne just did not complete the conjugation assignment that was due yesterday. Dorothy Banks [another teacher] told me that she was one of her very best students last year and I suspect she will be for me as well because when she answers in class she doesn't use slang and she's always well dressed, so I decided not to give her an F for this assignment. That's just going to mess up her final grade and since, according to Dorothy, she's planning to go to a four-year college and study English and history, I'm not going to spoil her chances. So, I guess I'll give her a passing grade for the assignment and then at the end of the semester just not count it.[32]

Three things should be noted. First, both of these teachers generally counted all the test grades for each of the students in determining final grades for the course. Second, I observed that other students who were very competent, some even more competent than those whom Mr. Daniels and Ms. Leary favored based on cultural assets, did not receive the advantage of a negative test grade being suspended in their final evaluation. Third, many teachers I observed over the course of the research included in this book indicated that how a student dressed or spoke demonstrated the student's character and ability; and I observed many teachers who included these assessments in assigning final grades for courses.

In sum, students who may have been smart but displayed signs associated with lower-class culture were more vulnerable to having a negative assessment of their capabilities and desire for success, which in turn created obstacles to their progress. On the other hand, cultural capital associated with the dominant culture had the opposite effect, indicating that a student wanted to follow the dominant conventions, which in turn gained them a strategically positive reputation. Ultimately, positive and negative reputations influenced both a student's progress in school and their successful transition to the next stage of education.[33]

Factors Inhibiting Cultural Capital Development

Two factors inhibited the development of cultural capital among the students in this study. The first had to do with the existence of two types of cultural capital and the reputations associated with each; the second impediment was the existence of a complete counterculture that opposed the dominant culture. If there had been just one type of cultural capital that everyone needed to compete to acquire, the situation would have been different from the one prevailing in the high schools of this study.[34] Sociologists Michèle Lamont, David Harding, and Mario Small have argued that people from low-income neighborhoods use different cultural frames in different circumstances to get by, and education is one of the areas where this occurs.[35] In contrast, Stephen Vaisey has shown that a student's moral or value orientation is at the core of their culture and plays a particularly strong role in education.[36] Similar to what Vaisey found, in the schools of this study the students' personal moral and value orientations were more significant in shaping their efforts to secure cultural capital than any particular "cultural frame."

Therefore, to understand why students from low-income families have difficulty gaining cultural capital, it is necessary to understand the foundation that informs youth as to what is a cultural asset that can be used as capital and in what arena this capital can be used. It is impossible to avoid the cultural elements of morals, values, and beliefs since they are the lens for determining what and where a symbolic or practical resource becomes the capital that can be spent in attaining an objective. Although Small et al. argue that low-income youth can be nurtured to adopt cultural frames that enable them to succeed in high school, the world views, norms, and habits that students in this study brought to school were not as flexible as the cultural-frame approach would suggest. Students could express middle-class values, but these expressions had little consistent effect on gaining the skills they needed because their actions did not match their words. They understood what school officials and the broader American society wanted to hear, but did not invest the time required to realize those values because they were not central to their current value-orientation. The comments of Brian, a 17-year-old junior at Los Angeles's Chumash High School, were representative:

> Mr. Wallen [the assistant principal] always brings people around to show off what he's doing.... [W]hen those folks come by, we always tell them we're going to college and want to get a good job afterwards, but most of us ain't going to do that college shit. I know I ain't interested in college at all. I'm just finishing high school and getting a job. It's funny seeing all them smiling after we tell them we're planning to go to college—they're really fucked up with that shit. So, it's better telling 'em we're going to college so they don't see us as being retarded or something. [His friend laughs.][37]

This is not to say I didn't observe students from lower-income families who had integrated middle-class worldviews and orientations, but these students demonstrated that incorporating these values was not as straightforward as simply changing cultural frames. It required a significant commitment, and Alicia and Jamie were two representative examples. Alicia, a 17-year-old eleventh-grader attending Los Angeles's Chester Himes High School, was giving a prepared talk to a group of freshman in a study period during the first week of school:

> I wanted to tell you just what happened to me so you know the good and the bad so you won't make the same mistake I did and lose time in doing good in school. Before coming to high school, I got good grades, so when I got here and there was all the new people and things to do, I just thought I'll have fun and just get up early in the morning before going to school and do my homework. My first report card was really bad, and my mom said, "What is going on here? Whatever you're doing has got to change, or you won't be going to college!" And I knew she was right, so I started to religiously study and do my homework after school and on the weekends, and the next report card was really good. So, if you want to get good grades, it starts with changing everything that you are doing now and making a total commitment to study every day.[38]

Jamie was a 16-year-old eleventh-grader at Oakland's Kaiser High School:

> You complaining about not getting any good grades, but you just have to work harder, man. I used to tell you and Junior that I wasn't getting the grades I should, but when I told my mom she just said, "You got to work more than

you do or you won't get ahead in life." She's right, and you should do like me and work at school shit all the time, and you'll get good grades too.[39]

Many students do understand that they will need to change how they think and behave in order to be academically successful, but some of them will abandon the effort when they experience a setback. Terrence was an example of this dynamic. As a sophomore attending the Bronx's Lanape High School, he had been meeting with a school counselor he liked, and the two of them decided that Terrence was capable of going to college if he changed his study habits and committed himself to staying out of trouble with his friends. He took the counselor's advice and went home every day after school and studied. In order to stay out of trouble with his friends, he limited his social life to the time he was at school, including weekends, when he would leave the neighborhood and visit his older sister in Brooklyn. Over the following two semesters, his grades slowly but steadily rose in every subject. In the third semester, he studied hard for a geometry exam but received a C+. Although this frustrated him, his counselor told him not to let this setback affect his new habits because they would eventually prove successful. Terrence continued to study hard and received a C on his next exam. This demoralized him and, even though he told the counselor he would keep up his new work habits, he started to hang out with his friends each night, and in the third semester his grades fell in every course.[40]

The second impediment to developing a worldview associated with middle-class life was what many researchers have identified as a counterculture to that identified with the mission of the school.[41] Although it is described in different ways, this counterculture value-orientation is directly associated with the social environment of lower-income communities, and its appeal includes rewards from others in that milieu.[42] To some students I observed, the allure of cultural capital associated with their local lower-income communities was related to the additional social status and sociability it yielded in their neighborhoods.[43] For example, people who possess one element of this cultural capital are often referred to as possessing "street smarts" or a confident swagger that allows them to navigate the everyday interactions of a low-income community with social status and a minimum risk of harm to their body and finances. This capital involves presenting oneself in a way that resonates with local norms. L. Janelle Dance refers to this presentation as "tough fronts" and describes how it plays an important part in students' lives in and out of school.[44]

The finding that some students prized the cultural capital associated with their low-income communities presented a number of challenges to conventional thinking about students from low-income families. First, it challenges the position that, in general, youth from low-income families have overwhelmingly adopted the values of middle-class America. Second, it calls into question whether they are in the habit of switching between a variety of cultural "frames" to provide them with possibilities for advancement in both school and the community.[45] In fact, the low-income students I observed had difficulty translating the meanings and behaviors associated with their local cultural system to that found in their middle-class-oriented high school environment, and this hindered their ability to easily switch between them when the situation called for it.

Interestingly, this difficulty in what is generally referred to as "code-switching" or "culture-switching" was based on a number of factors that have been undervalued by researchers. First, some youths from lower-class neighborhoods preferred their local cultural values and norms to those found in the middle class and their schools.[46] Second, those who did see advantages to incorporating middle-class values found it difficult to know and master all the elements of middle-class culture. An example of this can be seen in Drew's comments about an interaction he had with three teachers:

> I just fucked up with Mr. Calhoun. He wanted me to talk to the two new teachers so I would do better in their classes, but while I was talking to them I got excited and said something ghetto. I didn't mean anything, . . . and they were like, "This is not appropriate" shit. So, I was like, "Ooh, sorry," but they seemed offended or something, so I just said, "I gotta go, see you later" and just left. I saw one of them an hour later, and he was, like, cold, you know, like nodding his head instead of saying "Hi" or something. Fuck it! It's too hard to guess all the time what these White middle-class fuckers want to hear and do![47]

When students exhibited aspects of middle-class culture that were partially developed or awkwardly executed, it caused difficulties for them successfully transitioning within their high school year of study, and Drew happened to be one of these students.

Before leaving the issue of cultural capital, it is necessary to address another element found in the literature. Some researchers have attributed the inability to navigate the formal education structure to a student's limited amount of middle-class cultural capital, particularly their knowledge of how to advocate for themselves in navigating the system.[48] However, for students in the present study this was not a problem. Students were able to advocate for themselves, but for those who experienced difficulty in navigating the formal educational structure, it was not the lack of internal middle-class cultural dispositions or capital that was the problem, it was their lack of knowledge of, and access to, people who could assist them.[49] Thus, it was not a lack of cultural capital that caused problems in navigating the formal structure but the character of a student's social capital portfolio.

In sum, the idea that most low-income students possess multiple cultural frames and can use them at different strategic moments to academically advance (i.e., code-switch) is insufficient for understanding the challenges they face. So too is the idea that cultural capital has singular power for students successfully transitioning to the next educational level.[50] Cultural capital was a resource in the academic transition process, but it was most effective when used in conjunction with a student's social capital.

SOCIAL CAPITAL

"Social capital" has been defined by sociologist Nan Lin as "resources embedded in social relations and social structure, which can be mobilized when an actor wishes to increase the likelihood of success in a purposive action." He goes on to say that social capital is "an investment in social relationships through which resources of other actors can be accessed and borrowed" and thus "embedded in social networks."[51] For sociologist Pierre Bourdieu, social capital is unevenly distributed not only among individuals but among social classes.[52] In fact, most researchers have come to see the advantage to having social capital and to understand that, while it is theoretically available to everyone, it is unevenly disseminated.

We know from economists that education is human capital, but we know less about social capital as a resource for accruing human capital during the high school years.[53] To understand the nature of social capital in the everyday lives of students, this part of the chapter will address how students from lower-income families accumulated social capital, what type of it they acquired, the difficulties they experienced accumulating it, and whether these experiences affected their various academic destinations. That is, many researchers see an advantage to having social capital, and this next section addresses the impact that varying amounts of it have on the ability to accumulate human capital.[54]

The types of social capital available among the lower-class students attending the high schools in this study, the difficulties that students experienced in accumulating it, and its implications varied for individual students. Accumulating resources that students could use for personal gain resulted from behavior instrumentally driven for that purpose, and these resources took the form of social relationships that evolved from everyday interactions. Like most high schools, the schools serving students from low-income families were places where students could seek and accumulate social capital and spend it for the purpose of individual gain. In the present study, and contrary to the framework provided by Bourdieu, a student's socioeconomic position did not predetermine such a limited amount of social capital that they realized no benefit from it.[55] The social capital that was available varied as to where it was most useful, but students did recognize the "use value" of social capital and did engage in accumulating it. The comments of Ellen, a freshman at Los Angeles's Tongva High School, and of Nicolás, a freshman at the Bronx's Van Twiller High School, were representative of this understanding. Ellen said:

> I've been so busy talking to people, you know, different students because it's nice to have a lot of contacts that maybe can help you with something. I think most of the people I met are like me so I'm happy with that, and I'm just going to keep going 'cause you can't have too many contacts.[56]

Nicolás said:

> Hey, Rick, would it be good to check out that honors group of students? [Talking to a friend, he is motioning to a group of students sitting near them.] They're definitely smart, and maybe they can help if I need it in my courses or something. I think we should definitely get to know them 'cause you never know when we might need some help and hit them up for it if they're friends. OK?[57]

High school was a natural environment for creating social networks because it was a place where individual students found other students who also were looking for friends who could benefit them socially and academically. In fact, almost immediately after arriving for freshman year, most students engaged in building their personal networks. One of the benefits of having a personal network was psychological in that it provided identity, self-esteem, and comfort; but there were other benefits related to social status, entertainment, and academic success. Thus, some of the students' choices in developing their peer networks were directed at short-term gains, while others were directed at gains that might occur in the future.

Obstacles to Developing Social Networks

High school was a natural place to develop personal networks, but as Oseguera et al. argue, school conditions can impact a student's personal network.[58] In the present study, the strength of each student's personal network in producing academic success was affected by three main factors and a number of complications related to each.

The first factor in building social networks was students' access to other students they identified as people they would like to associate with. In some cases, their class schedule made it difficult to find an opportunity to interact consistently to establish a friendship, a result of the schools' regimen systems (i.e., some form of tracking). There was, of course, the lunch period and time after school, but the limited time to develop a relationship of any significance challenged students' intent to expand their networks to include those participating in other regimens.

The challenge of interacting with students in separate regimens combined with the issue of creating trusting relationships had a significant impact on the students' network development. Like most high school students who were in the process of establishing an identity, students in this study relied heavily on trust, therefore any instrumental gain a student could foresee from having particular friends was based on an understanding that a relatively trusting relationship was involved. Because such relationships take time to develop, having to confront structural conditions associated with a tracking system that separated vocational and college-bound students constrained a student's ability to expand a trusting network. An example involved a ninth-grader named Corina who attended Brooklyn's Knickerbocker High School. Corina was interested in going to college but had experienced difficulty in math and was placed in the general academic regimen. She wanted to develop a relationship with honors students who she thought could tutor her in math so she could improve her grades and strengthen her applications for college. She was introduced to three honors students at different times and was excited about the opportunity to interact with them. After three weeks of trying, however, she was not able to arrange time to consistently interact with them because their course schedules conflicted with hers. Feeling frustrated, she stopped trying. When asked why she did not simply ask them for help, Corina said, "You don't just ask people for help and not know them. Who does that? You only ask friends for help, and if you're not friends you can't trust the other person."[59]

Another complication students faced in gaining access to other students who were advantageous to include in their personal networks had to do with being rejected by someone they identified as desirable to have in their network. In this situation, whether by articulating a rejection or by simply indicating no interest in being friends, members of the targeted group essentially said, "We, and only we, choose people in our group, and we have not chosen you."[60]

In this context, the obstacle was personal, in that the individual student was being excluded. An example of this occurred with Elvin, who was a tenth-grader at Los Angeles's Chester Himes High School. He was telling two friends that he knew a student who was part of the social group that was active in the advanced science program and presented projects at the annual city science fair. Elvin wanted to join the group so he could work with others on one of these projects because he wanted to pursue science in college and knew other student presenters had met college recruiters at the annual city science fairs who had helped them get into top universities. He told his friends how frustrated he was because the group would not let him associate with them due to two members saying he looked "too ghetto." He said he thought it was because of the clothes he wore and an old tattoo that his cousin had put on him with a pin when they were nine, but he was not sure.

Elvin never managed to associate with members of this group and, as a result, never presented a project at the local science fair. Most members of the group he wanted to join did help each other with their science and math projects and all went on to attend colleges and universities after high school. So, it was clear that Elvin had chosen an appropriate group, and it is very likely that he too would have been able to proceed directly to a college or university. Although the inability to gain access to this group and increase his chances for an immediate admittance to a four-year college was impeded, ultimately, he attended a community college where he met other students who had made contact with local university authorities who aided him in transferring to UCLA, where he earned a bachelor's degree in biology.[61]

Elvin's experience illustrates two important findings. The first is that simply identifying the need to develop a social network does not make it happen because there were aspects outside an individual student's control. The second finding is that being unsuccessful in one particular effort to accrue the social capital needed for successfully transitioning to the next educational stage did not mean a person would be unsuccessful at another time. Future success depended on both the individual's commitment to a goal and their accumulated social capital that helped them overcome obstacles.

A third complication students faced in gaining access to other students who might help them had to do with making disadvantageous decisions. A typical example of this involved Olivia, a ninth-grade honors student attending Los Angeles's Tongva High School who was considered by her peers to be smart, attractive, and a gifted basketball player. During her junior year, she was having trouble in math and wanted help. She spoke with her friend Dana about the situation.

DANA: Why don't you ask Tanya or Jenna? They're taking math. [She was taking French with Tanya and Jenna.]

OLIVIA: I would, but I really don't know them, and they're not going to want to spend time helping someone they don't even hang with.

DANA: We're all in honors classes together; how come you didn't get to know them and their group?

OLIVIA: I don't know, it was just that I liked to hang around girls who played sports, and they didn't play any.

This dynamic produced what sociologists McFarland et al. label "homophily networks" that constricted a student's social capital.[62] In Olivia's case, her reluctance to initiate a social connection with Tanya and Jenna reduced the resources that might have given her a better chance to improve on the C–grade she received in math.[63] In sum, the three complications just described related to issues of structure, culture, and self-efficacy, and together created impediments for the students of this study in creating and sustaining diverse social networks. Identifying these complications provides a better understanding of why the breadth of an individual's network may be truncated and may reduce the amount of social capital they can accrue.

The second factor affecting a student's capacity to build social capital was the weak obligations felt by some students to aid other members of their existing social network. Sociologist Sandra Smith has documented this tendency among African Americans who are seeking employment. She finds that a primary reason for a job-holder to withhold aid to job-seekers in their network is the assessed "trustworthiness" of the job-seeker to execute the employment responsibilities in a manner that does not reflect badly on them.[64]

Within the schools of the present study, the reluctance of students to aid other members of their social network was based on five considerations. The first was deciding whether what was being requested violated the granter's moral code. A typical example involved Debra, a sophomore attending Los Angeles's Chester Himes High School:

Jordan wanted me to check out the answers from the teacher's guide when I take the roll for Mr. Holder [the teacher]. I'm definitely not doing that 'cause it's cheating, and that's definitely wrong![65]

A second aspect of how students' sense of obligation affected their decisions about helping someone in their network was whether the request took unfair advantage of the relationship by asking for more assistance than had historically been reciprocated. Eugene, who was a sophomore at LA's Chumash High School, offers a typical example:

Jason is asking me to help him with his history paper. I've helped him so many times this year, but I've asked him to help me on a couple of things not related to school, and he never gets back to me. Why should I always help him and not get anything back? I'm not doing it this time. That's it![66]

The third consideration weakening the sense of obligation to help members of one's network was that requests for aid could not jeopardize the strategic position the potential benefactor had achieved. An example can be seen in the comments of Kim, who was a senior attending Brooklyn's Knickerbocker High School:

Sheila's been calling to ask for help on the next few chemistry assignments, but I don't think I'm going to help her out. I did help her once, but then I was thinking, "Hell, she got as good a grade as me last time!" Well, I ain't doing that anymore 'cause that could hurt me since I want to stay [at] the top of the class so that Mr. Allen gives me the top recommendation for college.[67]

The fourth consideration was whether the network member asking for aid merited the effort. A typical example of this consideration can be seen in the comments of Andrea, who was a junior attending the Bronx's Lanape High School:

Juanita asked me to talk to Steve about getting some help with writing the paper. This is fucked up. All she wants is for him to tell her what the book they're supposed to be writing the paper on is about. She's really lazy and won't do any work if she can avoid it. I haven't seen Steve in school the last three days 'cause we've got different schedules, but she's still pressuring me to spend my time tracking him down to save her from doing the work. Fuck it, I ain't wasting my time on someone like her! She just needs to stop being lazy and work harder, that's all.[68]

A fifth and final consideration in deciding whether to aid another member of one's network had to do with economizing favors. In this situation, if the benefactor had only one favor remaining from the person they would have had to approach to provide aid to another member requesting it, they may have wanted to save it. An example of this can be seen in the comments of Oscar, who was a junior attending Los Angeles's Polk High School:

> Francisco called me last night and wanted me to get Mr. Jay to ask Mr. Brennan to not count his last exam because there was trouble in his house. I know Mr. Jay would do it, but I've been having some trouble lately so if I ask Mr. Jay to help me he'll say, "I can just do this once, and I already did it before for you." So, I'm not going to use up my favor with Mr. Jay because then there's nothing for me, and I'm thinking I'm probably going to need a favor from him soon.[69]

The third factor affecting students' network development concerned decisions about how they were going to invest their time.[70] Students accumulated social capital in the high schools of this study through friendships, and the depth of friendships was predicated on the amount of time they spent with members of their network. Close friendships produced strength in one's network because they created tight bonds and the concomitant obligations to aid those with whom one was bonded. The strength of a network portfolio was based on the ability to count on receiving help when it was needed, and that was directly related to the amount of individual time invested in socializing with others in the group.

Dean, a sophomore attending the Bronx's Van Twiller High School, offered a good example of a student who decided to spend his time in ways that would help him broaden his social network. Dean was a good athlete who played football and, as a result, his primary network included athletes and students who liked athletes. He was also very good in math and science, where he consistently received A grades and scored high on achievement tests. He was friendly with most students in his math and science classes, but he did not nurture a close relationship with any of them. Although Dean was a good football player, he was not good enough to receive a scholarship to college on that basis, and in order to increase his chances of attending a top university he wanted to attend an advanced math class that was being offered after school by one of the school's young math teachers, but it was full.

Dean understood it would be necessary for a class member to ask the math teacher to let him in as a favor to that student. The problem was that he really did not know any of the students well enough to ask them to intervene. One day Dean was lamenting the situation to a fellow football player, who said,

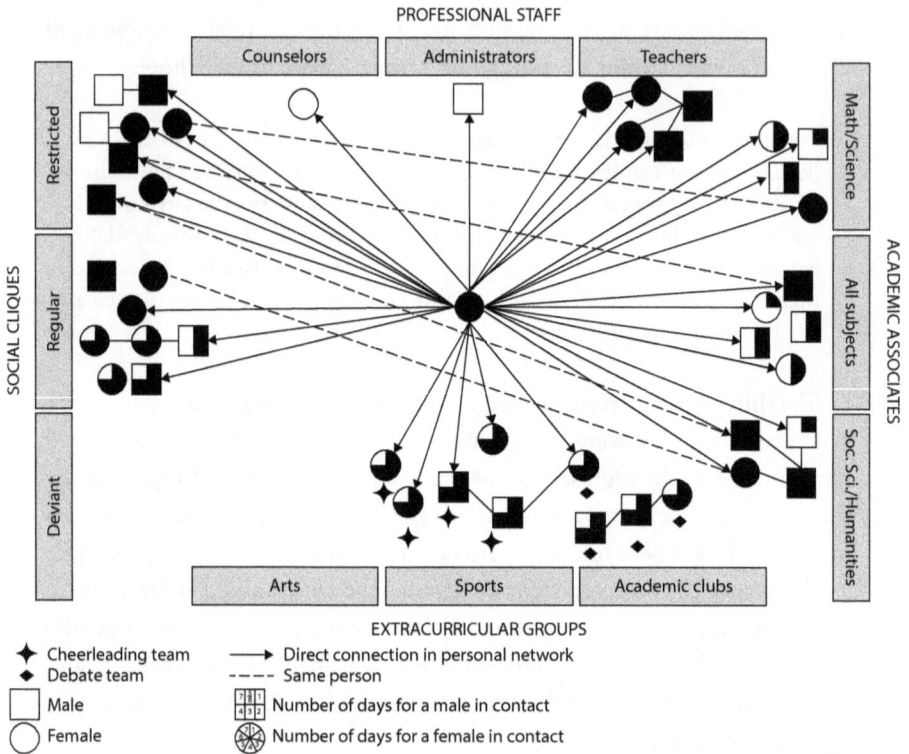

PROFESSIONAL STAFF

Counselors | Administrators | Teachers

Math/Science

ACADEMIC ASSOCIATES

All subjects

Soc. Sci./Humanities

SOCIAL CLIQUES

Restricted

Regular

Deviant

Arts | Sports | Academic clubs

EXTRACURRICULAR GROUPS

✦ Cheerleading team   → Direct connection in personal network
◆ Debate team   ---- Same person
☐ Male   Number of days for a male in contact
○ Female   Number of days for a female in contact

*Students may spend different amounts of time with the
same individual belonging to multiple groups in their network.

"You know Joyce. Why don't you ask her?" Dean replied, "Yeah, I know her but not well enough to have her ask for the favor." His friend retorted, "Well, if that's what you want, you better get to know her or somebody else, or you're going to be out of luck."

Over the next semester Dean made a deliberate effort to talk with Joyce and four or five other students before and after their math and science classes. At the start of the following year, Dean's junior year, he asked three of the students he had befriended, who were now part of his extended network, to ask the teacher to let him join their after-school group. Joyce and two other students did ask the teacher to let him join, the teacher consented, and Dean became a member of the group for his junior and senior years. He said to another friend after a football game, "Joining the math group really helped me improve my math and science achievement scores." Upon graduation,

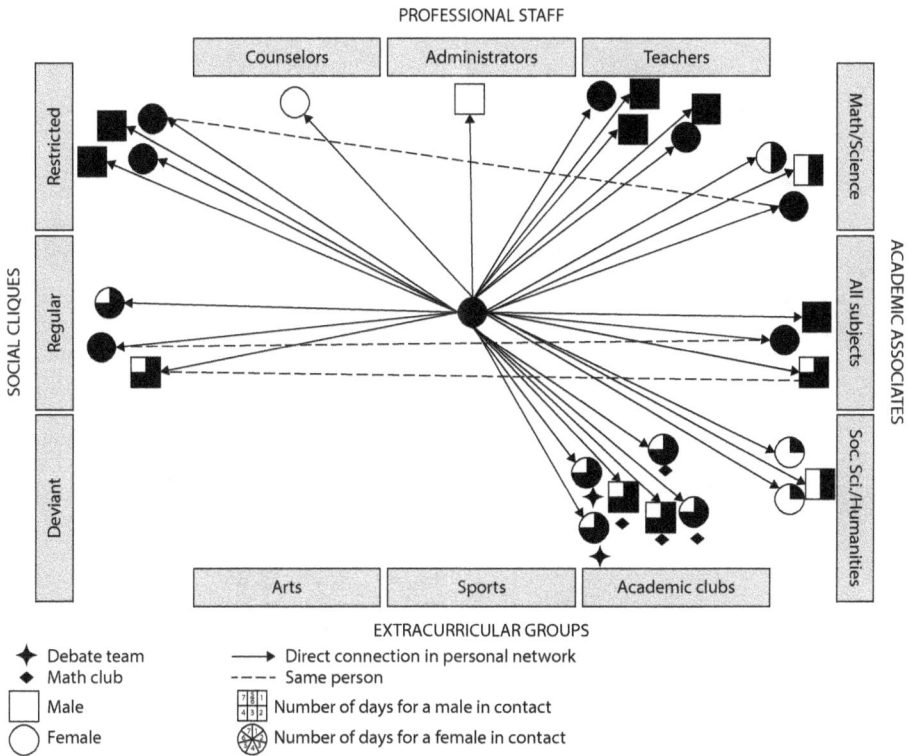

FIGURE 4.2. Network of female student who is not having academic difficulty in LA.

Dean was admitted to a top university where he majored in cell biology.[71] Whereas Dean succeeded, many students who faced an obstacle to transitioning to the next stage of their education discovered that they had not invested enough time in developing their networks and, as a result, did not have the necessary social capital to surmount the obstacle.

The Importance of Students' Social Capital Portfolio

Understanding how a student's network was constructed provides a critical understanding of the strength of their resources and their potential to obtain academic help from those resources. Figures 4.1–4.12 provide a visual representation of the general network configurations that helped students attain success and those found to be problematic. In essence, these figures need to

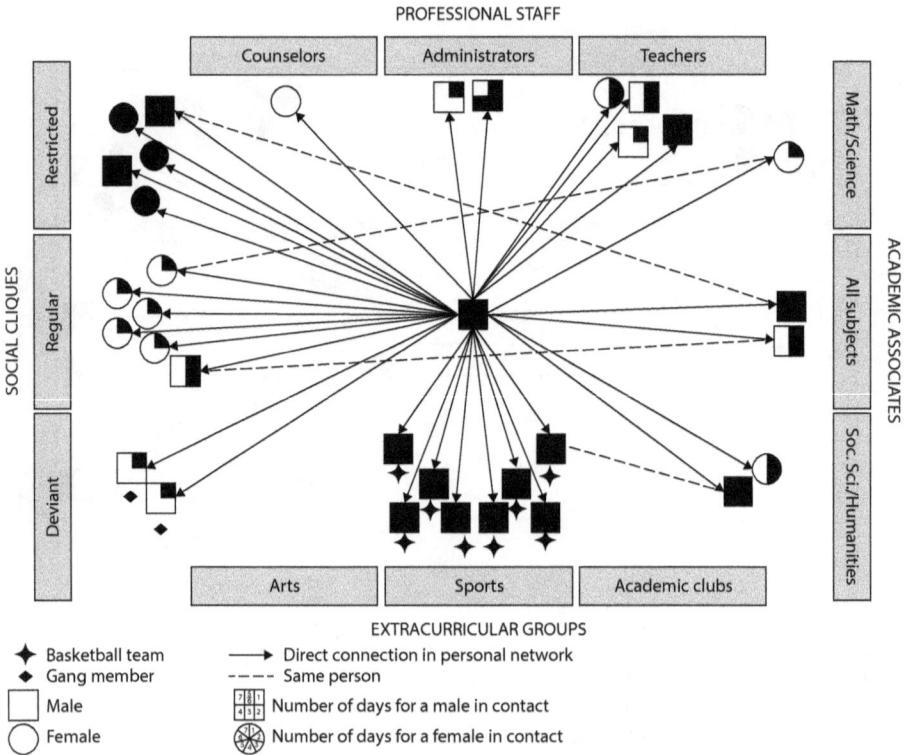

FIGURE 4.3. Network of male student who is not having academic difficulty in NY.

be understood like an X-ray. They depict what healthy and unhealthy social networks looked like in their ability to produce an effective social capital portfolio for aiding educational success.

The data in these figures include the personal networks of twelve individuals attending two different schools in New York (Lanape and Knickerbocker high schools) and two in Los Angeles (Himes and Polk high schools). The larger sample was arrived at by randomly selecting four students, one male and one female, from each of two required courses each year over two five-year periods (1993–97; 2006–10), and then following them periodically during the week, recording who they were spending time with before, during, and after school. All forty individual social network charts were composed and analyzed.

FIGURE 4.4. Network of male student who is not having academic difficulty in LA.

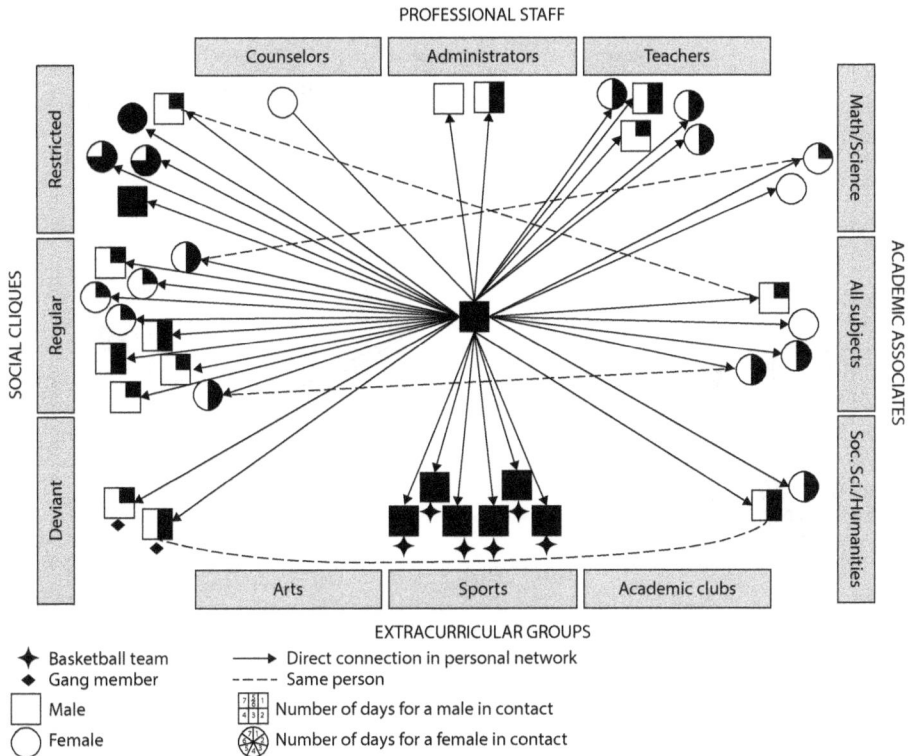

Figures 4.1–4.12 are examples of the two general resulting configurations. What is important to highlight is that while the data presented does not emanate from a random sample with a large "n," the patterns that emerged among the forty subjects who attended these four different schools in two different cities in two different time periods were remarkably alike. I offer them as illustrations of the strong social network and weak social network structure that existed for some students who experienced success and difficulties in their overall grade point average and standardized test scores.

In order to interpret the data in these charts it will be necessary to understand the symbols used in them. Technically, in network analysis, these figures would be considered egocentric, in that they chart the network for one individual, with a female being represented as a circle and a male a square.

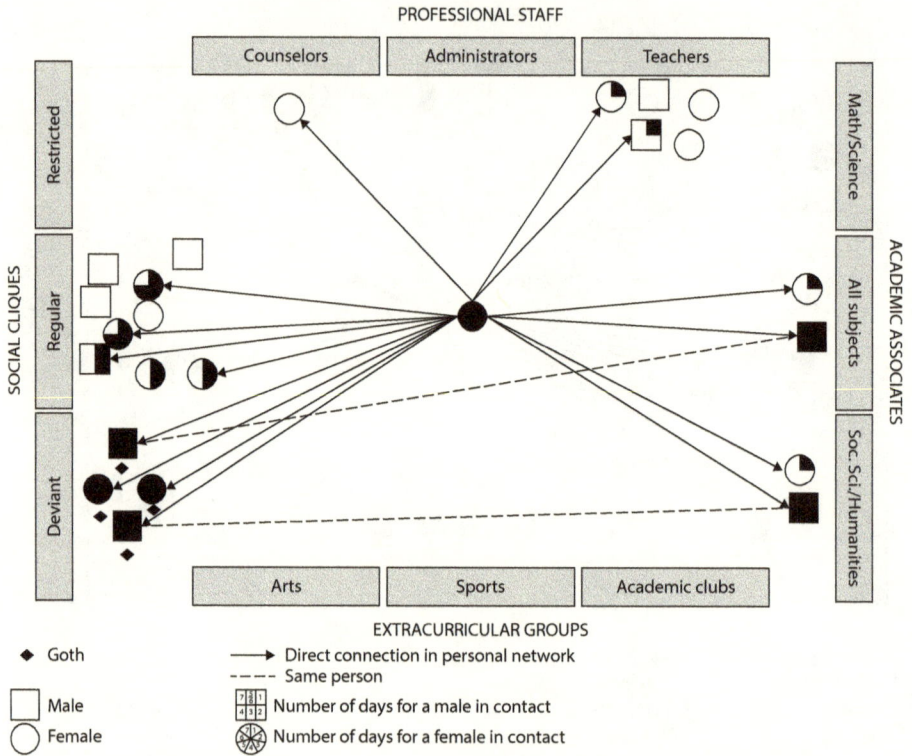

FIGURE 4.5. Network of female student who is having academic difficulty in NY.

PROFESSIONAL STAFF

Counselors   Administrators   Teachers

SOCIAL CLIQUES

Restricted

Regular

Deviant

Math/Science

ACADEMIC ASSOCIATES

All subjects

Soc. Sci./Humanities

Arts   Sports   Academic clubs

EXTRACURRICULAR GROUPS

◆ Goth   ⟶ Direct connection in personal network
              ---- Same person

☐ Male   ▦ Number of days for a male in contact
◯ Female   ✳ Number of days for a female in contact

*Students may spend different amounts of time with the
same individual belonging to multiple groups in their network.

There are four quadrants representing social groupings in which the individual has a relationship. These groupings are: professional staff (including teachers, counselors, and administrators); social cliques (including high-status groups that regulate who can be a member, regular social groups generally open to most students, and groups viewed by the school community as deviant); extracurricular groups (sports teams, arts groups, and academic clubs); and the individuals the student associated with in various academic areas.

The solid lines represent a direct connection; if there are members associated with the clique that the student does not have a direct connection to, there is no line pointing to the student. The dotted line indicates a person the subject is connected to happens to be in two separate groupings. The shaded area inside the circle or square indicates how many times that person, on

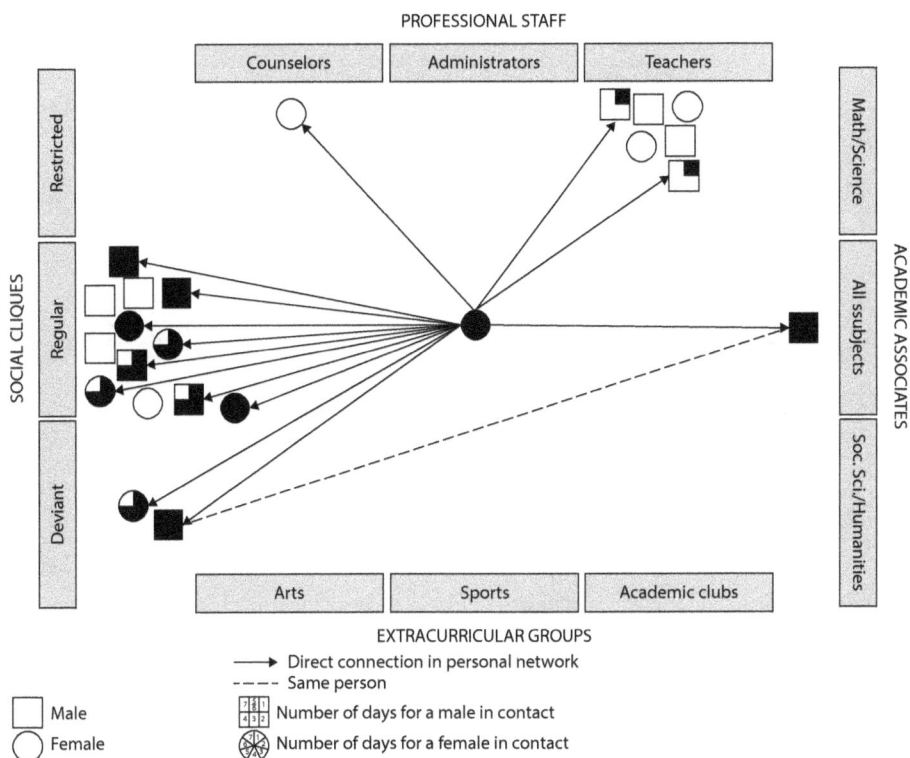

FIGURE 4.6. Network of female student who is having academic difficulty in LA.

PROFESSIONAL STAFF

| Counselors | Administrators | Teachers |

SOCIAL CLIQUES: Restricted, Regular, Deviant

ACADEMIC ASSOCIATES: Math/Science, All ssubjects, Soc. Sci/Humanities

EXTRACURRICULAR GROUPS

| Arts | Sports | Academic clubs |

→ Direct connection in personal network
---- Same person

☐ Male
○ Female

▦ Number of days for a male in contact
✳ Number of days for a female in contact

*Students may spend different amounts of time with the
same individual belonging to multiple groups in their network.*

average, interacted with the student. A quarter-shaded area indicates the two individuals would interact one day a week, a half-shaded area indicates meeting two or three days a week, a three-quarters shaded area indicates meeting four or five times a week, and a fully shaded symbol indicates meeting six or seven times a week.[72]

Before discussing the results, it is important to point out that figures 4.1–4.8 present networks of those male and female students having academic success and those experiencing difficulty; figures 4.9–12 do the same but also present the difference by grade 10 and 12 levels. When comparing the data for those who were successful in school with data for those who were having difficulty, the importance of having balance within one's network portfolio becomes apparent. The males and females who were successful in school

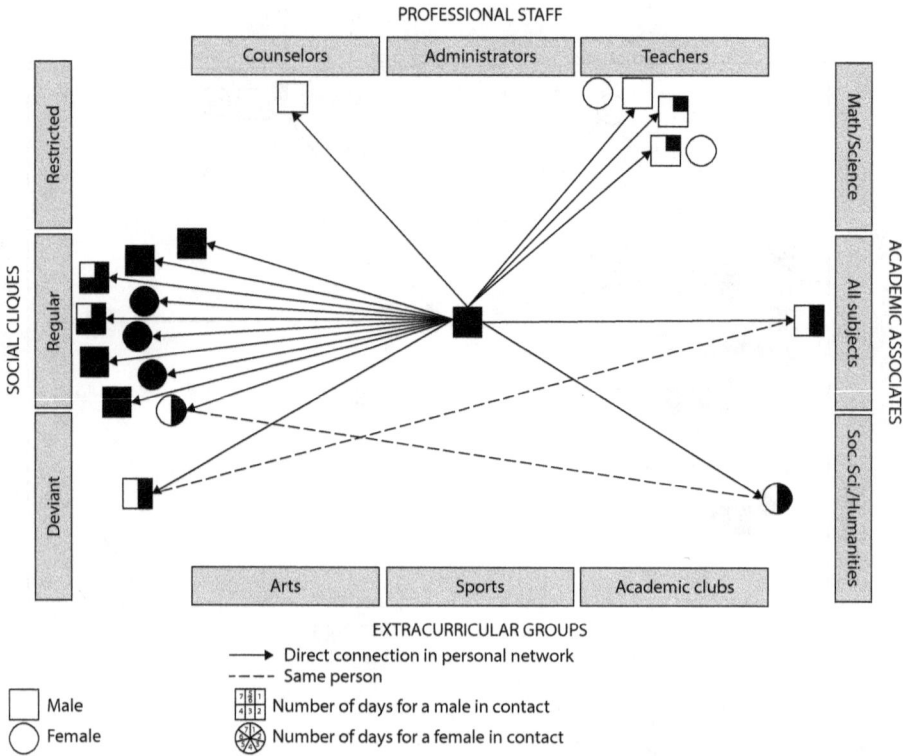

FIGURE 4.7. Network of male student who is having academic difficulty in NY.

(whose grades and standardized test scores were in the top 10 percent) had developed relatively extensive networks and were connected with individuals in each of the four quadrants (see figures 4.1–4.4). This gave them access to individuals who could aid them.

It is important to point out that successful students were associated with students who were in high-status groupings that restricted entrance and with students in regular groups where association was more open. It is also worth noting that successful females tended to avoid associating with individuals and groups the general school population viewed as deviant, while successful males did have associates who participated in deviant groups. Membership in a deviant group nearly always indicated a gang affiliation; because gangs were so prevalent where the schools were located, it was extremely difficult,

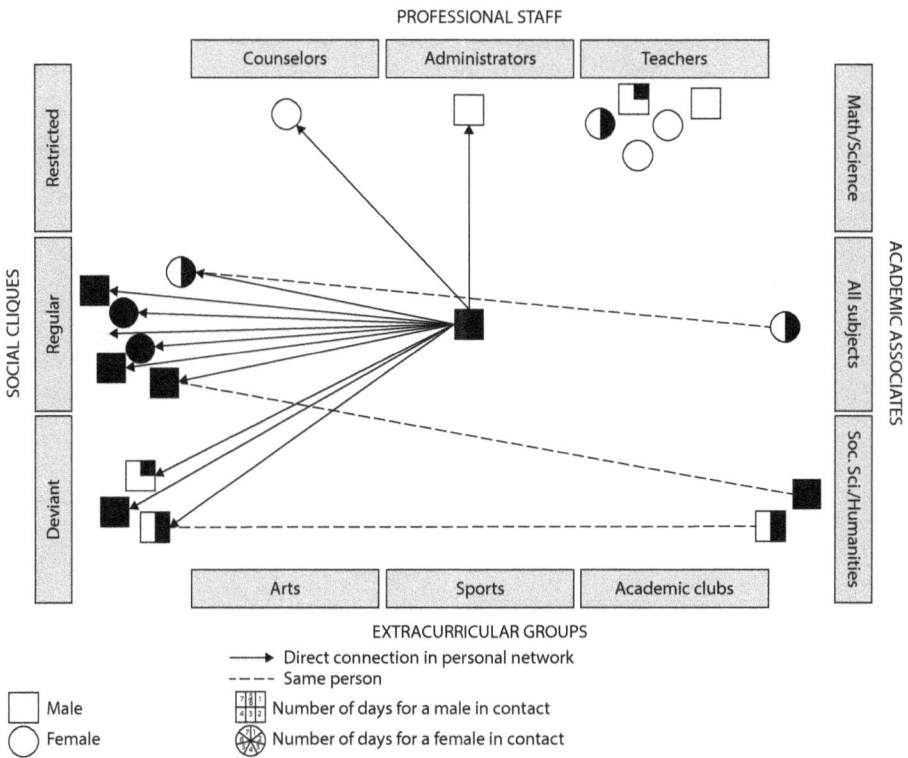

FIGURE 4.8. Network of male student who is having academic difficulty in LA.

if not impossible, for young males to avoid having some connection with a member of a gang—if for no other reason than self-protection.

If we look at the male and female students represented in these figures who were succeeding in academics and making a smooth transition from one grade to the next, their networks included both students they would regularly interact with in different social and academic areas as well as teachers and, to a lesser extent, administrators and counselors. Having a diversified network portfolio increased the social capital (i.e., personal resources) available in purchasing aid when necessary in successfully navigating the educational process.

The networks of students who had had academic difficulty in school were much more truncated, with the exception of having more associates in deviant groups (see figures 4.5–4.9 and 4.11). In particular, their networks

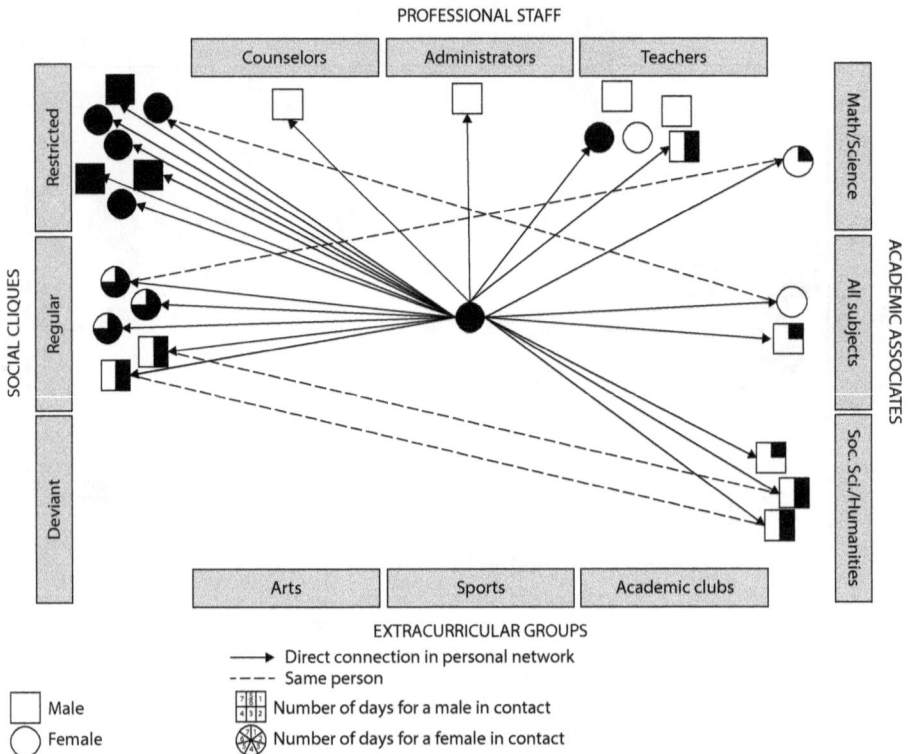

FIGURE 4.9. Network of female student who is having academic difficulty in grade 10 in LA.

demonstrate structural weakness in the "academic and professional quadrants." Obviously, not having people they could ask for assistance when experiencing academic difficulty left them at a disadvantage in progressing in a timely manner.[73] The comments of Sydney, a junior at the Bronx's Van Twiller High School, were typical of students in this predicament:

> I didn't do any homework last night because I couldn't understand it very well. So I said, "Fuck it!" . . . I did ask Kerry, who is the only one I know in the class, if he understood it and he said no. So, I just went and watched TV.[74]

It is important to point out that students having difficulty did have friends, and they did have a network, but this network most often was composed primarily of individuals who did not attend their high school. Thus, their resource portfolio was quite limited.

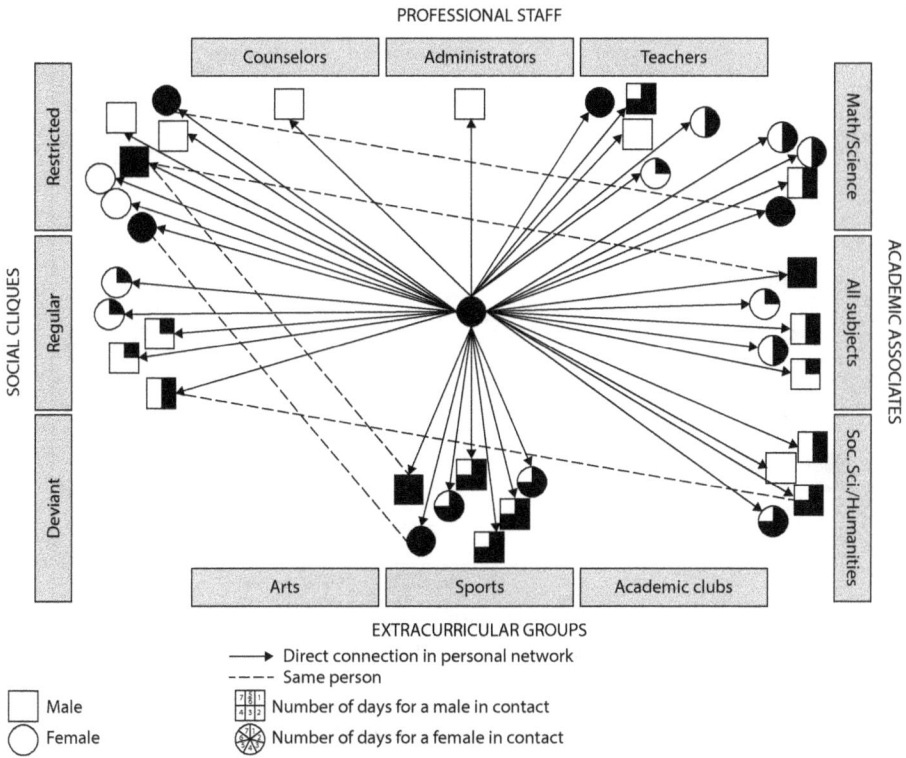

FIGURE 4.10. Network of female student who is having academic difficulty in grade 12 in LA.

The data in these figures suggest that the architecture of a student's network affects the level of resources available to them. How much of an effect each of these resources had cannot be answered with these data. Nonetheless, it must be noted that having a less-developed social network presented additional obstacles for students from low-income families as they made transitions within and beyond high school.

SOME FINISHING COMMENTS

This chapter has addressed cultural and social resources that might be used as capital in securing academic success, capital (i.e., resources) that traditionally have been identified as important to middle- and upper-income students'

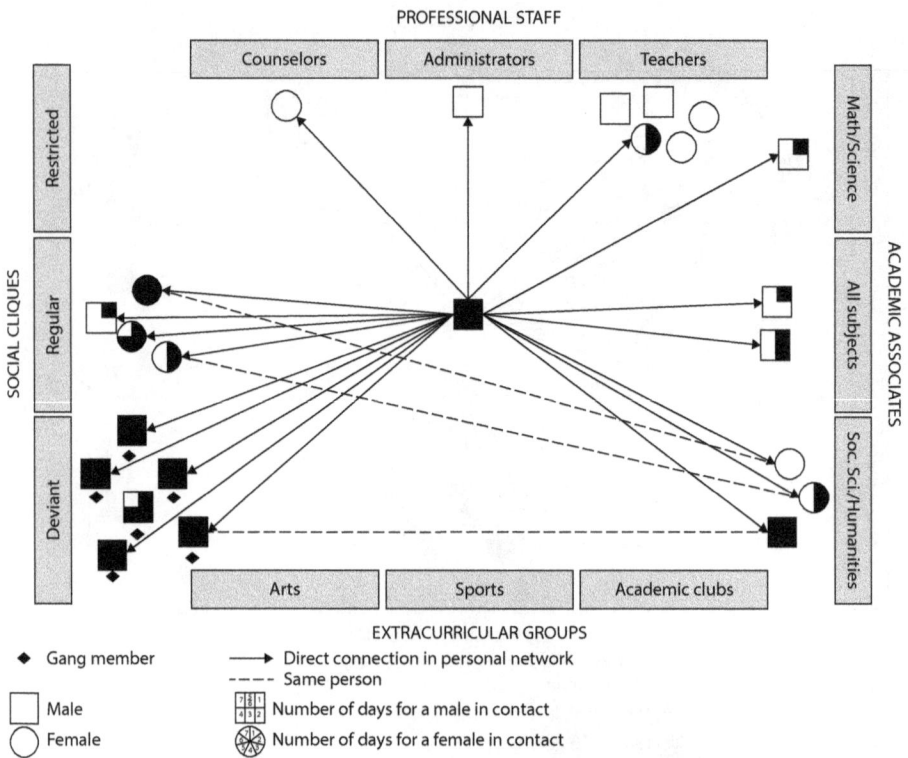

FIGURE 4.11. Network of male student who is having academic difficulty in grade 10 in NY.

success in high school and beyond. The corollary assumption has been that having less of these two kinds of capital leaves individuals vulnerable to failure in school and beyond.[75]

There has been little research, however, on how the lack of such capital negatively affects individuals' educational success. One reason is that the prevailing conceptualizations of cultural and social capital have been ambiguous. For example, sociologists' use of the idea of capital deviates, to varying degrees, from the way economists use the concept, although social and cultural capital, like financial capital, are generally taken as entities that produce "things"—with the "things" in sociology being resources to spend in the pursuit of status, mobility, or other socioeconomic goals. In addition, the concepts of social and cultural capital are too often assumed to operate with

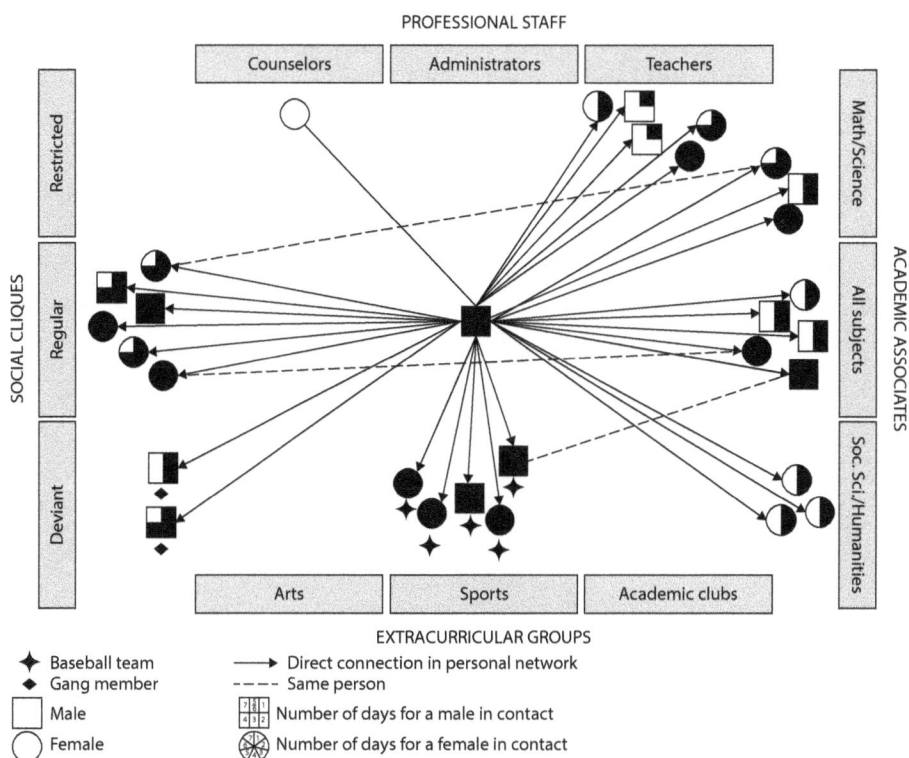

FIGURE 4.12. Network of male student who is having academic difficulty in grade 12 in NY.

PROFESSIONAL STAFF

Counselors   Administrators   Teachers

SOCIAL CLIQUES

Restricted
Regular
Deviant

Math/Science
All subjects
Soc. Sci./Humanities

ACADEMIC ASSOCIATES

Arts   Sports   Academic clubs

EXTRACURRICULAR GROUPS

✦ Baseball team   ⟶ Direct connection in personal network
◆ Gang member   ----- Same person
☐ Male   Number of days for a male in contact
◯ Female   Number of days for a female in contact

*Students may spend different amounts of time with the
same individual belonging to multiple groups in their network.

a zero sum rather than on a continuum.[76] It would be rare for an individual to have zero social and cultural capital without being totally isolated and significantly disabled, but researchers have done little to create instruments to investigate, or measure, the level of each that an individual possesses to determine the optimal amounts for producing success or failure. Finally, social and cultural capital needs precision because, as discussed throughout this chapter, the amount that a student has accumulated is not more important than its substantive composition, which can either advance or undermine the academic success of an individual.[77]

In sum, this chapter has attempted to address some of these issues by (1) bringing the concept of capital back toward its resource properties; (2) describing how varying amounts of each kind of capital as well as their content create challenges to academic success; and (3) showing how cultural and social capital can impact an individual's efforts to succeed in school and make a smooth transition to the next level of education. Thus, although the forms of cultural and social capital validated by institutions are in shorter supply in schools serving low-income students, the problems in accumulating resources and turning them into capital is not simply related to supply. There exist pools of social and cultural resources in low-income schools, but converting these resources into capital is filled with challenges. Those individuals who are able to overcome the challenges and accumulate both social and cultural capital are better able to academically succeed and successfully transition to their next educational level.[78]

CHAPTER 5

Social Tracking in the Educational Process

> The chimney smokes and I leave the room. Why do you think it
> a great matter? But while no such reason drives me out, I remain
> a free tenant and none shall prevent me from acting as I will,
> and I will what agrees with the nature of a reasonable and social
> creature.
>
> MARCUS AURELIUS,
> *Meditation V,* 170–180 CE

THE RESEARCH ON THE EDUCATION experience of youths from low-income families often focuses on structural impediments to their success in school, and the ways that many of those impediments affect low-income students have been discussed in previous chapters of this book.[1] However, one of the unfortunate analytic consequences of employing a singularly structural framework is that the subjects are represented as being in a constant state of responding to a preexisting set of fixed arrangements in much the same way that a guinea pig placed in a maze can exit only by successfully navigating the structures in place.

It is important to call attention to the fact that, despite having internal structures, the high schools in this study were not as constrained as a maze. We will see in this chapter that the structures within the high schools serving low-income students in the present study allowed them choices, and these choices had both positive and negative consequences for students as they progressed.[2] Thus, in contrast to previous chapters that focused on issues related to the structural and cultural factors affecting students' transitions from one stage of education to the next, this chapter will focus on student agency.

The analysis that follows will address what I have called "social tracking" and the structural burdens that accompanied it. Social tracking was similar to the official academic tracking. Both created social boundaries, and a generalized trajectory was associated with each. I use the term "track" similar to the definition found in the *Oxford English Dictionary*: "a rough path or a course followed by someone." Therefore, a "social track" should be seen as a substantive path chosen by students that had a set of behaviors commensurate with its intended destination.

As long as a student was engaged in a given path, there were limits or boundaries associated with the behaviors of others who shared in the path's aim. This produced a structuring effect in a student's self-identity and behavior, but what differentiated social from academic tracking was the amount of holding power associated with each system, as well as the degree of difficulty when moving from one track to another. Thus, the locus of holding power for a student's social track was internal to them as individuals, whereas for the academic track it was external. This made changing social tracks difficult, but less so than changing academic tracks.

It should be understood that both the social and academic tracks coexisting in the studied schools affected the content, scope, and value students placed on divergent types of relationships within the educational trajectories associated with each track. It is also important to note that academic tracking was established by education professionals to provide the skills for advancing in the academy, and students were required to adjust to the structured environment where they were assigned—i.e., to the curricular structure. In contrast, students chose a social track as their own individualized response to the system they encountered, a response they believed provided them the greatest opportunity to realize their current goals. This chapter describes the content of the four social tracks students chose to participate in and how they impacted their academic trajectories during high school.

SOCIAL TRACKING

A social track, not to be confused with a social clique, was associated first with a set of goals that an individual student had chosen to be most desirable for both their current socioeconomic and educational situation, as well as what they believed would be their situation in the near future. These goals were predicated on each student's evaluation of the quality of their current life and what might maximize their social well-being in the near future.[3] In addition to accumulating money and status, well-being for students involved a qualitative sense of social comfort, psychological security, and intellectual interest.

Students' general understanding of well-being in life was clearly linked to images and ideas associated with the American Dream, such as the idea that every American has the opportunity to attain economic prosperity and happiness—i.e., a sense of security and comfort.[4] It was rare to find any student, or their parents, who did not identify with, or acknowledge, some of these elements among their personal goals. What usually varied among individual students was how ambitious their personal goals were to those associated with the American Dream.

Students applied their efforts in achieving the American Dream based on a strategy that involved their own assessment of their (1) personality; (2) academic and social capabilities; (3) motivation to utilize these qualities in divergent domains during high school; or (4) willingness to invest time and effort to improve their capabilities in these domains. They did not use the word strategy, nor did all students realize they were engaged in actions that could be described as a strategy, but all students undertook some type of planning for goals they considered positive.

In observing the variety of strategic actions that students undertook, I discovered four strategy-type patterns that I have labeled the Bureaucratic Track, the Entrepreneurial Track, the Wandering Track, and the Drifting Track. For each student, these strategic pathways included boundaries associated with achieving their desired goals.

Because these pathways created the kinds of challenges for students that we generally associate with the concept of academic tracking, I treat these pathways conceptually as "social tracking" because they combined the academic and social aspects of students' lives during high school. A first impression might be that a "social track" is simply another name for a social clique, but that would be inaccurate because the social tracks I describe involved groups of individuals all sharing a set of behaviors intended to satisfy their dispositions and goals. So, within each social track there were numerous social cliques.

The Bureaucratic Track

The general ideology underlying American education policy is that every individual has a right to receive the tools required to become economically self-sufficient. US presidents have used evocative titles for their policies like "No Child Left Behind" and "Every Student Succeeds" to reinforce this formal commitment.[5] Fundamentally, this philosophy supports the American Dream that is at the ideological foundation of the republic, and most families in the United States have been introduced to the idea that, by successfully completing high school and perhaps additional education, individuals can attain socioeconomic success.[6] Every school professional symbolically reinforces this principle by virtue of occupying an official position in the education hierarchy and by executing their everyday tasks and requiring student compliance with their directives.

School professionals in the studied schools all abided by some variant of a phrase used by Ms. Thomas, a social studies teacher at Brooklyn's Knickerbocker High School: "Being successful in school will provide you with what you will need to be successful in the future."[7] Most students and their families knew the standard arguments for complying with the established curricular aims of their school district, though not all conformed. Those who consistently conformed were following what I am calling the "Bureaucratic Track." I am using this term because the standard educational structure is a bureaucracy of some proportion—large in metropolitan districts and small in rural ones—and like all bureaucracies, the bureaucracies of the districts that included the schools I studied required students to assume a role and fulfill specific duties associated with that role.

The role that youths assume in the education bureaucracy is that of a student, and although this role remains the same for four years, the duties associated with it change as the individual navigates the curriculum during each year of high school. To be successful, students were required to execute their assigned duties and were rewarded with bureaucratic promotions (i.e., promoted to the next grade level) based on the assessment of their job performance by their immediate supervisors, who happened to be called teachers. Thus, the individual who commits to a position in this bureaucracy does so by submitting to the internal demands associated with following its codes and concomitant rewards and penalties.[8]

There were four reasons students from low-income backgrounds pursued the "Bureaucratic Track." The first had to do with the general process in the United States where youth are socialized by parents, siblings, peers, and professionals in education, business, trades, and religion toward the belief that fully participating in the formal system is the "normal" and best way to be occupationally and financially successful throughout life. Because this perspective represents the cultural ethos of American society, it was not surprising when students assumed this position since it represented what most authorities in the US characterize as the only legitimate way to realize goals and minimize negative encounters in the process of being educated.[9]

Following the Bureaucratic Track had both positive and negative consequences, however, depending on the circumstances a student encountered.

The behaviors most closely associated with the Bureaucratic Track were following the rules, attending class regularly, paying attention in class, and completing homework. Students understood that following this path did not guarantee success, but there was a companion belief that doing so provided a greater chance of success than pursuing any alternative. The comments of Lawrence, a 15-year-old sophomore at Oakland's Miwok High School, were representative of students who chose the Bureaucratic Track:

> Yea, I'm going to class and studying and stuff. I'm doing what everyone says is the right way to go to school 'cause I think it's best for me if I want to get a good profession and life. Plus, if you don't do it this way, you got to deal with all kinds of shit from school people and your parents.[10]

The second reason students chose the Bureaucratic Track was that all the peers they were socially involved with also had chosen it. Joining them not only reinforced what they believed were the future rewards of adopting this social track but facilitated their social relationships as well. The comments of Dora, a 16-year-old junior at Brooklyn's Knickerbocker High School, were typical:

> Oh, you say we should have more fun and not study like what the teachers tell us, but all our friends in school do it so how can we change without looking stupid? . . . and if we didn't do what we're doing, we'd have to meet all new people and stuff, and that would be really a mess.[11]

Despite the efforts of education officials to promote the positive returns to investing in the Bureaucratic Track, a number of stresses associated with it could impede a student's chances for advancing economically and socially. The first was a feeling of vulnerability that emanated from disappointment and insecurity due to a loss of confidence after expending a good deal of effort on being successful and not receiving the high grades or aptitude test scores that everybody expected. This affected students more than if they had not put effort into passing the course or standardized test because it challenged their sense of intellectual competence and altered their sense of self. I often observed students who felt vulnerable in this way resorting to the defense mechanism of articulating that the Bureaucratic Track they had committed to was a hoax. This defensive response significantly inhibited these individuals from seeking and committing to the remedial academic aid that was available. The conversation between 15-year-old sophomores Felton and Nathaniel, who were attending Los Angeles's Chester Himes High School, was representative of this group:

FELTON: No, I don't feel great right now 'cause I really put a lot of work into this course, and I just got C+ grades on all my exams. Maybe I just can't do A work.

NATHANIEL: Well if you're not getting it, why don't you ask Mr. Underwood if you can attend his "help class" after school?

FELTON: I don't know, maybe; but right now I'm feeling that what I've been working at is a big joke, and if I did ask for help it wouldn't make a difference.[12]

Felton did not attend any of his teacher's remedial lessons but did manage to receive a B– in the course. He was disappointed with the grade, but he carried on and received a B the next semester. He told another friend that he was "feeling depressed."[13]

The second observed cost to some students pursuing a Bureaucratic Track was an unintended consequence of teachers being so enamored with students abiding by the educational ethos that they used a moderated grading system or presented less demanding academic material, or both. Although these were teachers' actions, they could result in students receiving lower scores on the school district's or state's standardized tests than would have been expected, given the students' grade point average and success in class. Thus, the costs that these students incurred were a reduction in their self-confidence and an added burden of remedial work to bring their scores up to a level that would make them competitive for admission to a college of their choice.

The Entrepreneurial Track

The second social track students pursued was what I have labeled "Entrepreneurial" because the goals and behaviors of students who adopted this track resembled those of people participating in entrepreneurial activities. These were students who aimed to finish high school and then look for local business opportunities to make money.[14] There were clear differences between the ways that these students and those of the Bureaucratic Track related to school. The first difference was in how students viewed the world. Instead of seeing the local community as something to escape from, students in the Entrepreneurial Track saw it as a place where they not only could continue to live but could make a significant amount of money. These students tended to accept the social and cultural traditions of their poor neighborhood and the opportunities it offered, though limiting, to be socioeconomically mobile. Before continuing, it is essential to note that within the "Entrepreneurial" social track there existed a significant gender difference. I did not observe any female students choosing to participate in this social track during the twenty-three years covered in this study. At the end of the chapter I will discuss the reasons I found for this, but it should be understood that until then the discussion throughout this section will involve male students solely.

The students who adopted the Entrepreneurial Track had a strong sense of self-efficacy even though it often was misplaced. There was a confidence in one's agency, and that the poor economic circumstances they found themselves confronting were surmountable. Thus, these students believed they could be socioeconomically mobile within their neighborhoods and, with luck, within the larger society. The example they often used was of early rap musicians who began by performing for their local community and achieved status within it and then were "lucky" that their music crossed over to middle-class society, which produced socioeconomic mobility for them in the larger society. The comments of Cooper and Cesar were representative of this attitude. Cooper was a 15-year-old student at the Bronx's Lanape High School:

> Yea, you got it! I am going to do business for myself 'cause I know you can make money that way. I got some ideas about how to do that, and I'm going to try to see what I can do next year. . . . I'm going to start running dope for [the local syndicate] and save my money, then go into something else like selling high-end tennis shoes online. If you get the right kind of shoes, then you can make real good money, but I got other ideas, too, because there's opportunities here that I can turn into money.[15]

Cesar was a 17-year-old student at Los Angeles's Chumash High School:

> I ain't interested in that college shit they talk in school; and I ain't spending time doing stuff that don't give me money now. There's all kinds of stuff you can do to make real-good money, and that's what I'm trying to do. . . . My brother works for a construction company, and it's a crap job that I ain't doing any time at, but he told me that a lot of stuff they use gets stolen and he thinks resold. So that's what I'm checking out real fast, 'cause you can make real good money doing that; and with that money you can get a real nice home in this neighborhood. If that don't work, I'll be looking to see what other business I can get involved with to get money.[16]

A second way that students in the Entrepreneurial Track differed from those in the Bureaucratic Track in relation to school was an immense dislike of authority. Although many adolescents have some dislike of authority, students who chose the Entrepreneurial Track exhibited an extreme form of it. They focused on avoiding environments like school where they had to take orders from someone, and the only way they could see sustaining this over the long term was to develop an occupation where they could be self-employed. The comments of Stewart and Joaquin were representative of students in the Entrepreneurial Track. Stewart was a 15-year-old sophomore attending Brooklyn's Knickerbocker High School:

> All those fuckheads that sit there in class and do whatever the teacher told them to do is just fucking robots! I ain't into that shit, oh no, that ain't it for me. I'm about working for just me now and in the future, 'cause taking orders leaves you always catching up to somebody else's choices. So that's why I'm trying to talk to people here [school] and see what's possible and who might want to work on the same projects to make money.[17]

Joaquin was a 16-year-old junior attending Los Angeles's James K. Polk High School:

> I'm not interested in school stuff really. I just ain't. I want to work for myself and so even if we did go to college, we'd have to work for a company that we took orders from, and I really don't like to do that. My mom does that, and she's always worrying about her boss, so why would I want to do that? No, I'm going to do my own business. We just need some good ideas to make money and see who else wants to be a part of it. That's what we need to do while we're in school, 'cause it's a great place to meet people.[18]

The third difference between students who chose the Entrepreneurial Track instead of the Bureaucratic Track involved a desire to gain access to as many monetary and material resources as possible over their lifetime, and to rely on skills and strategies not provided by their high school. For these students, the strategy was to learn who was working in the illicit sector, how individuals in this sector worked, and what possibilities existed for them gaining access to participate.

Those who decided on the Entrepreneurial Track directed most of their attention toward people and practices in their neighborhoods. At the same time, they knew that attending high school could provide benefits for future projects that were not related to the curriculum. For example, they wanted to develop an extensive network of people who could aid them in businesses they might pursue in the future. They understood that people could provide information about what opportunities were available to make money, who was currently involved, and who were the competitors. Students who chose this track were open to seeing who they might meet that could be helpful in their pursuit of making money. This required spending a great deal of time both in meeting new people and maintaining ties within their network so as to maximize the number of people who might be able to provide assistance later. The comments of Junior and Manny were representative of students in the Entrepreneurial Track. Junior was a 16-year-old student at the Bronx's Van Twiller High School:

> You need to do what I do if you're going to be successful later. I check every-body out and make time to meet up with all kinds of folks because they may be able to help me get what I want from whatever business I want to do. I'm friendly to everybody and I keep contact with people so nothing gets dull. You know what I mean? . . . If you and me is going to do the business stuff we've talked about, we got to have lots of friends 'cause it's going to be about who we fucking know, not what we fucking learn in this school.[19]

Manny was a 15-year-old student at Oakland's Miwok High School:

> I've been talking to a whole lot of people about getting together and seeing if we can start some street business. This [school] is a great place to do this 'cause there's lots of people who might be interested. The more people we meet, or I guess the more I meet, the more contacts I got to help me later. All business is like this, you know? You got to have lots of people that know you and can help you when you need it. . . . I work every day on ideas to make money and adding to my list of people who can maybe help me with businesses I want to start. You should too, or hook up with me.[20]

Not all students who chose the Entrepreneurial Track focused solely on the illicit economy. Some student-athletes assumed an Entrepreneurial Track per-spective because they felt their work as an athlete and not as a student would make them successful and provide socioeconomic mobility. Many of those who wanted to be professional athletes assumed traits identical to the students who wanted to make money in the illegal economy because both occupations were considered viable professional pursuits with high status in their lower-income neighborhoods. The comments of Tremaine, a 16-year-old sophomore attend-ing the Bronx's Van Twiller High School, were an example:

> Hey, you got it, man. I be paying attention to getting a basketball scholar-ship, not getting no academic one. I don't want to be no egghead 'cause who

around here thinks eggheads is anything? ... I want to be known here as one of the guys who made it in basketball—and that's righteous respect. You know? So, I'll try to do what I have to so I'm eligible to play, but my real work is basketball.[21]

In brief, students in the Entrepreneurial Track constantly talked about schemes to make money in ways that many people in the local community believed were legitimate. They were preoccupied with discussing possible ventures whenever an idea came to their minds. Basically, a money-making scheme could come while they were in the classroom and the teacher was presenting educational material, in the hallway before or after class, in the cafeteria during lunch, or while traveling to and from school. Very often, a conversation about one scheme or another that had started before class would be resumed during instructional time through whispering or passing notes while the teacher was presenting material or when they were expected to be finishing an assignment. Students who chose the Entrepreneurial Track did not prioritize work related to their formal education, though many did try to complete it. What they did prioritize was educating themselves in the resources they would need to be successful primarily, though not exclusively, in the informal economy.

Now, let us return to the finding mentioned in the beginning of this section that no female students in this study participated in the Entrepreneurial Track. Information emerging from student discussions surrounding the Entrepreneurial Track indicated that females simply did not find the mission or focus of the track attractive. They viewed it as dominated by males whose interests and activities were centered around competition for resources. They saw participation in these entrepreneurial ventures as unattractive because they wanted to have positive social interactions with their male cohorts and avoid competition and conflict with them over what they saw as dull low-level economic activity. The comments of Lois, Vilma, and Erica were representative of this view over time.

Lois was a 16-year-old junior attending Brooklyn's Knickerbocker High School in 1993:

I don't like Jimmy and Darek's friends, you know the [Entrepreneurial] group they hang around with 'cause they just talk about who is doing what and how much money they made. That's really boring shit. Who wants to be around guys like that all the time?[22]

Vilma was a 15-year-old sophomore at Oakland's Miwok High School in 2006:

Yea, I like Donnie, but we don't see each other that much because he spends a lot of time with his [Entrepreneurial] group of friends. He asks me to hang out with them, but they're always talking business stuff and I really don't find that stuff at all interesting.[23]

Erica was a 17-year-old senior attending Los Angeles's James K. Polk High School in 2013:

No way I'm running around with that [Entrepreneurial] group! They got some really good-looking guys there, but they're arguing about like who cheated somebody and how they would get back at them; and I'm just not interested in being around them and all that conflict all the time over dumb stuff.[24]

In sum, the lack of female participation in the Entrepreneurial Track was not the result of males excluding them from associating, but rather the assessment by the young female students that this grouping had no social or practical benefit for them.

The Wandering Track

It is often thought that students wander in school when their attention is interrupted by a new thought, but in observing high school students for the studies incorporated into this book, I found considerable evidence that wandering involved more than inattention to a particular scholastic assignment. I observed two forms of behavior in the various high schools I studied that could be considered wandering. The first involved a deliberate search for something that inspired the student intellectually, though not necessarily something in the school's academic curriculum. The second was associated with a student physically walking in the hallways and other public spaces while classwork was occurring. In the present analysis, I include only the first form in the "Wandering Track"; the second behavior is substantively different and is part of the social track discussed next.

The students who chose the Wandering Track generally did not lack academic skills. They were in quest of topics and courses that excited their interest. Their quest involved constantly responding to what was being presented in class. They generally challenged the material as uninteresting, and their focus would fluctuate between the material and concepts quite tangential to it.

An example of this involved Barbara, a 16-year-old attending Los Angeles's Chester Himes High School. During her English class the teacher was describing how the proper use of language in the text they were reading elicited a particular feeling. Barbara said, "I don't get why we need to know what is proper language or use it." The teacher responded, "Well, it is important to use language in its proper form because that is the way we will best be able to express ourselves." Barbara retorted, "It doesn't seem to be a big deal at all to me. I mean, it's just as interesting to me how music sounds that have no words can make meaning too, and we come up with different sounds all the time to make feelings. I think that needs to be checked out." The teacher responded, "Well, that's true, but the whole issue of sounds and how they relate to language is something that we cannot get into right now."[25]

Individuals who chose the Wandering Track did not know what they were interested in, but they did have self-awareness as to when they were interested in something. So, they wandered from one subject, topic, or vocational goal to another looking for intellectual stimulation. This behavior was observed in these students' getting excited with a particular course's material in the beginning of the semester, losing interest generally after a month, and then moving on to something outside of the course's parameters. The comments of Dalin and Alex are examples. Dalin was a 16-year-old junior at Oakland's Kaiser High School:

> I was into the astronomy stuff we were learning in science, but then in class someone asked something about biological stuff in space; and I thought, 'That's pretty interesting.' So, now I'm reading stuff on biology even though I know that's not what we're studying, but hey, that's what I'm interested in now.[26]

Alex was a 16-year-old junior at Brooklyn's Knickerbocker High School:

> The stuff on the Civil War was real interesting, but after the teacher mentioned the civil war in France, I thought, 'That's pretty interesting.' So, I don't know why, but I went off and got a book on the French civil war and I'm reading it instead.[27]

When Wandering Track students exhibited interest in a course's material, the interest was real, and teachers often recognized the excitement and attempted to build on it, believing the student had a future in school if only the material could be made interesting enough to "grab them." However, regardless of the teacher's efforts, what most often occurred was the student's interest faded after they learned more about the subject matter. Jerry was a 15-year-old sophomore at Los Angeles's Chumash High School is an example:

> I was really interested in biology and cutting into the frogs and seeing all the parts that were part of their bodies, but then we have to memorize all the different parts of other animals and stuff, and I just can't get excited about memorizing that stuff. It just ain't for me, but I'm interested in checking a lot things out and seeing what's really interesting.[28]

As mentioned earlier, students following the Wandering Track path often got bored. When this happened, they tended to get into small amounts of classroom trouble, such as engaging in a disruption, even though they were unlikely to have initiated it. In addition, they were regularly viewed by the teacher as totally detached and reprimanded for not paying attention. In both of these situations, the student had simply lost interest and their mind was looking for a new stimulus.

Lastly, like students in all the social tracks, the students in the Wandering Track did not prefer to be alone. They sought out others who felt the way they did. These associations reinforced their sense of being "deviant" from the average student in their high school, but they thought this deviance made them "superior" to their peers. The comments of Julia and Bryan were representative. Julia was a 16-year-old junior at Los Angeles's Polk High School:

> I see all those other students just sitting there dealing with boring stuff and not trying to check other stuff out that might be really interesting. I check new things all the time. If I don't find the stuff the teacher's doing interesting, I try to see what's interesting in the whole area, even if it's not what everybody else is doing. I just keep changing, but most of the other people I meet here in school just either totally check out and do nothing or act like some kind of science fiction clones or something [her friend laughs]. . . . I guess we're just smarter, or got it more together than them [her friend nods in agreement].[29]

Bryan was a 15-year-old sophomore attending the Bronx's Lanape High School:

> My mother always is saying to me, "You're changing your mind all the time about what's great in school and what's shitty, and you need to settle down and just do what is required in the school." But she don't see that some things is interesting to start and then really, really boring. So, you got to keep looking for stuff that's interesting, or your mind's going to dry up. You and me is

doing it different, but it's years ahead of the ones that be just going along with everything. Right? [His friend nods in agreement.][30]

Finally, it is important to emphasize that among students in the Wandering Track the pattern of searching, finding, and searching again continued for large portions of each grade and sometimes for multiple grades. They could remain in this track well into their senior year of high school and beyond. All of the students I observed in this social track did graduate, although those who transitioned to college most often did not do so immediately.

The Drifting Track

A fourth social track existed among students attending the schools in the present research. I call it the "Drifting Track." It included students who had a propensity to roam the hallways during instructional time to escape the demands of the classroom. These students were not like those in the Wandering Track, who "wandered off" mentally from the content being presented in class but stayed in the room.[31] Students in the Drifting Track had no particular goal other than to have no academic goals. This was accomplished by avoiding situations where one had to, or was expected to, declare a goal.

Students in the Drifting Track had no specific interest in any educational subject or in what formal education might provide them. They were disengaged from the school's formal curriculum and unconcerned about what they might do in the distant future. Most students in this track would say they knew their parents and teachers were concerned about what they would do in the distant future, but these students did not want to think about their future. The comments of Sally and Alfredo are examples. Sally was a 16-year-old student at the Bronx's Van Twiller High School:

> Fuck Mr. Stanton [the English teacher]! He's bothering the shit out of me! Every time he sees me in class, he's asking if I'm ready to start concentrating on schoolwork. And every time I say, yes, but then he goes on and on about me floating around and not taking school serious enough for anything good to happen in the future. It's getting tiring because I'm in tenth grade, and the future is a fucking long way off, you know?! He wants me to be some fucking follow the donkey shit! I just want to cruise. I'll figure out the future later. [The two students she is talking to shake their heads in agreement].[32]

Alfredo was a 16-year-old student at Los Angeles's Chester Himes High School:

> My mom and dad keep wanting me to tell them what I want to do in the future. You know, like, am I going to college and stuff. But I really don't know what I'm going to do, and I wish they'd stop bothering me about it. I'll think about it later. What about you? [His friend shrugs, and they enter their next class.][33]

It is often thought that students like Sally and Alfredo are adrift because they were academically challenged, but this was difficult to assess because students in the Drifting Track did not indicate any interest in academic work. The examples of Sally and Alfredo were chosen because they both drifted throughout high school and, although both minimally satisfied state requirements and graduated with their classes, they took different paths after high school. A year after graduating, Alfredo was attending community college, while Sally was working as a clerk in a department store. Three years later, Alfredo transferred as a psychology major to a state university, while Sally was working in accounts receivable at a mail-order clothing store.[34]

What separated students in the Drifting Track from those in other social tracks was a myopic focus on the present. They were concerned with the experiential "now" and determined to resist being forced to think about the future. Some professional observers at the schools I studied characterize these students as "disengaged," believing their situation was caused by a failure of the school's professionals to engage them in a way that would ignite their interests and provide them the opportunity to maximize what economic philosopher Amartya Sen calls their "individual capabilities."[35] However, this was a misdiagnosis.

In the schools I studied, the Drifting Track accumulated students lacking interest in academics, although they had a heightened interest in pursuing a fun social experience while at high school. I observed these students drifting from one experience to another, and their walking in the hallways was an extension of them simply responding to an immediate impulse to experience something different from what was occurring in one of their classes.[36] What differentiated the individuals in this social track from those in the Wandering Track was their constant state of responding to whatever new stimulus occurred. In essence, they were in a state of drifting in the same way that an object responding to a current in a river drifts, whereas the students in the Wandering Track were pursuing something that would interest them.

Ultimately, individuals in the Drifting Track were in a constant state of reacting, and those in the Wandering Track were in a constant state of acting.

CHANGING SOCIAL TRACKS

The academic literature on academic tracking has highlighted how students are constrained from moving from their original placement to a more demanding curricular track.[37] Thus, it would be appropriate to ask whether a student in one of the social tracks I have described could decide to change tracks and do it successfully. The immediate empirical answer is "yes," but three aspects to that answer loom most important in understanding such a change and its significance for the student's educational transitions: (1) the factors that influenced a call for change; (2) the factors influencing a student's ability to make a successful change; and (3) the choice patterns that existed between the origin track and destination track.

To begin it is important to understand that there were students in each of the high schools studied who were attracted to a particular social track because they were either excited about participating in it, they doubted they were capable of participating in another track, or they became complacent in it because they neither wanted or could not decide what they wanted to do in their near- or long-term futures.

The most prevalent factor that influenced students to want to change social tracks was related to obstacles they met in their current track that sparked doubt that they could realize their goals if they remained there. This was particularly prevalent among students in the Bureaucratic Track who lost or did not acquire the academic skills needed for their current classes, or who lacked confidence in their ability to garner these skills soon. The comments of Alejandra, a 16-year-old junior at Tongva High School in Los Angeles, were representative:

> I'm having a real difficult time in math and science. I just can't understand the stuff like I used to. I mean, I understand some stuff, but not everything like I was doing before, and I got two bad grades on my tests. I don't know if I can make stuff up, you know? I think I just need to check out some other things in school and see what I like and [might] be better at.[38]

The second-most-prevalent factor spurring change was among the students who had opted into the Entrepreneurial Track and consisted of an inability, or a limited ability, to generate new projects that they could influence others to join; or a realization that their personality was not conducive to establishing the social contacts required for their business plans to work. The comments of Aurelio and Damon were representative of these thoughts. Aurelio was a 16-year-old junior at the Bronx's Lanape High School:

> You know, I think I'm going to just stop putting the effort into coming up with good ideas for making money. Ain't none of them been interesting to anybody. I'd just be better off studying and doing my homework. That's fucked up, but my mom would be happy! [His friends laugh.][39]

A month after making this comment, Aurelio started consistently trying to study and complete his homework. Two months after that, he joined an after-school chess club. All indications were that he had switched tracks, and he began to socialize primarily with students who were in the Bureaucratic Track.

Damon was a 15-year-old attending Los Angeles's Chumash High School:

> Fuck, I been trying to make friends with people I need for getting a project going and ain't making no headway. I just don't think people like me enough. Whatever, it ain't working, and I got to do something different with my time than trying to come up with making money. I really don't know what that is, but I guess I'll figure it out.[40]

For the remaining two months of the fall semester, and for the entire second semester, Damon did very little and hung around with other students who were looking for something that interested them—i.e., they were in what I have labeled the Wandering Track.

Two other factors spurred students to initiate a change of social tracks. The first was discovering they had a talent they had not recognized, and the second was becoming bored with what they were doing and wanting a break from something they considered dull. For the individuals who discovered a talent, which could be in sports, arts, academic writing, or math, this new reality presented both opportunities and dilemmas as to what they should do next. Similarly, students who were simply bored also were searching for something that excited them. Thus, when they chose to make a change, the pattern of behavior for both inspired and bored students was to seek out individuals who were active in the new vocation and develop relationships that could act as conduits to the new social track. The comments of Jackie and Evron were representative of the students making changes for the two reasons just given. Jackie was a 16-year-old attending Los Angeles's Chester Himes High School:

Did you ever do something that you were just playing around with and say, "Hey, I'm pretty good?" I mean, I was just drawing some stuff, and all of a sudden, the lesson in geometry today was just really clear. So, then I went to the other lessons and I could do all the questions, and they were right. I don't know, I just think I can see this math stuff, 'cause I got a B+ in algebra and really didn't study anything.... I'm going to check out some more of this math stuff and start thinking about college.[41]

Jackie had been in a Drifting Track, but after this conversation she associated primarily with students who were in what I have labeled the Bureaucratic Track. She had discovered a talent that she had not been aware of, and this stimulated her to change social tracks to see how far it would take her. By the time she reached her senior year, she had received mostly A grades in math and science and B grades in her other courses. Further, all but one of her friends was in the Bureaucratic Track. After graduating from high school, she attended University of California at San Diego and was majoring in math.

Evron was a 15-year-old student attending Brooklyn's Knickerbocker High School:

... [I'm] just plain bored at the moment and got to find something different to do. I been thinking about checking out stuff and seeing what's out there. I don't know, maybe there's nothing, but I'm going to check.[42]

Observing Evron after he made this statement, I noticed that almost all the students he had been associating with in school during his freshman year were in the Bureaucratic Track. Two of his teachers told me that he was a B student. Three weeks after he made this statement at the beginning of his sophomore year, I observed him with a group of students in the Entrepreneurial Track. Another two months later, he was socializing primarily with students interested in partying, drinking, and smoking marijuana who were in the Drifting Track. Then, another month later, he began an association with students in what I have labeled the Wandering Track. On numerous occasions, I was invited to join their group, and the conversations were permeated with comments about exploring new academic subjects that "might be interesting." By his senior year, Evron was interested in environmental science and back associating with individuals in the Bureaucratic Track. After graduating, he enrolled in a community college and was studying environmental science.

Figure 5.1 displays the trajectory of forty students from my participant-observation notes for 1997 to 1999, 2003 to 2006, and 2009 to 2011. I made

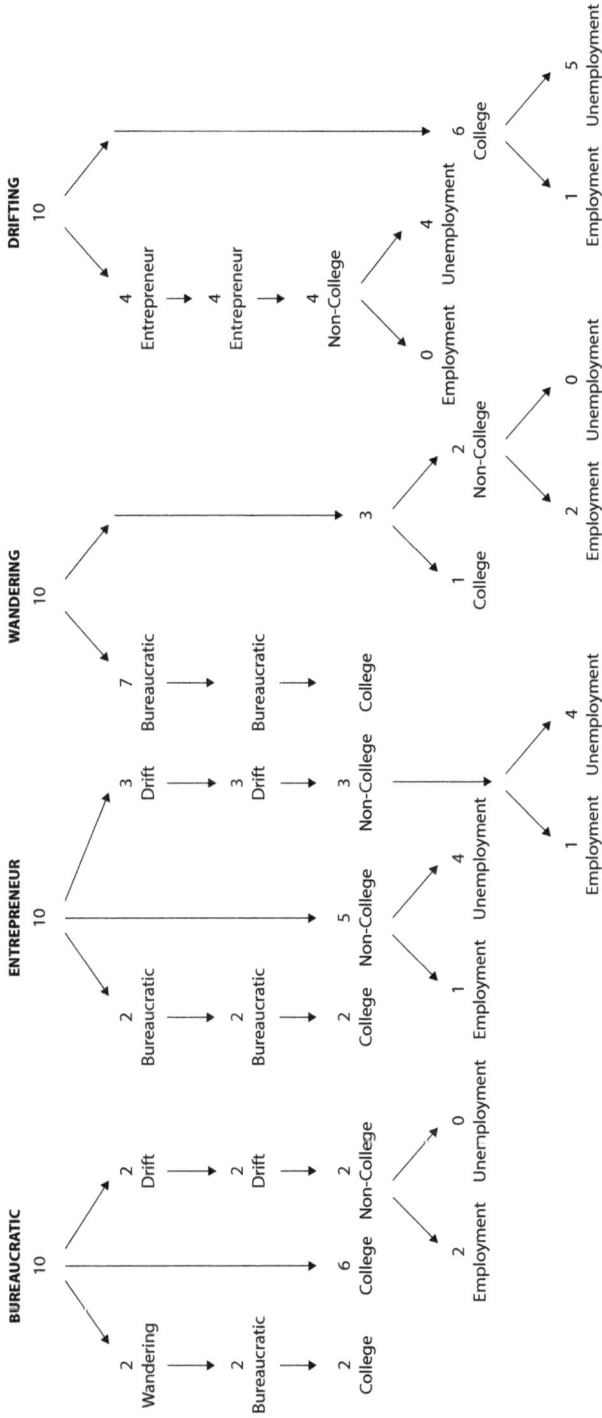

FIGURE 5.1. Trajectories of individuals in various social tracks.

NOTE: Fifty students were randomly chosen in 2003 to be followed for five years. The intent was to follow each from their beginning year in high school through one year beyond graduation, 2008. These 50 students are not the total number of students identified and recorded as being in one of the four social tracks. The total from my notes is 680. The figure reports the results of 40 students, as 10 of the original 50 selected dropped out of school. Of the 10 who dropped out, 6 were identified as "Entrepreneurs," 3 as "Drifting," and 1 as "Wandering." See text for a description of the "Entrepreneur," "Drift," "Wandering," and "Bureaucratic" categories used in the study.

substantial field notes pertaining to the 169 students categorized in the various social tracks, but selected only forty to follow closely to see if changes occurred. This sample of forty includes students from all the high schools in the study: five males and five females in the Bureaucratic Track; ten males in the Entrepreneurial Track (I did not find any females who adopted this social track); five males and five females in the Wandering Track; and five males and five females in the Drifting Track.

This figure displays data on the forty students' trajectories when they decided to change social tracks by presenting the raw number of students in each category and the destination of change when it occurred. The students in the figure had a tendency to follow particular patterns when changing social tracks. Those who were in the Bureaucratic Track tended to stay in that social track, but if change occurred it was in two different directions. When individuals in this track lost their focus on academic subject matter, it was associated with a loss of interest in academics more generally, and this was followed by a search for an interesting replacement. They tended, as their search continued, to switch to what I have called the Wandering Track, where they joined others in search of something worthy of their full attention. The comments of Adriana, a 17-year-old junior at Oakland's Kaiser High School, were representative of both this attitude and behavioral change:

> No I ain't been hanging with them [her previous friends] anymore. I'm hanging with Jay, Catia, and Lori now 'cause we all kind of been looking around and checking out what's interesting to do here at school. . . . yeah, I was doing OK in my studies, but I just wasn't that interested in the stuff so I thought it'd be good to just start seeing if there is something else that would be interesting, you know? I been checking out some things like shop and art, but I kind of like to check out some stuff like astronomy, you know?[43]

In assessing Adriana's comments, I asked three teachers about her and the new people she was socializing with, and each one confirmed that all of these students were very capable academically but were not focused on anything in particular. All three teachers said that these students seemed to be "looking around trying to find something that really interested them."[44] It is important to point out that all the students who remained in the Bureaucratic Track and all those who switched to the Wandering Track and then back to the Bureaucratic Track went on to college. So, all had a significant foundation in academic skills.

The second pattern involved changing from the Bureaucratic Track to the Drifting Track, which generally occurred when a student experienced failure in one or more academic courses and lost confidence that they could be academically successful. The comments of Victor, a 15-year-old sophomore at the Bronx's Van Twiller High School, were typical:

> . . . I don't know, it was just that I was not getting the math and English stuff, and don't know if college is for me. So, I been going to classes and stuff, but mostly just been hanging with friends and seeing what's up here and there. We been cruising around checking out all the partying stuff.[45]

The new people Victor socialized with the most in school were described by three different teachers as "not focused on anything but having fun."[46]

Of the ten students who were in the Entrepreneurial Track, half (five) remained there throughout high school. Five students who had started in the Entrepreneurial Track decided to change social tracks, including two who switched to the Bureaucratic Track. When that occurred, the student had experienced the risk of being physically hurt or killed in their entrepreneurial activities or they had suffered a bad outcome in one of their ventures and lost a considerable amount of money. These occasions influenced them to conclude that the successes associated with entrepreneurial activity were not worth the risks, or that they would not succeed as entrepreneurs. However, contact with a school counselor nearly always preceded a decision to switch to the Bureaucratic Track.

All of the students I observed who wanted to change from the Entrepreneurial to the Bureaucratic track were bright but needed remedial help. The example of Murphy, a 16-year-old attending Los Angeles's Chester Himes High School, was representative. Murphy approached a counselor and asked to meet. At the meeting, he stated clearly that he wanted to commit to his studies and wanted the counselor to help him develop a plan so he could graduate from high school and go to college. The counselor indicated that he had passed his courses with Cs but that his aptitude test scores showed he was "very capable" of higher grades.

When asked why he had not done better and why he was changing his attitude, Murphy said he had previously devoted most of his time to "a number of business ventures" that he believed would produce "a very large sum of money" for him, but that one had turned bad and his partner had been shot in the arm. Murphy said he feared he would be killed because he had been shot at, and that made him feel like he needed to change what he was doing. After meeting with the counselor, Murphy took some additional after-school remedial courses. The counselor reported to me that he got all Bs that year, improved his grades the following year to a B+ average and graduated. The next year after graduating he was admitted to California State University–Pomona.

The second move made by individuals who had been in the Entrepreneurial Track was to the Drifting Track. This was motivated by the same reasons that spurred students in the Entrepreneurial Track to move to the Bureaucratic Track: They had a negative experience in pursuing their business interests. These students did not try to move to the Bureaucratic Track because they were not confident they would be successful. They expressed a low self-assessment of their academic abilities and, given this and their desire to leave the Entrepreneurial Track, they gravitated to the Drifting Track, where students let school activities take them in a direction that fostered enjoyment. The comments of Reynaldo, a 16-year-old attending Oakland's Miwok High School, were representative:

> Shit, the police came and busted up the after-hours place that me, Tomás, Wilber, and Luis had set up. We were making good money, but that's over now because Wilber and Luis got caught, and probably they're going to get some years for it. Me and Tomás were lucky, but I got to get out of any spotlight, you know? I went to school and talked to one of my teachers about trying to study hard and trying to maybe go to college or something. . . . He was supporting me, but I really ain't study-smart, so I'm just going to have fun and see where things take me while I'm here [in school]. At least I won't get into trouble, 'cause me and jail ain't good! [Two of his friends nod and laugh.][47]

The next general change in social tracking involved students in the Wandering Track who were looking for something which would interest them enough that they could commit to it. Of the ten students in this social track, seven moved to the Bureaucratic Track. In brief, while wandering, they came across a subject that interested them and then committed their energy not only to their new interest but to all of their academic subjects. They typically said they now understood that, if they wanted to pursue their new subject of interest, they needed to do well in all their academic subjects. So, even though their passion focused in one subject area, they devoted the time required to do well in all their subjects. The comments of Norma, a 16-year-old junior at Los Angeles's Chumash High School, were representative of this group:

> You know, I really am interested in the stuff I'm learning in chemistry. It's amazing, it's just so incredibly interesting. Most school stuff is boring and I really couldn't get into it but this I find great! ... Well, I told my history teacher how interested I was in chemistry, and she said, "Well, if you're wanting to keep studying it, you're going to have to do good enough in the other classes, or you won't be able to go on." I heard her, and that's why I've been working hard in my other classes and getting good grades. I really think I want to keep with chemistry. [After she graduated from high school, Norma attended UCLA and still planned to major in chemistry.][48]

This particular change is understandable because the students in the Wandering Track were academically skilled but lacked intense interest in any of their subjects. So, they looked around for a subject that would fascinate them. I followed all the students I observed in the Wandering Track for a year after they graduated, and the seven who changed to the Bureaucratic Track all went immediately on to four-year universities. Of the three who kept wandering throughout high school, one went to a four-year college, and the other two were unemployed a year after graduating.

The last switch in social tracks involved students who were in the Drifting Track. Although most students I categorized in the Drifting Track stayed there throughout high school, when students moved out of this track they generally went to the Entrepreneurial Track. Four of the ten students I followed in this track changed to the Entrepreneurial Track. In their cases, while drifting, they had made friends in the Entrepreneurial Track who convinced them there were opportunities for them to make money while still having fun. This was particularly attractive to them because they had skill deficiencies and found academic work difficult and unpleasant. The comments of Dario, a 17-year-old junior at the Bronx's Lanape High School, were representative of those who made this change:

> Nah, I was just doing nothing and hanging with a few friends having fun when this guy came and was hanging. When we was alone, he just started talking, and I was just listening. Well, you know, I was surprised that it was not a bunch of shit that I thought it would be. He got an idea about selling this distilled liquor that his uncle and cousin make to kids here at school when they party. I went with him, and the stuff is good and potent, so I said I'm in, and I put a little money in and a lot of time, but we been getting

about ten or fifteen kids from school to buy the stuff each week. He's got another idea that I like too, and so I'm going to keep doing stuff with him. Ain't no question there's a lot of money to be doing this stuff in the future. [A year after he graduated from high school, he was selling marijuana out of an abandoned building and prostituting two women, one of whom he was living with.][49]

Of the ten students I observed in the Drifting Track, six stayed, including one who went on to junior college four years after graduating from high school and five who were unemployed a year after graduating. Of the four students who switched from the Drifting Track to the Entrepreneurial Track, none attended college and all were unemployed a year after graduating.

In sum, most students I observed did not change social tracks during high school, but if change did occur, the primary requirements for it were (1) a change in goals, (2) a new commitment in focus and allocation of time, and (3) the development of peer friendships in the new track. While change was occurring, the students experiencing it felt like they were in a social limbo, in that while they were adjusting to a new set of norms and behavior they simply did not feel a part of either their old or their new group. Figure 5.1 reports the trajectory of students who successfully fulfilled a desire to change social tracks. It should be noted that I recorded a significant number of students who experienced difficulty in adjusting to a new group's norms and behaviors, aborted their effort to switch tracks, and reverted to their original social track. So, while students could change social tracks, the process was fluid.

SOME FINISHING COMMENTS

Most sociological research on education has been concerned with the impact of structures on student performance. In these analyses, as in all structural analyses, the student becomes an object responding to the prearranged formations they confront. However, if structures were all-powerful, we would not see variation in the behaviors and outcomes of people who interact with them. What became evident in the current study was that, within the various school structures, individual students had agency and exercised it in ways that either aligned or resisted official school structure; and their actions moved them in varying directions.[50]

There were a number of reasons that exercising their agency did not yield uniform results for students. First, there were two parallel sorting processes within the schools: an official curricular tracking system and a parallel social tracking system that students formed through the choices they made. This second system had a profound influence on student behavior and, in turn, a meaningful impact on students' academic trajectory. It is important to emphasize that there was enough flexibility in the social tracking structure for students who seemed fated or channeled to certain life outcomes to dramatically change their trajectories. This speaks to the importance of agency, the sense of self-efficacy, and the potential for a chance intervention to make a difference in an individual's academic trajectory.

Conclusion

Prosperity is not without many fears and distastes; and adversity
is not without comforts and hopes.

FRANCIS BACON,
Of Adversity, 1625

AMERICA HAS LONG RECOGNIZED the importance of education in promoting financial security and status. It has depended on the public education
system to provide the opportunity for socioeconomic mobility. This study
focused on schools servicing low-income students, asking: What obstacles do
students from low-income families face while attending a high school in a
low-income area?; and when obstacles are confronted, how do they affect an
individual's trajectory in high school and their ability to successfully transition to college? In this concluding chapter, I address the contributions this
book provides for understanding the school challenges that low-income
youth confront by (1) discussing the issues associated at the micro level of the
educational transition process involving individuals and their families; (2)
moving to issues at the meso level involving the various educational administrative tiers, teachers, counselors, and curriculums; and (3) ending with a
discussion of those at the macro level involving the importance of education
in the maintenance of the American Dream ideology and society. In addition, I offer various policy recommendations to address the issues presented
in particular sections. However, before proceeding, I want to emphasize that
although I will address various aspects of education at the micro, meso, and
macro levels, for analytical and policy clarity it should be remembered that
they are all interconnected and work together in generating the outcomes
seen in American society.

INDIVIDUAL, FAMILY, AND EDUCATION
CHALLENGES

The data presented in this book has identified many, though certainly not all, of the obstacles faced by youth attending high schools serving mainly lower-income communities, and how they presented challenges to their progress during high school and beyond. These obstacles came from a number of sources: (1) the national and state political agendas associated with providing educational opportunities to all the nation's youth and the local school district's responses to these agendas; (2) the school district's official plan and strategy (i.e., the formal curriculum); (3) the goals of school administrators with responsibility for providing a quality education to these youth on a daily basis; (4) the competence, creativity, and commitment of teachers and staff (counselors and deans) charged with implementing the plan; (5) the technical, resource, and emotional support provided to each student from parents, siblings, and peers; and (6) each individual student's interests, goals, and skills at various stages in the process. Further, I charted how these played out at the micro level in shaping the actions and experiences of the youth in the study.

To begin, we learned that no one student confronted all of the obstacles addressed in the book, but many confronted a considerable number of them, and some dealt with certain obstacles multiple times during their time in high school. We also learned that in most cases no single incident would limit a student's ability to make the transition from high school to the next educational stage of their life, although it was possible for one incident to have a critical impact on a student successfully transitioning from one semester or grade to the next. The most important finding about the nature of the obstacles faced by students did not concern the potency of any single obstacle that was critical for the transition process, but the number of obstacles that students encountered and how successful they were in overcoming them.

It is important to note that youth from middle-income families also encounter problems, a few of which are similar to those faced by the youth from low-income families, but they do not face them in the same way. Research has shown that middle-class youth have additional material and social resources, particularly those associated with their parents, that can eliminate an obstacle or reduce its adverse effects.[1] However, for low-income students whose families lack the resources to mitigate the educational challenges they encounter, these challenges have a profound impact on their ability to make a successful transition. Remember, the meaning of "transitioning" as defined in the introduction of this book is not simply "advancing" from one grade to the next or from high school to college; "advancing" simply implies that a person moves from one location to the next, whereas "transitioning" means that a person moves from one level of learning to the next and is able to both understand the new material and competently execute the concomitant operations associated with it. Therefore, at the micro level—and it should be remembered that factors at the meso and macro levels also shape the individual—a decisive factor for low-income youth in successfully managing obstacles toward transitioning was a person's internal determination, which was composed of three elements. The first was an individual's character and whether they had a clear sense of self and confidence in the qualities understood as making up who they were. If they did, then no matter what obstacles were presented to them, they did not feel inferior or lose the conviction that they were a person of value. The second element of internal determination was confidence in their ability to understand what was necessary to surmount an obstacle, where to seek assistance, and how to use the assistance they received. The third element was a resolve to push on in addressing current and future obstacles, irrespective of any history of being unsuccessful in negotiating past ones.

Another factor found to affect a student's ability to overcome obstacles and successfully transition was some form of luck. Two forms of luck made a decisive impact. The first had to do with a teacher, counselor, or administrator intervening to aid a student encountering one or more obstacles. What made the aid "luck" had to do with the fact that individuals offered it outside of what would be required or professionally expected of them. Thus, the teacher, counselor, or administrator providing the help, the timing of the help, and the help's effectiveness in overcoming the obstacle were, when considered as a whole, perchance. The second form of luck was an event that changed a student's focus and enabled them to find a way to overcome the obstacle. What made this "luck" was that the fortuitous event was unexpected and indirectly related to the change it stimulated in the student to improve their educational performance and make a successful transition.

Improving educational outcomes for individuals from low-income families requires a significant number of counselors, and each of the schools studied needed many more counselors than they currently had. Students from low-income backgrounds faced obstacles that their parents, siblings, and peers were unable to mitigate, so greater responsibility fell on school personnel. Teachers can certainly aid in maximizing the competency of students in various skills to advance academic achievement, but because many obstacles that low-income students face fall outside the classroom and a teacher's ability to intervene, counseling staff are in a more strategic position to help students address them. Therefore, a general assessment of how likely a student is at any given stage during high school to make an effective and smooth transition would help determine both whether intervention was necessary and what interventions promised the best results for the student's success.[2] Thus, a suggested policy intervention to address this situation would be for the counseling staff in high schools serving low-income students be increased, and that they have greater interventional authority—i.e., that they have authorization to intervene in determining why students are experiencing difficulty without having to wait for an official referral from school administrators or teachers.

Of course, the above discussion assumes that counselors have the necessary training in academic support, social-psychological guidance, and career advising to provide the assistance and intervention low-income students often require. Consequently, increasing the number of fully trained counselors in each of these areas and improving the student-counselor ratio is as important as improving the student-teacher ratio.

A useful heuristic for understanding the high school experience of youth from low-income families is to revisit the title to this book, *Potholes in the Road*. Having been told that everyone must attend school and that there are benefits if they progress to the completion of their schooling, the young people in this study entered school for the first time like a new car off the production line. By the time they reached high school they had logged some miles to be sure, but they knew they were near the end of a twelve-year drive. However, despite the end being in sight, the last four years of the drive were particularly challenging and served as the proving ground for the education system's assessment of both the student's and the system's merits.

Using this automotive metaphor, all the students in this study faced obstacles in pursuing the completion of high school. These obstacles have been described throughout the empirical chapters of this book and, for students, they were like the potholes that automobiles confront. For example, if a car is going fast a pothole presents a greater shock to its frame than if it is traveling more slowly. The analogous situation is a student cruising along in a particular course and then confronted with material they could not master. This could result in a poor exam grade and cause a greater shock to their self-confidence system than if they had been experiencing some difficulty in understanding the material before taking the exam.

Despite the fact that a sudden pothole shock could be greater for some students than others, most important was the number of pothole shocks that any one student absorbed and whether they received any periodic maintenance (academic or counseling support) to mitigate the impact of these potholes. It should be added that the potholes themselves can be addressed with policy, but the individual's and system's will to fix them has not been consistently present.

Students who were more likely successful in completing high school and transitioning to college needed not only to make a commitment to succeed but to absorb disappointments, insecurities, hazards, and detours during their travels. Of equal importance was their ability to seek aid when they felt vulnerable to breaking down and surrendering their goal of completing high school and attending college. When students sought assistance, it was the equivalent of a driver taking their car to a mechanic for maintenance. The difference is that the mechanic for the student was a counselor, teacher, or dean, and those students who met with one or more of these individuals and explained their problems were more likely to receive the aid necessary to effectively carry on. Of course, there were no guarantees that the consultant the student approached was competent. When students encountered incompetent "mechanics," it was those who continued to seek out professionals more capable of effective assistance who were more likely to carry on and succeed in their academics than students who did not.

For those students who never made a commitment to academics (i.e., doing well in their coursework) or who succumbed to obstacles and became demoralized, the most likely outcomes were (1) dropping out of high school; (2) looking immediately after graduation for local job opportunities that required few skills, paid low to moderate wages, and offered unreliable employment and no benefits; (3) taking on the high-stakes risks associated with activity in the illicit economy; or (4) being unemployed and receiving some form of financial assistance.[3] However, for the low-income students who made the commitment to succeed in high school so they could continue their education at college, the ability to not let the obstacles they confronted affect their sense of self or sense of competence was likely to lead them both to finish high school and to experience the first step toward a successful transition to college—i.e., gaining official admission.

Let us now turn to the meso level of the education process. Max Weber identified bureaucracies as a central feature of complex societies and described their tendency to perpetually expand their personnel and responsibilities.[4] This certainly occurs in US educational bureaucracies at the federal, state, and large-city levels. Sizeable bureaucracies require large financial, material, and workforce support, and with that come important political decisions as to who gets what, when, and how.[5] Further, as resources and political decisions regarding their allocation increase, so too do the responsibilities associated with choosing educational goals, how they will be achieved, who will be accountable for achieving them, and what the means will be to determine whether they have been reached. Given, as described in chapter 1, that members of the education bureaucracy and society have their own interests, politics often plays a significant role in the education transition process. Attempting to satisfy the wants and needs of various interest groups associated with national, state, and local education authorities can lead to corruption, compromise, and impediments in the effort to provide every student the opportunity to receive the skills and knowledge they need for a successful transition to their next stage of life.

Although it would not be possible to eliminate politics in education, I suggest the way to minimize its impact would be to establish independent review boards composed of education specialists from outside the districts. These boards, similar to corporate boards of directors, would have authority to review the policies for filling administrative vacancies, developing and implementing curriculum, and recruiting and retaining teachers. Probably the most pivotal decisions confronting these boards would have to do with teacher recruitment and retention because the focus would be on establishing procedures for evaluating teachers' expertise in the substantive areas they are presenting to students and the likely effectiveness of their presenting methods. The importance of recruiting high-quality teachers cannot be overemphasized because students from lower-income families depend more on classroom instruction than students from middle- and upper-income families, who often have parents, or tutors the parents have hired, to supplement what they are learning in the classroom.

Programs to aid in retaining high-quality teachers, such as periodic year-long sabbaticals to attend courses providing new information in their instructional areas and the most effective ways to deliver it, would need to be an integral part of teacher contracts. Further, pay for teachers who work in schools in low-income areas would need to be higher because these positions require more on-hands instructional work than does working in schools in middle- and upper-income areas. What is more, teachers who work with low-income students experience more stress because they are entrusted with providing these students with both the academic skills and scholastic material necessary to transition to the next stage of education. Plus, they must do it with less familial support than if they were teaching middle- or upper-income students, and sometimes with less student cooperation. Not recognizing this aspect of the job and financially compensating for it has historically threatened the ability of school administrators to retain high-quality teachers throughout their faculties.

High-quality faculty are indispensable to students making a successful transition, but a structural problem that administrators faced was the lack of a whole teaching staff with the expertise, commitment, and stamina to provide the instructional support low-income students typically require. As reported in chapter 3, teaching in low-income schools is challenging; thus, when teachers in these schools have gained the experience required to be effective, they often opt to transfer to schools serving middle- and upper-income communities, where there is less work and stress. This has left the students from low-income families with teachers who are usually newly graduated from university and enthusiastic but less experienced in providing education in the most effective ways; and teachers who feel "burned out" and commit less instructional effort as a result. So it is imperative that financial and sabbatical incentives be provided to teachers who demonstrate they are effective so they remain in schools that serve low-income communities.[6]

Although high-quality teachers are necessary for improving the educational transitions for youth from the poor inner-city communities, they alone are not sufficient. The data presented throughout this book show that students from low-income neighborhoods faced social and psychological challenges that emanated from outside the school, and that these problems were carried to school where they mixed with problems associated with the learning process. Given this finding, the next policy suggestion is the need to significantly expand the number of professionals trained in psychological counseling. As mentioned earlier, this would require a ratio of counselors to students high enough to make a significant difference in students' abilities to cope with exterior problems, allowing them to concentrate more fully on mastering academic material.

The findings reported in chapter 3 also clarify problems in schools' official curricula. In brief, the overarching problem was that official school curricula often did not operationally link the fields of language arts, science, math, social sciences, and cultural arts to make them fully integrated. While some schools had a curriculum integrating various fields, this often was the result of efforts by specific principals or teachers and not of a programmatic initiative throughout the school district. Therefore, an additional policy suggestion would be to establish such an approach. An integrated curricular approach would demand that the school's educational objectives at every stage of each year and between years be known by all the professionals in the school (administrators, teachers, and staff) and be logistically coordinated through weekly planning meetings so that objectives and activities in each course complement and build on the instruction being presented in a student's other courses. This would not merely unite teachers' efforts but also significantly reduce the temptation after they close their classroom doors to create their own curriculum because they find it is more interesting, less difficult to present, or easier to control student behavior. In brief, an integrated approach in which teachers are constantly consulting and coordinating their instructional plans limits the profusion of curricula that can undermine the efforts of the school's various instructional staff.

The changes I just suggested would have the potential to provide students a more consistent learning environment because the professionals creating it would be in constant dialogue and would be required to synchronize their approaches.[7] However, coordinating instruction in this manner will not be easy as teachers often resist changing the way they run their classrooms. Plus, teachers in most public schools in the United States are represented by labor unions, which generally aim to protect their members' job security from political whims, as well as thwart excessive demands on their workloads. There is obviously a need to work cooperatively with teacher unions. This is an area that is critical but difficult. Although wages, benefits, and hours worked are clearly very central to any contract that unions and school districts negotiate, the more difficult issues have to do with the areas of teacher discipline and dismissal. Like with any profession, there will be some individual teachers who are delinquent or incompetent in the execution of their duties. Clearly, there is no effective way to judge how well a teacher is teaching by simply looking at student academic achievement criteria because teachers are not in control of all the areas of individual learning that would provide evidence as to whether they were adequately executing their professional duties. For example, it is quite possible for a teacher to be prepared, organized, and present the necessary material to students and still not have them do well on assignments and in-class or standardized tests because the student did not commit enough attention to studying. Therefore, some type of formal cooperation between the district and the union would need to be initiated to handle parent, student, and teacher grievances in an effective and equitable way. One suggestion would be to mandate that school administrations (principals and vice-principals) consistently make random observations of each teacher in the school. If problems were identified, they would be brought to the attention of a formal school committee consisting of administrators and teachers who were union members to hear and make recommendations concerning the need for remedial assistance, disciplinary action, or dismissal that would then be forwarded to the district and local union headquarters to be sanctioned or adjudicated. The one structural problem that school districts must confront is that unions do not have a strong internal mechanism for disciplining members who are derelict in their formal duties. Therefore, the district and the union must negotiate means by which teachers who are derelict in their teaching duties (ill prepared, not presenting in class, and not consistently evaluating student progress), and administrators who are blaming teachers for results they cannot reasonably be expected to accomplish and requiring more work from them, are adjudicated. The best policy would be to create a procedure agreed upon by both the union and district whereby an outside arbitrator would decide each case.

Assessing Student Achievement

In each of the schools in the present study, the district officials were aware of the criteria used by their state to assess students' competence and eligibility to advance to the next educational stage, but they showed less interest in determining whether the criteria accurately indicate whether students are capable of transitioning. One might ask, are not the competency measurements for high school students standardized? The answer is they generally are, but the politics surrounding maximizing matriculation numbers encourages school personnel to focus on meeting the minimum requirements, which can be problematic for the transitional process. In brief, concentrating on simple matriculation focuses the criteria on the first half of the transition process—becoming eligible to leave the current educational stage—but not on the capability of being successful in the succeeding stage. This may leave a student who is successful in one stage of the transition process vulnerable to struggling or failing in the next. As mentioned in the text, an A grade in one high school is not necessarily an A in other schools.

This variation is a direct outcome of pressure on teachers to produce students eligible to graduate from high school and enroll in college, which often leads them to assess a student's competency and assign a grade in relation to others in the course or school rather than to standardized state or federal criteria. Whether in math, science, social science, language, or cultural arts, it is important to assess an individual in relation to standardized criteria because it is impossible to remediate deficiencies without that information. For all students, academic success involves a constant process of assistance and practice.[8] Because in each high school every student engages in a separate four-year process, there is no definitive way to ensure that all will proceed at the same pace. Therefore, maintaining state and national standards, and intervening with intensive assistance when students fall below these standards, is imperative, even if that means creating a new policy of extending the school year for students who fall behind.

The next issue confronting schools in low-income neighborhoods is the choice of criteria to use in assessing a student's ability to succeed at the next stage of the education process. Should it be grades in each substantive subject? SAT scores? High school exit exam scores? Or all of these? This is a very important question because it is not only the student who is being evaluated, it is the teachers and administration through their execution of the formal curriculum that are being assessed. Thus, among a school's administration and faculty, there will be concern about how to concentrate their efforts so they and their students have a greater chance of being evaluated as "successful." For example, should they stick strictly to the formal curriculum, which is nearly always intended to produce a student with a broad range of knowledge and skills necessary to confront and solve new intellectual and social problems?; or should they teach what they know will be on standardized tests like the SAT or high school exit exams in order to increase the student's chance of scoring well?[9]

There are tradeoffs with each approach, and this creates a pedagogical dilemma for the teacher, principal, and superintendent. If they focus on the formal curriculum, they strengthen the pupil's general knowledge and skill set, but this does not consistently translate into doing well on standardized tests where individuals must determine what is being asked of them, cognitively retrieve the relevant information, and neutralize any insecurities about their ability to be successful.[10] For students who are taught the exam and do reasonably well answering its questions, the result can be the accumulation of a more narrow range of information that leaves them without the skills to answer questions they are likely to encounter in college that require more breadth.

The obvious answer to this dilemma would appear to be to teach each student the exam and the broad curriculum, but this can leave students vulnerable on both fronts if time constraints inhibit teachers from fully executing both approaches and students from effectively mastering the material for both. Clearly, there is a need to determine what is best for the individual, on the one hand, and for molding the next generation, on the other, but there is a serious question as to whether the use of standardized tests to assess student competence fairly and effectively does this. Currently, they remain in use by some colleges and universities in the US not so much to assess the capabilities and promise of individuals but, in line with Max Weber's prediction early in the twentieth century, as a convenient mechanism to allot resources and opportunities.[11] One suggestion would be for state education departments to set up an ongoing committee that included representatives from various universities in their state as well as the nation to assess what information students should be required to know as well as the required scholastic skills to be mastered in various substantive areas for them to be successful in college. Once established, this criteria would be a basis for the construction of two "official state tests," one to be administered after completion of grade 10 that school administrations would use to direct interventions with those students needing remedial assistance, and one at the end of grade 12 that school administrations would use to assess what is working, what is not, and what needs to be changed. These exams would not be used to determine "competency among students," but rather provide information that educators, students, and parents could use in providing students with an increased chance to make a successful transition to their next educational stage.[12] Obviously, criteria for a successful transition will continue to evolve, but with such a committee the tests could also evolve.

STRUCTURE AND CULTURE IN
EDUCATIONAL OUTCOMES

Throughout the twentieth century, education systems across the United States generally increased their bureaucracies and budgets. This was in part a response to the growing need for an educated populace that could provide technical expertise for a manufacturing economy.[13] Accompanying this demand for expertise was the idea that the education system was the primary instrument for Americans to attain the expanding socioeconomic rewards available. This stimulated the development and spread of human capital theories in the fields of economics and sociology.[14] The empirical research that followed produced consistent evidence that higher levels of education for individuals in the United States were associated with higher personal incomes.[15] This had the consequence of elevating the education system to be seen as the institutional engine for both individual success and society's continued economic growth.

The problem has been that while the education system can be thought of as an engine that produces knowledge and analytic skills, it is not education alone that generates individual socioeconomic success. The expansion of the labor market and the incomes associated with specific occupations do that. Thus, while a great deal of responsibility has been placed on the educational institution to both educate and create socioeconomic success, it has become less capable of producing successful results for all the nation's youth, and this is especially true of those who start their lives in families with low incomes.[16] This has created ongoing concern among sociologists, economists, and educators about how to increase opportunities for low-income students to obtain educational and socioeconomic success.[17]

The present book has been a study of the obstacles that low-income students encounter in the pursuit of educational success. Those who are concerned with improving academic achievement and increasing the rates of college eligibility among students from low-income families have stressed the need to address structural inequities by increasing the operating budgets for school districts.[18] Most professionals would agree that students from low-income families face different obstacles in education than students from middle-income families.[19] As a result, the topic of structure receives a great deal of attention because it is assessed, often in error, that these obstacles can be overcome by increasing the amount of money allocated to address them. Troubles in the education system cannot always be redressed by increasing government funding to stimulate structural changes that will produce increasing benefits for students and society as a whole. There is evidence that increased spending in specific areas like teacher development, programs for students with academic disabilities, and continued availability of up-to-date educational materials and equipment does produce individual and societal benefits.[20] However, there is also evidence that higher spending on education does not necessarily make low-income students more competitive for subsequent economic and professional opportunities, even if it reduces structural gaps in schools' resources.[21] This book argues that more is involved in tackling the educational problems confronted by school systems serving large numbers of youth from low-income families than merely increasing their budgets, and this can be seen in the evidence presented in chapters 3, 4, and 5, where issues of structures, human resources, and personal decisions regarding "success" were analyzed. Thus, some increases in school spending must occur to accommodate rising costs in retaining quality teachers, adding counseling personnel, and providing additional instruction for any increases in the numbers of students who need remedial assistance, but the continual development of strategic pedagogical planning is also essential.

In addition to structural issues associated with the politics of managing school districts, such as the quality and effectiveness of supervisory and instructional staff, cultural issues related to the individual persist in creating problems for some low-income students making a transition to the next stage of their education.[22] Researchers who have addressed culture argue that, in order to improve academic achievement and college admissions among low-income students, serious inquiry is required into the contribution of culture to disparities in educational success.[23] Some scholars argue that differing cultural backgrounds, including values, norms, and styles, help explain why students in some low-income groups succeed in schools and those in other groups do not.[24]

There has been a long history of connecting culture to a variety of social areas like region, nation, profession, and, as shown in chapter 1 of this book, politics. However, it is important to turn to its association with both ethnicity and a subcultural variant related to social class. Both ethnic culture and a social class subculture can be shown to be impactful in the educational transition process. For example, many students from Jewish, Japanese, Korean, and Chinese backgrounds have stressed formal educational success as an integral part of their cultural norms. They have also seen large numbers of their respective groups succeeding in achieving high educational levels.

Even among members of these ethnicities' lower-income families, there are significant numbers who do well in high school and go on to achieve advanced college degrees.[25] Obviously, ethnic culture is playing some type of positive role for those groups.[26]

Nevertheless, regardless of a person's ethnic background, a subculture emanating from a person's social class background can also be a factor in influencing academic advancement. One example involving the immigrant experience makes clear the role that social class culture can have. Many ethnic immigrants came to the United States with the goal to improve their economic lives. Upon arrival they relied on the cultural norms of their country of origin to establish themselves in America and then slowly adopted the cultural norms of America the longer they lived here.[27] In general, most of these immigrants, as well as their first-generation relatives, did experience socioeconomic mobility, and the more they integrated American cultural norms into their everyday lives the less they identified with their country of origin's culture. As social integration into American culture progressed and economic mobility stalled, the dominant cultural orientation of the successive generation became more associated with their social class standing than that associated with their ethnicity. The progression of this social dynamic created larger numbers of youth from these generational backgrounds with cultural characteristics analogous to other lower-class individuals in America and dissimilar to the characteristics associated with the middle class of their respective ethnicities.[28] For a current example of this dynamic as it relates to education, there is evidence of academic improvement among Mexican and Central Americans from immigration through the second generation, but in succeeding generations when socioeconomic mobility is stalled, so too is academic improvement, suggesting that along with structural issues, subcultural ones related to social class are operative.[29]

Finally, there is evidence as reported in the present study and others that there are youth from low-income families who exhibited a lack of interest in formal education, a finding that is often ascribed to their receiving a less stimulating educational experience than students from middle- and upper-income families.[30] Some researchers who hear of students not being interested in school and deciding as a result to physically or intellectually drop out choose to look for some educational "gimmick" that will shock them out of their malaise and ignite their interest in striving for academic excellence. The problem is that some of these students, not all, are trying to tell anyone who is listening that they are really not interested in formal education because it is something they do not currently value and believe will improve their lives (see chapter 5).[31] Such sentiments are so antithetical to the accepted American norm, however, that many observers refuse to take these students at their word. For to do so would require interested observers to confront the possibility that formal education is not a sacred component of the cultural norms among some social groups of Americans.

Various researchers respond to evidence that culture may partly explain why some students do not succeed academically by charging that these observations are biased and that they "blame the victim" for structural inequities like a lack of family resources, inadequate school resources, and insufficient instruction. However, the use of culture as an explanatory variable does not inherently blame the victim, for similar to structure, a person's culture is not chosen, at least in the earlier stages of life, and thus is very different from the variable "agency" where choices are made and an individual's responsibility is clear.[32]

When culture is used as an explanation, it is certainly true that it would be too simplistic to say that not valuing education explains the failure of particular individuals. Clearly differences in the value that particular groups place on education is not determinative, but it can help explain group outcome differences in academics. On this point, it is understandable that there can emerge the uncomfortable feeling among all those interested in educational equity that culture is so personal that to deal with it confronts normative values and the rights of individuals—in other words, that people have the right to think, value, and legally act however they choose, regardless of whether it may be detrimental to their socioeconomic interests. Basically, the politics surrounding social problems are so volatile that people usually want these problems resolved quickly without violating anyone's personal rights; and because everyone recognizes culture as having taken a long time to develop, and thus requiring a long time to change, there is a tendency to either dismiss or ignore it.

There have been many signs that culture has been a powerful influence, both positive and negative, on academic performance, but as discussed above, negative impacts have proven difficult to address.[33] Clearly the factors that produce and reinforce culture's negative impact need to be addressed, and this requires confronting the workings of parents, peers, neighbors, community leaders, and education officials, and the socialization they provide youth.

An important aspect of the unease and reluctance to fully address culture is not simply one of short-sightedness or avoidance. It also relates to the lessons that have emerged from a radical experiment in attacking the issue of culture in American educational history. This experiment occurred in the nineteenth and twentieth centuries, when Native American children were removed from their families and communities and placed in boarding schools like Carlisle Indian Industrial School in Carlisle, Pennsylvania, whose founder General Richard Henry Pratt wrote of the need to "Kill the Indian and Save the Man." The program was designed to culturally transform children from being Native Americans with values associated with their ethnic group to values associated with White Anglo-American culture. The idea was for graduates of these schools to be transformed sociologically (i.e., to become non-Indian) and take these values back to their reservations and contribute to the process of their tribes adopting modern White Anglo-American culture. It would be fair to say the schools successfully removed from many Indian children much of their tribes' cultures and values, but at a very high psycho-social price to students, their families, and their tribes. For when they returned home they often were unable to communicate with their families or communities, and the White Anglo-American values they had been socialized to accept were so antithetical to their communities that the youth were marginalized. Thus, the program changed the cultural orientation of many of the children under its charge but produced individuals who were socially alienated, psychologically scarred, and had little if any impact on transforming the traditional cultural orientations of their tribes.[34]

The experience with Native Americans provides a stark warning about radical approaches to the issue of culture in the educational process, but it must not deter us from addressing those negative issues related to culture that exist in low-income communities, which in turn confront the education systems that serve them. To begin, it must be understood that educators during the American Indian experiment faced cultural systems that were entirely ethnically driven, whereas educators in low-income communities now often encounter problems emerging from the cultural orientations emanating from a student's social class background. Unfortunately, a class-based cultural system is often misconceived as being shared by an entire ethnic group,[35] but the cultural system that exists within lower-class communities includes morals, values, and norms that have developed from the experience of having had to live with limited income and resources for a sustained period of time, sometimes even for a generation or more.[36] While the concept of culture is still seriously studied in sociology, when it has been extended to include social class or race, it has in more recent times been treated as a factor to be avoided, opposed, or changed to make it more politically palatable by distancing it from its role as a normative force in creating negative outcomes in social life.[37] The result has often been to generate conceptual schema that mistakenly present products of culture (e.g., frames) as culture itself.[38]

The historic reason for apprehension surrounding cultural elements emanating from social class can be found in the controversy surrounding Oscar Lewis's introduction of the "culture of poverty" concept in the 1950s and 1960s.[39] Few concepts have been more attacked than the "culture of poverty," and those scholars who in any way are construed to be associated with it have often been thought of as "ideologically suspect researchers,"[40] whose work is to be avoided because of what their critics argue is either an ignorant use of the culture concept, or because it glosses over the real structural causes of poverty and leads to the disparagement of an already downtrodden group of people.[41]

Despite assertions that a "lower-class culture" concept faults the poor for their plight, use of the concept does not require one to see poor people as creating their own misery. People adapt to the environment they live in, and lower-class people are no exception, particularly when there is limited or no opportunity to significantly change their situation. So, like any social group, lower-class individuals develop a social life with the morals, values, and norms that have emerged as appropriate for that environment. For example, although there is cultural variation in poverty, a persistent worldview found to be prevalent among the lower class is to see the world structured in such a way that it acts on them, and because they have no, or very limited, opportunity to change this, they are required to adapt in order to negotiate the inevitable bad things to come. Compare this to the prominent worldview found in middle-class culture of seeing individuals as having the ability to change structures when they are producing negative results for them, i.e., they see an ability to act on the world as opposed to the world acting on them.[42]

Lower-class individuals also have value-orientations that emerge from their particular circumstance, such as placing a high value on physical objects like the body and how these objects can produce power, control, and status within and outside of their social class community.[43] In general this value-orientation has resulted from the precarity of the historical experience of having outside forces utilize their bodies for the work that produces the material benefits for others while using physical force to control them in the process.[44] In addition, lower-class individuals tend to focus on immediate goals and the rewards that come from successfully fulfilling them. There tends to exist among lower-class individuals a reticence to believe in rewards that are deferred too far into the future.[45] This makes complete sense; most of their current life is so unpredictable that being able to have faith that they will get some reward in the future for a current effort is easily seen as having a low probability of success.

Significant numbers of teachers reported in the present study that "most of the students [they have contact with] simply do not care about [i.e., value] formal education enough to commit themselves to constantly study for success."[46] This does not mean that all of the students from low-income families do not value education, but there is enough evidence to suggest this element of culture (not valuing education) in low-income communities is present and must be addressed if educators are to improve the academic achievement, college eligibility, and competitive admission rates of many students from these backgrounds.[47]

Some readers might question whether the valuing of schooling or the "discipline to study" is not better understood from an individual rather than a cultural orientation. There is evidence, however, that many low-income students either express ambivalence about the value of a formal education or say they are interested in receiving an education but do not prioritize a college degree nor behave in a way that would promote academic success such as paying attention in class, reading all the assigned material, completing all the assigned exercises, studying for tests, and seeking remedial help when needed.[48] This cannot, and should not, be dismissed. The number of people who do not value the formal education offered in high school has varied over time, but the sentiment has persisted for decades. In other words, this sentiment within low-income communities has varied within and between time periods, but it persists. Thus, there is a serious need to address whether not valuing education is the result of a persistent rational assessment by individuals that education will not produce an economic benefit for them, or is passed down as part of a cultural value-orientation.[49]

The fact that there has been a general decline among American youth in their attitudes toward the value of a college education would seem to suggest that the current "tracking systems," regardless of their forms, need to be reimagined. Certainly, systems that have included academic and vocational tracks could be revised to include within the vocational regimen highly technical skills associated with the expansion of the digital, advanced mechanization, and artificial intelligence segments of the economy. It is quite likely that educating youth in the technical aspects of these various sectors of the economy would prove particularly effective in transitioning students from high school to various economic sectors. Clearly a revision of what the "Vocational Track" should or could productively entail for the future is required.[50]

For those who object to raising culture as a factor in transitioning to college, it should be pointed out that most sociologists and educators would not find culture problematic in accounting for the success of middle- and upper-income youths' academic achievement and acceptance rates to universities.[51] Clearly, if culture is working in a positive way for middle-class students, it should work, if there is no difference between them, for those from low-income families, and it is not.[52] Therefore, while structural issues have been impactful, they do not account for all of the variance between the two social class groups, and this points to assessing the influence of culture for different lower-class groups over varying time periods.

Recently, Orlando Patterson and his colleagues have reasserted the need to evaluate the role of culture in the lives of African American youth from different social classes.[53] As mentioned earlier, many researchers and educators have shied away from the issue of culture for three primary reasons: (1) wanting to avoid offending people from various ethnic groups, particularly those who have suffered social stigmatization and poverty; (2) averting radical policies that produce negative results, as the American Indian Schools Program did for students, their families, and their communities; and (3) preferring to spend money on structural issues related to school inequality that they believe are more likely to be resolved more quickly.

The most important takeaway from this discussion of culture is that lower-class culture does not create academic failures; rather, it is better to understand that elements within lower-class culture can hinder the ability of students from lower-income families to overcome the structural challenges they face from the goals and internal operations of an education system based on the worldviews and values of the American middle class. Therefore, efforts must be made to confront the scars that poverty has left on the beliefs, norms, and practices of people who must continually confront it.[54]

On the cultural front, one policy initiative that would be worth pursuing to aid in undermining culture's impact is the establishment of a "buddy system" in schools serving low-income families whereby students in their freshman year could be assigned mentors such as successful upper-grade students or college student volunteers. This mentoring program would need to be ongoing until such time where the student being mentored was doing so well that they could then take on the role of a mentor themselves. The mentoring would include establishing the goal of a college education as well as specific suggestions for successfully overcoming whatever current academic challenge the mentee was confronting. The ultimate goal of such a program would be to change the entire culture of the school whereby it was expected that every student would go on to college and be successful, or be vocationally trained in a manner to expect a successful transition to a technical part of the economy.

Which future policy initiatives need to be implemented will vary depending on time and circumstances, and changing our approach to culture cannot solve all of the problems low-income youths experience in education. A multilevel policy that simultaneously confronts structure and culture will be required to reduce the number of obstacles low-income youths face. However, it should be remembered that reducing educational obstacles faced by low-income youth in high school does not guarantee that any one of these students will transition successfully; it will only mean that they will be in a better position to do so.[55]

Researchers and policy advocates have increasingly focused on individuals from low-income families who make transitions to higher education. What needs to be remembered is that a transition includes both being admitted to an institution of higher learning and successfully completing the requirements for a degree from that institution. Not satisfying the second part makes the accomplishment of the first part only partially meaningful, and this could produce personal financial debt resulting in a "net negative experience" for those having come from low-income backgrounds. Given there is evidence to suggest low-income youth have experienced difficulty in completing college, policy advocates must switch their focus to address what areas of competency development in a student's high school education make them vulnerable to experiencing difficulty in completing college.[56]

AMERICAN SOCIETY AND EDUCATION'S AMERICAN DREAM PREDICAMENT

Now to address macro-level issues associated with the education process. The education establishment that I have been discussing exists at the pleasure of society, and it will be society's various interest groups that evaluate how well it accomplishes their goals. However, there is general agreement that the education system needs to support society's dominant ideology and provide students with the technical skills required to support the well-being of the general population. So, the US education system has focused on (1) socializing youth to the values and norms associated with being good citizens; (2) providing the knowledge and expertise to expand technological development and compete creatively for the limited resources within various economic markets; and (3) promoting the required skills for the occupations that create socioeconomic mobility and security. What is unmistakable about the American system is that it is geared toward competition, though with a preference for rule-abiding competition.

This book has focused on the trials and tribulations affecting the education of youth from low-income families, and it raises important questions concerning the relationship between American education and society. Let's begin with the issue of competition for limited resources in the education arena. As with all competitive encounters, there is an understanding that some parties will win and others will lose, perhaps not totally as in an all-or-nothing contest, but certainly in a way that one might win or lose in comparison with others. Competition is a given in the US system and it has evolved into a revered element because it produces the inequality believed to be a positive driving force for society. Americans have often thought this part of capitalism made it superior to the socialist systems where there was no built-in incentive to not only become economically successful but to be more successful than others in society.[57]

Of course, every system includes endemic inequalities and, as Fischer et al. have shown in their book *Inequality by Design,* American society has chosen to treat these inequalities in a particular way.[58] In that regard, there are two facets to Americans' understanding of inequality. The first is that winning and losing can be positive forces in stimulating individuals to strive for success. In essence, success for individuals and society is accomplished through positive and negative forces. The positive force, the chance to win, creates energy and focus that brings out an individual's creativity, which in turn produces actions and products for a healthy society. The negative force of losing, in which exists both the fear of failure and experiencing punishments associated with failing, is thought to have the positive potential to strengthen an individual's resolve to compete and win the next time, thereby nourishing in the process the quest for "excellence" that generates positive actions and products for a healthy society. In sum, society's honoring of winners requires that someone lose because the identity of winners is predicated on having losers.

The second major facet of Americans' understanding of inequality is that a democratic political system is based on creating the opportunity to succeed, and this is best done by maintaining institutions that promote markets and arenas in which everyone has the ability to compete equally for the objects of success. Thus, in the United States, the legal system has been historically charged with monitoring any discrimination that might limit the chance to compete equally, and the education system has been historically charged with producing participants who are capable of competing equally for the limited resources that determine and symbolize success.[59] Herein lies the problem confronted by the education system, and the one with which this book has dealt: How does the education system create individuals with academic competence to compete equally in professional arenas and economic markets?

One of the best ways to see the predicament faced by the US education system is to use the analogy of competitive sports similar to the one suggested by Fischer et al. in *Inequality by Design*: It is not merely the field one plays on that must remain level, it is also the training facilities, coaching, and support personnel.[60] Social research has consistently shown that historically each additional year of schooling can produce financial advantages for an individual, and this has given the education system the appearance of being the primary engine in creating socioeconomic mobility and societal security.[61] Yet it is more realistic to see education as an important component in accomplishing the American Dream (socioeconomic success) but insufficient by itself.[62] Many more elements of a person's life must align for them to capture the American Dream, and the more they can successfully align these elements, the more aspects of the American Dream they will experience.[63]

US society is arranged to support an individual's freedom to pursue the American Dream, to "compete" in the various markets for the spoils they offer, and the education system has been designated to train individuals for that combat. Thus, the dilemma facing the education system is how to provide every student with equal training to compete for finite rewards.[64] When attempting to provide equal opportunity within the education system, academics and policy makers have focused on making structural changes. However, as we have seen in this book, students from low-income families and neighborhoods face a number of obstacles. Some of them would not be particularly problematic for students from middle-income families, but they can significantly limit the chances low-income youth have to make successful transitions toward the American Dream.

It is clear that creating and maintaining a level playing field for low-income students to compete for society's rewards would require significant changes in the current structure and culture of schools, and the United States may not have the political will to make those changes. Society would have to support a significant overhaul of the education system's training procedures. It also would have to change the criteria that indicate individual competence, and the way "competence" is used in allowing individuals access to compete for subsequent opportunities in education.

An education system that remains decentralized, with state and local authorities designing and implementing instruction, will inevitably produce unequal results because there will be too much variation from one locale to the next to create a level playing field. Even if it were possible to establish a single national education system, it would contain significant pros and cons, and a full discussion of them would require its own book, so I will simply mention one of each here. On the "con" side, many Americans might object to a national system because it would take control out of the hands of state and local authorities, even though the current decentralized system includes no effective way to get all participants to abide by the same rules and provide the same resources. Of course, national systems have the capacity to create their own forms of corruption, coercion, and incompetence, but a "pro" is that it can lay the foundation for a type of standardization that could support more equitable competition.[65]

This book has shown what will persist without a major national change.[66] Large numbers of students from low-income families and neighborhoods will continue to face significant obstacles that will limit their ability to move to subsequent competitive arenas and to succeed once they arrive. What should be unsettling is that these students from low-income families and neighborhoods will be the descendants of individuals who already experienced losing in the various competitive arenas; otherwise their families would not have low incomes. Thus, these young people will gain their socioeconomic disadvantage the old-fashioned way: They will inherit it.

For those who would say American education is doing all it can to reduce inequality, there is evidence to suggest otherwise.[67] Continued racial and income discrimination in the housing market has produced districts where schools are racially and socioeconomically segregated.[68] We know that middle- and upper-income Americans recognize that lower-income youth continue to face disadvantages, but they have shown a persistent unwillingness to do anything that would reduce the advantage they are able to pass on to their own children.[69] This leaves the nation's education system facing the task of educating youth who are largely segregated by their parents' socioeconomic status based on income and race.[70]

Thus, schools where a majority of students come from lower-income families become heirs to a situation of inequality that increases the probability that they will reproduce succeeding generations of low-income individuals. In general, the professionals at these schools do not pursue mediocrity for the students under their charge; it is simply that the structure, culture, and politics of the situation create obstacles for both educators and their students. It is the obstacles documented in this book that increase the chances that a student from a low-income family will not make the educational transitions necessary for a middle-class lifestyle. This situation presents society with a number of challenging moral dilemmas. The main one is: If we know that the presently constructed system is not able to provide all its youth with an equal playing field to compete, shouldn't we begin to make all the radical changes required to create one? Or should we simply admit to structural inequality and lament that some individuals, by virtue of who they inherited as parents, are just unlucky and must run a race in which their competitors get a head start and additional sustenance all the way to the finish line?

Methodological Appendix

The data for the analysis found in this book come from a number of previous studies that I carried out between 1991 and 2013. There were two foundational studies for the present analysis. The first was a study of social change in low-income neighborhoods that began in 1991 and finished in 1999. The second was a study of ethnic violence in high schools that began in 2000 and finished in 2003. Subsequently, I conducted follow-up studies of the same high schools included in the two main studies (see table MA.1 for each year that each specific school was studied). In these follow-ups, I focused exclusively on the educational process and the factors potentially preventing low-income students from making a smooth transition to their next educational stage.

The high schools that form the basis for the analysis in the present book come from the sampling designs associated with the two foundational studies. The first study included five schools from five low-income New York and Los Angeles neighborhoods that were randomly chosen. For the specific details involved in the sampling design strategy and selection, the reader should consult the methodological appendix in my book *Cracks in the Pavement*.[1] The second foundational study included three randomly chosen high schools in three different neighborhoods of Los Angeles and three randomly chosen high schools in three different neighborhoods of Oakland, California. For specific details of the sampling design strategy and selection for this study, the reader should consult the methodological appendix in my book *Burning Dislike*.[2] Specifically, nine of the eleven schools in the combined data set taught students overwhelmingly from low-income families, and two taught students from predominantly middle-income families. This allowed me to identify factors directly associated with race and social class composition.

Briefly, the first study addressed neighborhoods and their institutions, which included the high schools, and I visited each high school three to five times each week. The second study involved schools themselves as the primary site of observation because it was focused on student violence, and although I was in attendance

TABLE MA.1 Schools and Dates of Projects in Present Study

School	1991–99[a]	2000–03	2006–08	2007–09	2010–11	2013/14[d]	# Years
Los Angeles							
Chester Himes	X				X[b]	X	11
James K. Polk	X				X[b]	X	11
Tongva		X	X		X[c]	X	7
Chumash		X	X		X[c]	X	7
De Neve		X	X		X[c]	X	7
Oakland							
Miwok		X		X			5
Kaiser		X		X			5
Ohlone		X		X			5
New York							
Lanape	X				X[b]	X	11
Van Twiller	X				X[b]	X	11
Knickerbocker	X				X[b]	X	11

a = Research covered the school year from fall 1999 to June 2000.
b = Research covered only the year 2010.
c = Research covered only the year 2011.
d = Research covered the school year from fall 2013 to June 2014.

at these schools five days a week, I focused on the internal educational operations of one or two schools every day of the week. For the subsequent follow-up studies, I visited both the schools involved in the first project on neighborhoods, as well as those in the second project on school violence, every day that I was in the area. As indicated in table MA.1 of this appendix, the follow-up studies began in 2006 and ended in 2013. The participant-observation data-gathering method employed in the follow-up studies was the same as that in the original study and did not include in-depth interviewing.

For the entire time that I was conducting the data gathering, I was provided total access to all areas and activities of each school. This included classrooms, administration offices, counselors' offices, nurses' offices, faculty lounges, and student and faculty lunch rooms, on-campus police offices, and custodial offices. In addition, I was given access to the central and district administrative offices where I followed administrators as they went about their duties and meetings with others. I did not participate in any of the official business of the administrators (i.e., by making comments), and I jotted notes only after individuals finished speaking and as quickly as possible. Finally, I sought out permission from families of students who were attending the various schools to spend time interacting with them in the everyday activities in their homes, particularly after school was officially ended.

Participant-observation methodology requires that the researcher be a part of their research subjects' environment. When I first arrived at each school, I was viewed with caution. As time passed, however, my presence had no discernable effect on any of the daily routines. I simply became another "normal" part of the environment. This allowed me to observe behavior and subtly record it. I observed physical behavior, including times when individuals were alone and when they interacted with others. I also observed verbal and nonverbal communications. Most of the time I did not intrude on the students' activities or conversations. I consciously tried to blend into the surroundings. Occasionally, I engaged in conversation and made notes of it, but for the most part I simply observed. In brief, I was primarily a "watcher" and "listener" and not an "interrogator."[3]

I initially recorded all of the field data in small 3 × 5 memo notebooks using Gregg shorthand. Each evening, I coded these notes and transferred them to a computer-assisted qualitative data program. I used two programs, askSam and Folio Views.[4] In the analysis stage, I looked for general patterns indicating consistency, as well as novel patterns related to particular circumstances. Thus, my descriptions should be taken as representative of consistent patterns, unless they are identified as being idiosyncratic.

Again, detailed information concerning the two primary research projects used in this book can be found in the methodological appendices to *Cracks in the Pavement* and *Burning Dislike*.

NOTES

INTRODUCTION

1. There is a vast literature that reports on this premise, and I will simply provide a few examples. See Leonard Dinnerstein and David M. Reimers, *Ethnic Americans: A History of Immigration* (New York: Columbia University Press, 2009); Alejandro Portes and Rubén G. Rumbaut, *Immigrant America: A Portrait*, 4th ed. (Berkeley: University of California Press, 2014); and Roger Waldinger, *Still the Promised City? African Americans and New Immigrants in Postindustrial New York* (Cambridge, MA: Harvard University Press, 1999), who examines whether the immigrant's and migrant's dream of securing a prosperous life in America is still a realistic goal.

2. For a discussion of the elements that constitute the "American Dream" see Lawrence R. Samuel, *The American Dream: A Cultural History* (Syracuse, NY: Syracuse University Press, 2012); and Jennifer L. Hochschild, *Facing Up to the American Dream: Race, Class, and the Soul of America* (Princeton, NJ: Princeton University Press, 1995), 15–38.

3. Raj Chetty, David Grusky, Maximilian Hell, Nathaniel Hendren, Robert Manduca, and Jimmy Narang, "The Fading American Dream: Trends in Absolute Income Mobility since 1940," *Science* 356, no. 6336 (December 2016): 398–406.

4. For current problems see Raj Chetty et al., "The Fading American Dream"; and for past success see Claude S. Fischer and Michael Hout, *A Century of Difference: How America Changed in the Last One Hundred Years* (New York: Russell Sage Foundation, 2006), 8–22.

5. See Raj Chetty, Nathaniel Hendren, Maggie R. Jones, and Sonya R. Porter, "Race and Economic Opportunity in the United States: An Intergenerational Perspective," *Quarterly Journal of Economics* 134, no. 2 (2019): 647–713; and Greg J. Duncan and Richard J. Murnane, "Introduction: The American Dream Then and Now," in *Whither Opportunity?: Rising Inequality, Schools, and Children's Life Chances*, ed. Greg J. Duncan and Richard J. Murnane (New York: Russell Sage Foundation, 2011), 3–8.

6. See Jonathan Kozol, *Savage Inequalities: Children in America's Schools* (New York: Crown, 1991); Sean Corcoran, William N. Evans, Jennifer Godwin, Sheila E. Murray, and Robert M. Schwab, "The Changing Distribution of Education Finance, 1972 to 1997," in *Social Inequality*, ed. Kathryn M. Neckerman (New York: Russell Sage Foundation, 2004), 433–66; Linda Darling-Hammond, "Inequality and School Resources: What It Will Take to Close the Opportunity Gap," in *Closing the Opportunity Gap: What America Must Do to Give Every Child an Even Chance,* ed. Prudence L. Carter and Kevin G. Welner (New York: Oxford University Press, 2013), 77–98, esp. 84–91; and Samuel Roundfield Lucas, *Tracking Inequality: Stratification and Mobility in American High Schools* (New York: Teachers College Press, 1995).

7. There is a great deal of work in the area of cultural and social capital. Some studies deal with oppositional culture and others with culture more broadly. See Signithia Fordham and John Ogbu, "Black Students' School Success: Coping with the Burden of 'Acting White,'" *Urban Affairs* 18, no. 2 (1986): 176–206; George Farkas, Christy Lleras, and Steve Maczuga, "Does Oppositional Culture Exist in Minority and Poverty Peer Groups?," *American Sociological Review* 67, no. 1 (February 2002): 148–55; Prudence L. Carter, *Stubborn Roots: Race, Culture, and Inequality in US and South African Schools* (New York: Oxford University Press, 2012); Simone Ispa-Landa, "Effects of Affluent Suburban Schooling: Learning Skilled Ways of Interacting with Educational Gatekeepers," in *The Cultural Matrix: Understanding Black Youth*, ed. Orlando Patterson (Cambridge, MA: Harvard University Press, 2015), 393–414; Martín Sánchez-Jankowski, *Cracks in the Pavement: Social Change and Resilience in Poor Neighborhoods* (Berkeley: University of California Press, 2008), 306–14, 329–39; and Stephen Vasiey, "What People Want: Rethinking Poverty, Culture and Educational Attainment," *Annals of the American Academy of Social and Political Science* 629 (May 2010): 75–101. There is a great deal of work in the area of social and cultural capital in assessing inequalities in educational attainment. See, for example, Pierre Bourdieu, "Le Capital Social: Notes Provisoires," *Actes de la Recherche Science Social* 31 (1980): 2–3; James S. Coleman, "Social Capital in the Creation of Human Capital," *American Journal of Sociology* 94 (special supplement, 1988), S95–S120; Nan Lin, *Social Capital: A Theory of Social Structure and Action* (Cambridge: Cambridge University Press, 2001); Susan Saegert, J. Phillip Thompson, and Mark R. Warren, eds., *Social Capital and Poor Communities* (New York: Russell Sage Foundation, 2001); Annette Lareau, "Social Class Differences in Family-School Relationships: The Importance of Cultural Capital," *Sociology of Education* 60 (1978): 73–85; and Annette Lareau and Elliot B. Weininger, "Cultural Capital in Educational Research: A Critical Assessment," *Theory and Society* 32, no. 5 / 6 (2003): 567–606.

8. See Gama Zamarro, Collen Hitt, and Ildefonso Mendez, "When Students Don't Care: Reexamining International Differences in Achievement and Student Effort," *Journal of Human Capital* 13, no. 4 (Winter 2019): 519–634.

9. Mads Meir Jaeger and Kristian Karlson, "Cultural Capital and Educational Inequality: A Counter Factual Analysis," *Sociological Science* 5 (2018): 775–95; Ethan Fosse, "The Values and Beliefs of Disconnected Black Youth," in Patterson,

The Cultural Matrix, 139–66; and Tina Wildhagen, "Why Does Cultural Capital Matter for High School Academic Performance: An Empirical Assessment of Teacher-Selection and Self-Selection Mechanisms as an Explanation of Cultural Capital Effect," *Sociological Quarterly* 50, no. 1 (2009): 173–200.

10. The question of decision making is most often predicated on the individual using some form of a cost-benefit analysis, which of course does not guarantee that in using this form of calculus a person makes a bad decision. See Michelle Jackson et al., *Determined to Succeed?: Performance Versus Choice in Educational Attainment* (Stanford, CA: Stanford University Press, 2013), 3–5.

11. The work of Robert D. Mare in the area of transitions is particularly important. He wrote a number of articles on the subject, so I shall only reference two: "Social Background and School Continuation Decisions," *Journal of the American Statistical Association* 75 (1980): 295–305; and "Statistical Models of Educational Stratification: Hauser and Andrew's Models of School Transitions," *Sociological Methodology* 36 (2006): 27–37.

12. Many of the studies in Yossi Shavit and Hans-Peter Blossfeld, eds., *Persistent Inequality: A Comparative Study of Educational Attainment in Thirteen Countries* (Boulder, CO: Westview Press, 1993), build on Mare's work and use econometrics to assess the transitions from grade school to high school, high school to college, and college to graduate work. The models which Mare suggested that sociologists and economists use in order to measure probabilities for transitions and the role of family background in their making have been the subject of some debate; see, for example, Steven V. Cameron and James Heckman, "Life Cycle Schooling and Dynamic Selection Bias: Models and Evidence for Five Cohorts," *Journal of Political Economy* 106, no. 2 (April 1998): 262–333; and Robert Hauser and Megan Andrew, "Another Look at the Stratification of Educational Transition: The Logistic Response Model and Partial Proportionality Constraint," *Sociological Methodology* 36 (2006): 1–26. An important addition to these debates is the work of Christiana Kartsonaki, Michelle Jackson, and David R. Cox, "Primary and Secondary Effects: Some Methodological Issues," in Jackson, *Determined to Succeed?*, 34–55.

13. There has been consistent evidence that inequality among social groups exists in the number who go on to attend and successfully complete college; and this was particularly the case before the present study began. See Thomas J. Kane, "College-Going and Inequality," in Neckerman, *Social Inequality*, 319–53.

14. The role of intelligence in determining a person's success in life has always been a hotly debated issue. Richard Herrnstein and Charles Murray in *The Bell Curve: Intelligence and Class Structure in American Life* (New York: Free Press, 1996) argued that intelligence (i.e., IQ) was the most important factor in determining where individuals will end up in the equality queue. This was challenged by many scholars, most notably by Claude S. Fischer et al., *Inequality by Design: Cracking the Bell Curve Myth* (Princeton, NJ: Princeton University Press, 1996), who argued that the choices made at the policy level, as well as other environmental factors, had more to do with where individuals ended up in the occupational hierarchy than did "native" intelligence. It was not that intelligence did not have an

effect on school performance, but that it had less impact than social factors on educational performance and where individuals landed in the job market.

15. See Alisa Szatrowski, "Pathways to Graduation and Beyond: Practices From Two High Schools for Low-Income Students" (PhD diss., University of California, 2019); Barnett Berry, "Good Schools and Teachers for All Students: Dispelling Myths, Facing Evidence, and Pursuing Right Strategies," in Carter and Wilmer, *Closing the Opportunity Gap,* chap. 13; Carter, *Stubborn Roots,* chap. 2; and Gilbert Q. Conchas, *The Color of Success: Race and High Achieving Urban Youth* (New York: Teachers College Press, 2006).

16. See Russell J. Skiba, Kavitha Medirata, and M. Karega Rausch, eds., *Inequality in School Discipline: Research and Practice to Reduce Disparities* (New York: Oxford University Press, 2012).

17. Jackson, *Determined to Succeed?,* 3–55; and the various empirical chapters that follow.

18. See Stephen L. Morgan, Michael W. Spiller, and Jennifer J. Todd, "Class Origins, High School Graduation, and College Entry in the United States," in Jackson, *Determined to Succeed?,* 279–305, esp. 299.

19. The 1991–99 study was focused on understanding social change in low-income neighborhoods. The results of this study can be found in my *Cracks in the Pavement.*

20. The results of the 2000–2003 study can be found in my *Burning Dislike: Ethnic Violence in High Schools* (Berkeley: University of California Press, 2016).

21. For a full discussion of the principles and procedures utilized by me for these two studies, as well as all the others that I have been involved with, see Martín Sánchez-Jankowski and Corey M. Abramson, "Foundations of the Behavioralist Approach to Comparative Participant Observation," in *Beyond the Case: The Logics and Practices of Comparative Ethnography,* ed. Corey M. Abramson and Neil Gong (New York: Oxford University Press, 2020), 31–56; and Corey M. Abramson and Martín Sánchez-Jankowski, "Conducting Comparative Participant Observation: Behavioral Procedures and Techniques," in Abramson and Gong, *Beyond the Case,* 57–87.

22. Sánchez-Jankowski, *Cracks in the Pavement,* 355–57; and Sánchez-Jankowski, *Burning Dislike,* 203–5.

23. I am not able to provide specific data concerning the median income levels and ethnicities of the students attending each school, due to school officials requiring that such data not be reported by me because it would be possible to identify the school and that would violate the protection of students', faculty's, and staff's confidentiality.

24. See Abramson and Sánchez-Jankowski, "Conducting Comparative Participant Observation."

25. All the research was approved by the institutional review boards of UC Berkeley and each school.

26. See Daniel Dohan and Martín Sánchez-Jankowski, "Using Computers to Analyze Ethnographic Field Data: Theoretical and Practical Considerations," *Annual Review of Sociology* 24 (1998): 477–98.

27. See Sánchez-Jankowski and Abramson, "Foundations of the Behavioralist Approach," and Abramson and Sánchez-Jankowski, "Conducting Comparative Participant Observation."

28. See the discussion in Vaisey, "What People Want."

CHAPTER 1. THE POLITICS OF EDUCATIONAL MANAGEMENT

1. See Meredith Phillips and Tiffani Chin, "School Inequality: What Do We Know?," in *Social Inequality*, ed. Kathryn M. Neckerman (New York: Russell Sage Foundation, 2004), 467–520.

2. There is a great deal of research on this topic, so I will mention some, not all, of the more influential research: Phillips and Chin, "School Inequality"; Kathryn M. Neckerman, *Schools Betrayed: Roots of Failure in Inner-City Education* (Chicago: University of Chicago Press, 2007); Samuel Bowles and Herbert Gintis, *Schooling in Capitalist America: Educational Reform and the Contradictions of Economic Life* (New York: Basic Books, 1976); and Kenneth J. Saltman, *The Politics of Education: A Critical Introduction* (New York: Routledge, [2014] 2016).

3. See Sean Corcoran, William N. Evans, Jennifer Godwin, Sheila E. Murray, and Robert M. Schwab, "The Changing Distribution of Educational Finance, 1972 to 1997," in Neckerman, *Social Inequality*, 433–66; and W. Norton Grubb, *Money Myth: School Resources, Outcomes, and Equity* (New York: Russell Sage Foundation, 2009).

4. The conversation was taken shorthand as Edward was talking to a principal while conducting an inquiry into some complaints leveled at the school's poor test scores and graduation rates. I was in the adjoining room waiting for a meeting called by the principal for department heads to begin.

5. The quote was taken shorthand as this administrator was briefing an associate on what they should pay attention to that day. I was in the room talking to this administrator when the associate arrived.

6. The quote was taken shorthand as this administrator was talking to two of his associates while having coffee during lunch. I was invited to accompany them and was seated with them.

7. The quote was taken shorthand. The administrator, who is Mexican American, was talking to two other administrators during lunch. I was sitting with them as they had invited me to have lunch with them.

8. See William A. V. Clark, "Residential Patterns: Avoidance, Assimilation, and Succession," in *Ethnic Los Angeles*, ed. Roger Waldinger and Mehdi Bozorgmehr (New York: Russell Sage Foundation, 1996).

9. Raphael J. Sonenshein, *Politics in Black and White: Race and Power in Los Angeles* (Princeton, NJ: Princeton University Press, 1993).

10. Sometimes tensions can reach a very intense level and violence breaks out. See Martín Sánchez-Jankowski, *Burning Dislike: Ethnic Violence in High Schools* (Oakland: University of California Press, 2016).

11. When it came to the everyday functioning of schools, the result of these political maneuvers was the establishment of a culture where central administrators did not consistently examine the schools' everyday operations to see where instructional problems existed, what accounted for them, and how they should be addressed.

12. Albert K. Karnig and Susan Welch, *Black Representation and Urban Policy* (Chicago: University of Chicago Press, 1980).

13. Katherine Tate, *From Protest to Politics: The New Black Voters in American Elections* (Cambridge, MA: Harvard University Press, 1993).

14. US Census for years 1990, 2000, 2010, and the 2015 Current Population Statics for Los Angeles and the Bronx, New York.

15. See Georges Sabagh and Mehdi Bozorgmehr, "Population Change: Immigration and Ethnic Transformation," in Waldinger and Bozorgmehr, *Ethnic Los Angeles,* 79–107.

16. It should be remembered that in the segregated South, there was the establishment of "Negro Colleges," which trained a significant number of professional teachers. A number of these teachers migrated to Los Angeles and provided professional resources to the Los Angeles Unified School District.

17. See Nicolás C. Vaca, "When Blacks Rule: Lessons from Compton," in *The Presumed Alliance: The Unspoken Conflict between Latinos and Blacks and What It Means for America* (New York: HarperCollins, 2004), 127–45.

18. For the demographic changes in what had been traditional African American schools see Manuel Pastor, "Keeping It Real: Demographic Change, Economic Conflict, and Interethnic Organizing for Social Justice in Los Angeles," in *Black and Brown in Los Angeles: Beyond Conflict and Coalition*, ed. Josh Kun and Laura Pulido (Berkeley: University of California Press, 2014), 37, 40–45.

19. I am not specifying the exact location of the subdistrict in order to protect the anonymity of the subject.

20. The quote was taken shorthand as Willard talked on the phone to a principal of a school that was experiencing violent confrontations between Mexican and African American students. He was visiting one of the schools that I was studying (not the one he was making the phone call to) and made the call from his cell phone in the assistant principal's office where I was sitting talking to a counselor. Willard did not have any inhibitions about talking in front of us. He and the assistant principal were friends and he assumed that what he was saying was not controversial and thus I posed no threat.

21. I am not naming the school in order to protect the anonymity of the subject.

22. The quote was taken shorthand as the principal was talking to the assistant principal at a meeting they were having after school. I was at the meeting, having accompanied the assistant principal on his after-school rounds that included reporting to the principal before they both went home.

23. Even though I have been using pseudonyms, I am not naming the specific school in New York in order to provide additional anonymity for the subject.

24. The quote was taken shorthand as this principal was talking to three of his teachers while they were out patrolling during lunch time. I was walking with them while the conversation was occurring.

25. Even though I have been using pseudonyms, I am not naming the specific school in Los Angeles in order to provide additional anonymity for the subject.

26. The quote was taken shorthand as the principal was talking to three teachers at a party for a candidate running for the Board of Education. I was with two teachers who were standing immediately behind Horace and the teachers he was talking to.

27. I am not naming the school, even though I have been using pseudonyms for them, in order to provide additional anonymity for the subject.

28. The quote was taken shorthand as this principal was talking to a colleague at a teacher workshop. I was sitting behind them as they were conversing.

29. I have chosen not to use a pseudonym for this assistant's name in order to provide additional anonymity for the subject.

30. The quote was taken shorthand as the subject addressed a group of administrators at a policy briefing before the start of the school year. I was invited to the meeting by one of the administrative analysts working on educational policy.

31. The quote was taken shorthand as the subject was reviewing each high school in the area and deciding on what to recommend in the way of personnel changes and resource allocations for the coming year. The group consisted of eight assistant heads within the administration. I was in attendance, having accompanied one of the assistants to the meeting.

32. The quote was taken shorthand as the subject was talking to a group of support staff at their weekly meeting. They were going over current planning for the next school year. I was invited to the meeting by the subject.

33. The quote was taken shorthand as the subject was talking to two other teachers while at lunch. I was sitting at the same round table, eating lunch.

34. The quote was taken shorthand as Larry was talking to two counselors during lunch hour. I was sitting at the table next to where they were eating.

35. The quote was taken shorthand as Casey was talking to a counselor and the attendance officer before a staff meeting.

36. The quote was taken shorthand as Nicolas was talking to his assistant principal and the head of his academic support staff. I was with all three as they were talking while standing and watching the students enter for the start of school.

37. The quote was taken shorthand as Dana was talking to another teacher in the faculty cafeteria dining room. I was at the table eating my food.

38. The quote was taken shorthand as Lara was talking to three other teachers at a school sporting event they were attending. They had just been told that a new principal would be taking over the school for the next academic year. I had gone to the game with them and was seated just behind them.

39. The quote was taken shorthand as Jeanie was talking to two male teachers after a faculty orientation meeting to begin the fall semester of the school year. I was walking with them as they went to their various homerooms.

40. Obviously, there are teachers over time who want to reduce their workload by being less flexible about where and when to meet and often less available to meet at all. However, the evidence presented in this section is focused on those teachers who were committed to resisting the changes that the current administration was trying to implement in the school.

41. The quote was taken shorthand as Lea was talking to five friends at lunch. I was at the table next to them.

42. The quote was taken shorthand as Darren was talking to three friends at the local grocery store on the way home from school. I was in the store talking to the owner.

43. The quote was taken shorthand as Lester was talking to a teacher in the faculty lounge. I was in the lounge reading the newspaper when the conversation started.

44. Harold Dwight Lasswell, *Politics: Who Gets What, When, How* (New York: Wittlesey House, 1936).

CHAPTER 2. THE INTERFACE OF FAMILY AND SCHOOL

1. There has been a voluminous amount of research which has found that an advantaged family background improves educational outcomes. I will simply name a few: Yossi Shavit and Hans-Peter Blossfeld, eds., *Persistent Inequality: A Comparative Study of Educational Attainment in Thirteen Countries* (Boulder, CO: Westview Press, 1993); John Ewisch and Marco Francesconi, "Family Matters: Impact of Family Background on Educational Achievements," *Economica* 68, no. 270 (May 2001): 137–56; and Ludger Woessman, "How Equal Are Educational Opportunities? Family Background and Student Achievement in Europe and the US," Center for Economic Research–Munich Working Paper Series, no. 1162 (April 2004).

2. See Annette Lareau, *Unequal Childhoods: Class, Race, and Family Life* (Berkeley: University of California Press, 2003), 233–57; and Marcia K. Meyers, Dan Rosenbaum, Christopher Ruhm, and Jane Waldfogel, "Inequality in Early Childhood Education and Care: What Do We Know?," in *Social Inequality*, ed. Kathryn Neckerman (New York: Russell Sage Foundation, 2004), 223–69.

3. See Michelle Jackson and Brian Holzman, "A Century of Educational Inequality in the United States," *Proceedings of the National Academy of Sciences of the United States of America*, July 27, 2020; Eric A. Hanushek, Paul E. Peterson, Laura M. Talpey, and Ludger Woessman, "The Unwavering SES Achievement Gap: Trends in US Student Performance" (Working Paper 25648, National Bureau of Economic Research, 2019); Greg J. Duncan and Ricard J. Murnane, "Rising Inequality in Family Incomes and Children's Educational Outcomes," *Russell Sage Foundation Journal of the Social Sciences* 2, no. 2 (May 2016): 142–58; Eric Grodsky, John Robert Warren, and Erika Felts, "Testing and Social Stratification in American Education," *Annual Review of Sociology* 34 (2008): 385–404; Bruce Bradbury, Miles

Cormak, Jane Waldfogel, and Elizabeth Washbrook, *Too Many Children Left Behind* (New York: Russell Sage Foundation, 2015); Sean Reardon, "The Widening Academic Achievement Gap between the Rich and Poor: New Evidence and Possible Explanations," in *Whither Opportunity? Rising Inequality, Schools, and Children's Life Chances*, ed. Greg J. Duncan and Richard J. Murnane (New York: Russell Sage Foundation, 2011); and Richard Breen and Jan O. Jonsson, "Inequality of Opportunity in Comparative Perspective: Recent Research on Educational Attainment and Social Mobility," *Annual Review of Sociology* 31 (2005): 223–43.

4. There are two lines of argument concerning parental background and its impact on a child's educational outcomes. One is based on biology and emphasizes the role of IQ and the genetic passing of it to offspring. The obvious example of this can be seen in the work of psychometricians, and for an excellent example see Richard J. Herrnstein and Charles Murray, *The Bell Curve: Intelligence and Class Structure in American Life* (New York: Free Press, 1994). The other line of argument is that parents have varying degrees of skills and resources, and it is these differences that account for most of the variance seen in school achievement. A good example of this line of argument is Claude Fischer et al., *Inequality by Design: Cracking the Bell Curve Myth* (Princeton, NJ: Princeton University Press, 1996).

5. The quote was taken shorthand as Victor was talking to two other teachers in the teachers' lounge. I was sitting with the group as they talked.

6. The quote was taken shorthand as Sherry was talking to three other teachers in the teachers' lounge. I was sitting at the next table drinking coffee.

7. The quote was taken shorthand as Emil was talking to three other students, two females and one male, while waiting to get into the gymnasium for gym class. I was waiting with the group and standing immediately next to them.

8. The quote was taken shorthand as Stacie was talking to four friends during her assigned homework period. I was sitting at the table next to the one they were occupying.

9. The quote was taken shorthand as Lena was talking to three of her friends at lunch time. I was sitting at the table immediately behind them.

10. The quote was taken shorthand as Lucas was talking to two male friends at the school's Friday varsity football game. I was sitting in the stands immediately to their left.

11. The quote was taken shorthand as Raleigh was talking to three friends. I was sitting at the next dining table to her and her friends during lunch.

12. The quote was taken shorthand as Micah was talking to his friend before his math class began. I was in the room, standing at the pencil sharpener next to their desks.

13. The quote was taken shorthand as Benjamin was talking to a new teacher at the school during lunch in the faculty dining room. I was sitting with a group of teachers at the table next them.

14. The quote was taken shorthand as Linda was talking to another teacher before a scheduled staff meeting at the end of an instructional day. I was sitting with a group of twelve teachers who were seated around one of the large worktables.

15. Martín Sánchez-Jankowski, *Cracks in the Pavement: Social Change and Resilience in Poor Neighborhoods* (Berkeley: University of California Press, 2008), 68–72.

16. The quote was taken shorthand as Mr. Stevens was talking to two other teachers in the teachers' lounge. I was sitting at the table with them.

17. The quote was taken shorthand as Ms. Randall was talking to two other teachers during lunchtime in the teachers' lounge. I was part of their group eating lunch.

18. The quote was taken shorthand while Donna was talking to one of her friends before the start of a study period. I was standing with a group of students behind them waiting for the door to open for the start of the study period.

19. When I had access to students in their homes, I would use the stopwatch function on my wristwatch to time various activities. The length of time that students started and completed their homework was something I would regularly time, and Steven was one of the subjects that I timed.

20. The quote was taken shorthand as Sheila was talking to four of her friends during lunch. I was eating at the next table.

21. See Paul G. Lehrmann, Timothy Z. Keith, and Thomas M. Reimers, "Home Influence on School Learning: Direct and Indirect Effects of Parental Involvement," *Journal of Educational Research* 80, no. 6 (1987): 330–37.

22. David E. Frisvold, "Nutrition and Cognitive Achievement: An Evaluation of the School Breakfast Program," *Journal of Public Economics* 124 (April 2008): 91–104; and Cesar Victora, Caroline Fall, Pedro C. Hallal, Reynaldo Martorell, Linda Richter, and Harshpal Singh Sachdev, "Maternal and Child Undernutrition: Consequences for Adult Health and Human Capital," *Lancet* 371 (2008): 340–57.

23. I recorded 164 out of 173 individuals who missed a morning meal and then became involved in disruptive behavior. This number reported in the text comes from observations that would start in the home and then the student would be identified in the classroom by me as being involved in disruptive behavior. These observations are consistent with the large literature on the positive impact that the current Federally Funded Breakfast Program has on learning achievement. See Peter Hinrichs, "The Effects of the National School Lunch Program on Education and Health," *Journal of Policy and Management* 29, no. 3 (Summer 2010): 479–505.

24. The observations were made by first being in the home of the student and noting when they went to sleep, then the next day observing their behavior. In addition, I carefully timed the behavior, in this case being tired and trying to sleep in class, to see how long it lasted throughout the day.

25. There is a great deal of research that finds a lack of quality sleep being an important factor influencing student performance in both elementary, high school, college, and medical students. I offer four such studies as examples: Reut Gruber, Gail Somerville, Lana Bergane, Laura Fontil, and Saukaina Paquin, "Sleep-Based Sleep Education Program Improves Sleep and Academic Performance of School-Age Children," *Sleep Medicine* 21 (May 2016): 93–100; Xue Ming, Rebecca Koransky,

Victor Kang, Sarah Buchman, and Christina E. Sarris, "Sleep Insufficiency, Sleep Health Problems and Performance in High School Students," *Clinical Medicine Insights: Circulatory, Respiratory, and Pulmonary Medicine* 5 (May 2011): 71–79; Ana Allen Gomes, José Tavares, and Maria Heena P. de Azenvedo, "Sleep and Academic Performance in Undergraduates: A Multi-Measure, Multi-Predictor Approach," *Chronobiology International* 28 (2011): 786–801; and Hanza M. Abdulghani, Norah A. Alrowis, Norah S. Ben-Saad, Nourah M. Al-Subaie, Alhan M. A. Haji, and Ali I. Alhaqwi, "Sleep Disorder among Medical Students: Relationship to Their Academic Performance," *Medical Teacher* 34 (2012): 37–41.

26. See Patricia Gándara and Frances Contreras, *The Latino Educational Crisis* (Cambridge, MA: Harvard University Press, 2009), 95; and Blanca Esthela Gordo, "What Planning Crisis? Reflections on the 'Digital Divide' and the Persistence of Unequal Opportunity," *Berkeley Planning Journal* 16 (2002): 4–23.

27. The exchange was taken shorthand as Taylor and Dida were talking before Geometry class began. I was in the classroom, sitting behind them, waiting for the teacher to begin.

28. Paul DiMaggio, Eszter Hargittai, Coral Celeste, and Steven Shafer, "Digital Inequality: From Unequal Access to Differentiated Use," in Neckerman, *Social Inequality*, 355–400.

29. The quote was taken shorthand. The conversation between Bernice and her mother was occurring in a small grocery store near their apartment. I was in the next aisle, listening to the conversation.

30. The quote was taken shorthand while Doris was talking to her beautician in the salon. I was in the backroom of the salon listening to the conversation. Doris knew I was in the salon because I had just come out and swept the floor of hair and then retired to the back room. Those interested in the specifics of how I conducted the research for this project should consult the methodological appendix in my *Cracks in the Pavement*, 355–65, where there is a discussion of the arrangement that I had to make with the owners of these hair salons.

31. The quote was taken shorthand. Courtney and her mother were having this conversation in the kitchen of their apartment. I was there as a friend of the family's and sitting in the living room where I could listen to their conversation.

32. This is consistent with the findings discussed in Alejandro Portes and Rubén G. Rumbaut, *Legacies: The Story of the Immigrant Second Generation* (Berkeley: University of California Press, 2001), 94–96.

33. The quote was taken shorthand while Homer was talking to three friends in a barbershop. The conversation was on education for their kids. I was sitting just behind them.

34. The quote was taken shorthand as Anita was talking to the hairdresser in the salon where she was getting her hair styled. I was in the backroom, having just come out and swept the floor.

35. The quote was taken shorthand as Chet was talking to a friend while drinking coffee at the counter of a local restaurant. I was at the counter with them when the conversation occurred.

36. The story of Elvi and her children came from the notes that I took shorthand while interacting with the family over a three-year period. I had been invited by one of Elvi's children to have dinner with the family, and while at dinner Elvi invited me to come by the house whenever I wanted. I accepted Elivi's offer and would periodically go to her apartment for coffee or dinner over a three-year period. Elvi and her children were one of the families that I had formally asked and was granted permission to be present in their residence.

37. The quote was taken shorthand as Elena was talking to a friend and the grocer at a small local grocery store. I was in the store socializing and listened to the conversation.

38. See Melvin Kohn, *Class and Conformity: A Study of Values* (New York: John Wiley and Sons, 1969), 93–103.

39. See Ivor Braden Horn, Jill G. Joseph, and Tina L. Cheng, "Non-Abusive Physical Punishment and Child Behavior among African American Children: A Systematic Review," *Journal of the National Medical Association* 96, no. 9 (2004): 1162–68; Howard S. Erlanger, "Social Class and Corporal Punishment in Childrearing: A Reassessment," *American Sociological Association* 39 (1974): 68–85; and Sánchez-Jankowski, *Cracks in the Pavement,* 28–29.

40. The incident with Suzanne and her mother took place in the family's small two-bedroom apartment in Brooklyn. As a result of an invitation from her older brother and husband, I was staying with the family during this time of the research. I was at the school when her mother arrived and got a ride with them back to their apartment. I observed the entire interaction, and after it was completed Suzanne's mother sat down, poured us both some coffee, said, "Kids, they just got to test you all the time," and then started to talk about something else. My shorthand notes were taken as best as I could manage while the incident was occurring.

41. Ricardo's family had befriended me and I was often at the house socializing with the parents. This example was recorded as I observed Ricardo at school, his father at the meeting with school officials, the incident that occurred in the home, and Ricardo's subsequent behavior at school. I recorded all behaviors when they were occurring.

42. The importance of peer group influence on the attitudes and behaviors of Black youth is discussed in various chapters of Orlando Patterson, ed., *The Cultural Matrix: Understanding Black Youth* (Cambridge, MA: Harvard University Press, 2015), chaps. 1, 2, 3, 13, 16. See also John Ogbu, *Black American Students in an Affluent Suburb: A Study of Academic Disengagement* (Mahwah, NJ: Lawrence Erlbaum Associates, 2003), who found that middle-class African American students would not work as hard as they could, and received underachieving grades, because they wanted to identify with lower-class African Americans who they thought were "more" African American than their parents. This must be seen as part of the general adolescent rejection of parental identity in the process of formulating a unique one of their own, albeit with a peer ethnic influence.

43. The work of Erik H. Erikson is most relevant for understanding the process of identity formation. See his *Identity: Youth and Crisis* (New York: Norton Press, 1968).

44. This is not a lower-class-specific response, but the consequences are greater for those in more tenuous structural circumstances as they generally get fewer second chances. In contrast, children of more affluent parents often turn their failures into a resource that they can use in their college admission essays for future success in obtaining access to additional resources.

45. The quote was taken shorthand while Cynthia was having a conversation with two of her friends during lunch period. I was sitting at the same table while listening to their conversation.

46. This finding is not specifically related to individuals whose fear of failure is so intense that it inhibits them from fully executing the skills necessary to be successful, i.e., their fear of failure creates the very outcome they want to avoid. Rather, the impact I am referring to comes directly from the effect of introducing doubt to the individual as to whether they are capable of successfully completing a specific assignment—i.e., introducing self-doubt about their capabilities that is based on what others have said comes from them having an inferior biological or cultural background. For a description of the "stereotype threat" see the work of Claude Steele and Joshua Aronson, "Stereotype Threat and the Intellectual Test Performance of African Americans," *Journal of Personality and Social Psychology* 69, no. 5 (November 1995), 797–811, who found that for African American students who had lived with the stigma that they were not as intellectually competent as White students, the mere suggestion before an exam of anything that could be construed as referring to race was enough to produce poor performances. There has been a great deal of subsequent research on the subject that has followed. See Cynthia Hudley and Sandra Graham, "Stereotypes of Achievement Striving among Early Adolescents," *Social Psychology of Education* 5 (June 2001): 201–21; T. Thomas Kellow and Brett D. Jones, "The Effects of Stereotypes on the Achievement Gap: Reexamining the Academic Performance of African Americans High School Students," *Journal of Black Psychology* 34 (February 2008): 94–120; and Jayanti Owens and Douglas Massey, "Stereotype Threat and College Academic Performance: A Latent Variable Approach," *Social Science Research* 40, no. 1 (January 2011): 150–66.

47. The quote was taken shorthand. The conversation was taking place during the lunch hour and I was seated at the table to the side of Carlos and Duane.

48. See Samuel Roundfield Lucas, *Theorizing Discrimination in a Time of Contested Prejudice*, vol. 1, *Discrimination in the United States* (Philadelphia: Temple University Press, 2009), 31.

49. For a very clear discussion of the issue see Lewis Anthony Dexter, *The Tyranny of Schooling: An Inquiry into the Problem of "Stupidity"* (New York: Basic Books, 1964).

50. See Gándara and Contreras, *The Latino Education Crisis,* 100–108; and Fischer et al., *Inequality by Design*, 171–204.

51. See Samuel Roundfield Lucas, *Just Who Loses?*, vol. 2, *Discrimination in the United States* (Philadelphia: Temple University Press, 2013), 138–73, who finds similar patterns of educational disadvantage to African American and women attributable to acts of discrimination.

52. Annette Lareau, *Unequal Childhoods,* 227–32.

53. The quotes were taken shorthand both during class and when Damian's teacher was talking to her colleagues during lunch period. I remained interested in Damian because I thought he was a student who had not received the remedial help he was entitled to. In addition, Damian kept in touch with one of the staff in the principal's office and she would pass on what he had reported to her. After being told that Damian had graduated from college, I made contact with him and accompanied him to his job in the accounting department of a large retail department store where he introduced me to his fellow employees.

54. See Paul Gorski, *Reaching and Teaching Students in Poverty* (New York: Teachers College Press, 2017).

55. One sees this reaction in regard to African American youth. For example, see Shelby Steele, *The Content of Our Character: A New Vision of Race* (New York: Harper Perennial, 1991); John McWhorter, *Losing the Race: Self-Sabotage in Black America* (New York: Harper Perennial, 2001); and Thomas Sowell, *Black Rednecks and White Liberals* (San Francisco: Encounter Books, 2005).

56. The category of "deserving" and "undeserving" poor is insightfully discussed by David Matza, "Poverty and Disrepute," in *Contemporary Social Problems,* ed. Robert K. Merton and Robert A. Nisbet, 2nd ed. (New York: Harcourt, Brace & World, 1966), 619–69; and James T. Patterson, *America's Struggle against Poverty in the Twentieth Century* (Cambridge, MA: Harvard University of Press, [1981] 2000).

57. There is a great deal of evidence supporting the position that there is positive economic returns to educational attainment. See Michael Hout, "Social and Economic Returns to Higher Education in the United States," *Annual Review of Sociology* 38 (2012): 379–400; and Michael Hout, "The Employment Patterns of Young Adults, 1989–2014," in *Youth, Jobs, and the Future: Problems and Prospects,* ed. Lynn S. Chancer, Martín Sánchez-Jankowski, and Christine Trost (New York: Oxford University Press, 2019), 19–34.

58. Cross Junior High is a pseudonym for the junior high that she does attend.

59. The quote was taken shorthand. The conversation was between Jeanne and two of her closest friends from the public housing building that the family lives in. I was at the table eating breakfast, having been a guest of her husband.

60. The quote was taken shorthand. The conversation was taking place between Teresa and her friend Julia on the telephone. I was in the house observing the entire interaction, and was sitting on the couch with Teresa as she talked to Julia.

61. The quote was taken shorthand as Emmett was talking to four men at a local grocery store while they are drinking beers after work. I was part of the group.

62. The quote was taken shorthand as David was talking to a friend at a football game. I was immediately behind him.

63. I was able to observe Ana-Luz because her family lived in my apartment building and as a neighbor I would often give her father a ride home and be invited in. As part of one of my research projects I also consistently went to the school that Ana-Luz attended to observe her and the others' educational behavior.

64. I was a friend of Gene's father who would regularly invite me to their home. During those times, there were numerous occasions when Gene's father and mother would get into an argument that involved them hollering and pushing each other. Since I had been there when the incident occurred, the next day, I would try to observe how Gene was doing. Every time I observed an incident at Gene's house, the following day I also observed Gene being quiet and uninterested in what was occurring in school. His behavior was unusual because he was generally a good student who received A and B grades and so his changed demeanor caught the attention of his teachers who would ask him if anything was wrong. He would always say no and return to drawing cartoons in a notebook.

65. I have used the word "refining" to describe the labors of individuals during the adolescent period because, much earlier in the life course, morals are initiated and in adolescence there is the effort toward refining their current array of moral principles.

66. I was a friend of Sara's parents for three of her four years attending high school. That placed me at the family home on numerous occasions where I documented Sara's interactions with her father and mother.

67. The interaction was recorded shorthand in the teacher's lounge of Chester Himes High School. I was sitting at the same table of the three teachers while they were talking.

68. Pierre Bourdieu, *Distinction: A Social Critique of Judgement and Taste* (Cambridge, MA: Harvard University Press, 1984).

69. A much more detailed discussion of lower-class culture can be found in my *Cracks in the Pavement,* chap. 1.

70. See Corey Abramson, *The End Game: How Inequality Shapes Our Final Years* (Cambridge, MA: Harvard University Press, 2015), 19–39, where he finds it is the body's function as a "resource," "locus of experience," and "signifier" that makes it a structure.

71. Students from middle-class families did not see physical aggression as being normal. They saw it as being unacceptable. However, they were willing to engage in verbal aggression when they utilized insults to leverage an advantage.

72. The quote was taken shorthand as Horton was talking to two friends in class while he was waiting for the teacher to finish giving him a pass to the principal's office with the formal reason for why he was being sent. I was in the classroom observing when the incident occurred.

73. I found that teachers who came from lower-class families as compared to those from middle class-backgrounds had more of an appreciation for the difficulties associated with a student's inability to sit for an extended period of time, but they faced the same problem of getting the student to focus on the activities designed for building their academic skill base and thus acted similar to middle-class teachers.

74. Jackson's story comes from one of the studies where I was living in high-poverty neighborhoods. In this particular case, I was close to Jackson's father and mother and often was in their apartment socializing. I had opportunities to talk and

observe Jackson both at home, school, and the local library. The events just described were directly observed. This also included times when Jackson would talk about school with his friends and family.

75. Jackson's ultimate success was certainly aided by his military experience, which built skills that benefited him in his future studies such as being precise in executing an assignment and practicing to improve at each level of activity. In addition, his "in harm's way" experience during the Afghanistan conflict was instrumental in him being clear as to what he wanted to do and its importance to what he considered his future.

76. The interaction was recorded shorthand while I was at Joan's house talking to her mother. I had come to know her mother and father while attending the school's parent-teacher organization. They occasionally invited me to their home for dinner.

77. The quote was taken shorthand as Miguel was talking to the dean of his class, who addressed student disciplinary issues. I was outside the dean's office sitting with other students who were waiting to see the dean.

78. See Lawrence S. Friedman, "Adolescence," in *The Child: An Encyclopedic Companion*, ed. Richard A. Shweder (Chicago: University of Chicago Press, 2009), 18–21; and Erikson, *Identity: Youth and Crisis*, 124–28.

79. Labeling is both a "normal" part of bureaucratic categorization and a problem for providing the appropriate service for those in need. It also creates a problem for those who have been labeled, either correctly or not, because the labels have a longer life in stimulating prescribed responses than is empirically appropriate. Thus, the labeled individual assumes a social stigma that is difficult to shed and this creates situations in which the stigmatized individual experiences inappropriate and counterproductive behavior from those reacting to the stigma. See Lewis Anthony Dexter, "On the Politics and Sociology of Stupidity in Our Society," in *The Management of Purpose: Lewis Anthony Dexter*, ed. Martín Sánchez-Jankowski and Alan J. Ware (New Brunswick, NJ: Transaction, 2010), 65–74.

CHAPTER 3. SCHOOL ORGANIZATION AND ITS CHALLENGES

1. There is a vast literature on school structures and their negative impact on low-income and racial / ethnic minority students, so I will simply mention a few examples. There is the older generation, represented by Jonathan Kozol's *Death at an Early Age* (New York: Plume, 1985) and *Savage Inequalities: Children in America's Schools* (New York: Crown, 1991); Samuel Bowles and Herbert Gintis, *Schooling in Capitalist America: Educational Reform and the Contradictions of Group Life* (New York: Basic Books, 1976). Among the newer work is Karolyn Tyson, *Integration Interrupted: Tracking, Black Students, and Acting White after Brown* (New York: Oxford University Press, 2011); Prudence L. Carter and Kevin G. Welner, eds., *Closing the Opportunity Gap: What America Must Do to Give Every Child an Even*

Chance (New York: Oxford University Press, 2013); and Greg J. Duncan and Richard J. Murnane, eds., *Whither Opportunity?: Rising Inequality, Schools, and Children's Life Chances* (New York: Russell Sage Foundation, 2011).

2. See Annette Lereau and Kimberley Goyette, eds., *Choosing Homes, Choosing Schools* (New York: Russell Sage Foundation, 2014), part II; Marybeth Shinn and Hirokazu Yoshikawa, eds., *Toward Positive Youth Development: Transferring Schools and Community Programs* (New York: Oxford University Press, 2018); and Heather Beth Johnson, *The American Dream and the Power of Wealth: Choosing Schools and Inheriting Inequality in the Land of Opportunity* (New York: Routledge, 2015).

3. Many of the findings associated with the older work on tracking and its implications on issues of internal school stratification and inequality remain present. See the work of Jeannie Oakes, *Keeping Track: How Schools Structure Inequality*, 2nd ed. (New Haven, CT: Yale University Press, 2005); Samuel Roundfield Lucas, *Tracking Inequality: Stratification and Mobility in American High Schools* (New York: Teachers College Press, 1995); and Karolyn Tyson, "Tracking, Segregation, and the Opportunity Gap," in Carter and Welner, *Closing the Opportunity Gap*, chap. 12.

4. See the recent work of Thurston Domina, Andrew McEachen, Paul Hanselman, Prijanka Agarwal, NaYoung Hwang, and Ryan W. Lewis, "Beyond Tracking and Detracking: The Dimensions of Organizational Differentiation in Schools," *Sociology of Education* 92, no. 3 (2019): 293–322, that describes how different strategies associated with tracking affect school achievement and inequality.

5. The curriculum of vocational education was the result of the congressional Carl D. Perkins Vocational and Technical Education Act, 1988, that was legislated to provide educational opportunities to those students not wanting to proceed on to college.

6. The quote was taken shorthand as Deidre was talking to three friends at a school assembly to celebrate Martin Luther King Day. I was sitting behind them as they were talking.

7. The quote was taken shorthand as Francisco was talking to five friends just before his scheduled study period. I was next to them waiting to enter the room for study period.

8. The quote was taken shorthand as Alejandra was talking to four friends while waiting to get a haircut. I was in the salon's backroom, waiting to come out and sweep the floors for the owner / beautician.

9. The quote was taken shorthand as Darcy was talking to a friend while at a mandatory school assembly. I was sitting immediately behind and slightly to their left.

10. The quote was taken shorthand as Ms. Yancy was making these comments at the start of the school year. Her presentation was part of the orientation presented to a group of new teachers at Chester Himes High School. I was in the group listening to the orientation.

11. The quote was taken shorthand as Mr. Mack was talking over coffee with a group of teachers who had just been given their respective assignments within the school's "quasi-tracking system." I was in the group listening.

12. Hector's first comments were recorded shorthand as Hector was talking to a friend at the local barbershop while waiting to get his hair cut. I was also in the barbershop. Later, I followed Hector's trajectory by inquiring about his progress with his teachers and counselors. After he graduated, I contacted him to keep track of his progress. The last contact was during his second year of medical school.

13. For how a rational system like "tracking" can be abused because of prejudice see the important work of Gilda L. Ochoa, *Latinos, Asian-Americans and the Achievement Gap* (Minneapolis: University of Minnesota Press, 2013); Patricia Gándara and Frances Contreras, *The Latino Education Crisis* (Cambridge, MA: Harvard University Press, 2009): 97–100; and Angela Valenzuela, *Subtractive Schooling: US-Mexican Youth and the Politics of Caring* (Albany: State University Press of New York, 1999).

14. Janice was one of the students who I followed during her high school years, and I recorded various statements and behaviors she engaged in. After high school, I made an effort to contact her to see what course her life had taken. The last time that I contacted her she had just received her degree from a four-year college majoring in graphic design.

15. For a discussion of problems associated with tracking judgments see Sabine Glock, Sabine Krolak-Schwerdt, Florian Klapproth, and Mathias Böhmer, "Beyond Judgement Bias: How Students' Ethnicity and Academic Profile Consistency Influences Teachers' Tracking Judgements," *Social Psychology of Education* 16, no. 4 (December 2013): 555–73; and Doug Archibald and Elizabeth N. Farley-Ripple, "Prediction of Placement in Lower Level Versus Higher Level High School Mathematics," *High School Journal* 96, no. 1 (October 2012): 33–55.

16. This example involving April came from notes I took shorthand. I began following April's situation upon hearing her complain to her mother after she had completed her homework. She told her mother that she found her math course too easy and that she felt she should be in the "advanced placement" course. Her mother listened and told her that she would make an appointment with the school to talk about her placement. I went with the mother to the school and then made an effort to follow April's progress. I was already researching the school and had access to April's teachers.

17. See Doug Archibald, Joseph Glutting, and Xiaoyu Qian, "Getting into Honors or Not: An Analysis of the Relative Influence of Grades, Test Scores and Race on Track Placement in a Comprehensive High School," *American Secondary Education* 37, no. 2 (Spring 2009): 65–81.

18. See Michelle Jackson, *Determined to Succeed?: Performance Versus Choice in Educational Attainment* (Stanford, CA: Stanford University Press, 2013), where the literature associated with educational transitions is reviewed. This is done in the introduction and in each of the empirical chapters.

19. Theo Klimstra, "Adolescent Personality Development and Identity," *Child Development Perspective* 7, no. 2 (June 2013): 80–84; and Velma McBride Murry, Cady Berkel, Noni K. Gaylord-Harden, Nikeea Copeland-Linder, and Maury Nation, "Neighborhood Poverty and Adolescent Development," *Journal of Research*

on Adolescence 21, no. 1 (March 2011): 114–28. Much of the current research is related to the classic work of Erik H. Erikson in *Identity: Youth and Crisis* (New York: Norton, 1968) and *Identity and the Life Cycle* (New York: Norton, 1980).

20. The fact that students were responsible for how well they did in their schoolwork and on the standard achievement exams provided them with input as to where they might be placed in the school's tracking system; however, their actual social identity was determined by other students' reactions to them and the track they were placed in.

21. The comment was taken shorthand as Calvin was talking to a barber who was cutting his hair. I was in the barbershop socializing.

22. This issue is taken up by Lewis Anthony Dexter, *The Tyranny of Schooling: An Inquiry into the Problem of "Stupidity"* (New York: Basic Books, 1964), 18–93, and his "The Sociology of the Exceptional Person," in *The Management of Purpose: Lewis Anthony Dexter*, ed. Martín Sánchez-Jankowski and Alan J. Ware (New Brunswick, NJ: Transaction, 2010), 75–80.

23. What is more, this occurs among most students in every high school regardless of their ethnicity. An example of this was reported for African American students who strived, and achieved, good grades that conveyed the identity of being a "good student," but which elements of their peers identified negatively as "acting White." See the work of Signithia Fordham and John Ogbu, "Black Students' School Success: Coping with the Burden of 'Acting White,'" *Urban Review* 18, no. 3 (1984): 176–206; and John U. Ogbu, "Collective Identity and the Burden of 'Acting White' in Black History, Community, and Education," *Urban Review* 36, no. 1 (2004): 1–35. There has been research challenging the generalizability of this finding by Fordham and Ogbu; for example, see Tyson, *Integration Interrupted*.

24. See Kathleen M. Collins, *Ability Profiling and School Failure: One Child's Struggle to Be Seen as Competent* (New York, Routledge: 2013), who documents the effects of stigmatization in the educational processing field.

25. The quote was taken shorthand as Travis was talking to two friends during lunch period. I was sitting at the table next to them.

26. The quote was taken shorthand as Dianna was talking to three friends during morning nutrition period. I was sitting next to them.

27. The conversation was recorded shorthand as Kenny was talking to his sister, who was a senior at the time, before a high school basketball game. I was sitting in the row in front of them and slightly to their left.

28. The quote was taken shorthand as Connor was talking to two classmates before the start of his "honors" English class. I was sitting two rows behind. There were no other students between Connor and myself and I could hear the conversation clearly.

29. There are other subcultures that youth during their high school years could become involved with, such as "Goth," "rave," or "punk" subcultures, but these, with the exception of Goths, were not present in the schools of this study. For a discussion of youth subcultures see Ross Haenfler, *Goths, Gamers & Grrrls: Deviance and Youth Subcultures* (London: Oxford University Press, 2015).

30. According to the school police report, Maria-Luz and the others said they had not participated in this act of school vandalism and no one was charged with a public offense.

31. The data for this example of Maria-Luz was drawn from conversations I had with teachers, conversations recorded shorthand between Maria-Luz and friends at different times throughout her four years at Chumash High School, and observations of her behavior during the four years at Chumash High School. In brief, she was one of the students who I attempted to follow throughout her four years.

32. See Roundfield Lucas, *Tracking Inequality,* who also documents the stratification effect of tracking.

33. See Claude S. Fischer, Michael Hout, Martín Sánchez-Jankowski, Samuel R. Lucas, Ann Swidler, and Kim Voss, *Inequality by Design: Cracking the Bell Curve Myth* (Princeton, NJ: Princeton University Press, 1996), 158–70.

34. The classical educator is one who develops in their students both a knowledge base and, most important, a means to examine substantive intellectual problems in a systematically rational manner. Often this approach has been associated with the Greeks and Romans, but it also has its contemporary version found in many private school curriculums and those public high schools that created "schools within schools" and separate courses for those placed in honors and advanced placement classes. In the case of the Greeks, it would be the *Gymnasium*, while in Roman times education was provided for boys between the ages of 7 and 11 by a single teacher provided by the father of the family who taught numbers, calculations, language, and some forms of rhetoric. For Greek education see Frederick A. G. Beck, *Greek Education: 450–350 B.C.* (London: Methuen, 1964); for Roman education see Stanley F. Bonner, *Education in Ancient Rome* (Berkeley: University of California Press, 1977); and for both see Teresa Morgan, *Literate Education in Hellenistic and Roman Worlds* (Cambridge: Cambridge University Press, 1998).

35. I was often in the study hall where Dyson and the two girls studied and I recorded the conversation one day before study hall session started. Dyson and the two girls were studying at a table that was immediately next to where I was sitting and observing study hall behavior. I followed Dyson through high school and afterward. My last contact with him was during the summer between his sophomore and junior year at the university he was attending. He was proud of the fact that he was on the dean's list and expected to graduate on time.

36. I took these notes shorthand while Casey was in high school. I kept in touch with Casey after high school, and my final contact with her was when she was in her final year for the bachelor of arts degree from Rutgers University.

37. The conversation was recorded shorthand as Lydia and Salvador were talking to each other at the school bus stop. I was standing with a group of students next to them.

38. I observed Adelita during some of her classes where she would do this. I also was in the counselor's office during his exchange with her. She was not there because she was being reprimanded for bad behavior, but because she was discussing her

course schedule for the next semester. It should be noted that Adelita was not a bad student. According to her counselor she maintained a B average.

39. The quote was taken shorthand as Paul was talking to his sister and a friend at a small grocery store. I was standing behind them as they waited to pay for the potato chips they selected.

40. All the teachers who would collect the student outlines at the end of class would review them that night and hand each back, sometimes with comments and other times without any, the next day. This allowed them to keep the students honest in outlining what they read, record if they completed the assignment, and reinforce that the assignment would be counted and therefore they should continue to complete the assignment in class.

41. There is a formal academic professional society focused on critical thinking entitled The Foundation for Critical Thinking. Further, there are a large number of books written about it; see, for example, Anne Thomson, *Critical Reasoning: A Practical Introduction,* 2nd ed. (New York: Routledge, 2002).

42. The quote was taken shorthand as Hugh was talking to two teachers who work at the same school while they socialized after work at a local restaurant. I was a member of the group by invitation.

43. Susan was talking to three friends while they were waiting for their gym class to begin. I was standing with another group of three students who were next to these four students. Everyone was waiting for the gym teacher to set up the net for volleyball.

44. The quote was taken shorthand as Melissa was talking to two of her friends while they were waiting to enter their English class. I was standing with another group of individuals immediately behind them.

45. The quote was taken shorthand as Mr. Tayes was talking to two other teachers during his preparation period in the teacher's lounge. I was at the same table with these teachers. I also observed Mr. Tayes's approach in a number of his courses.

46. The quote was taken shorthand as Ms. Vernon was talking to two other teachers in the school's faculty lounge. I was in the lounge drinking coffee immediately next to them.

47. The quote was taken shorthand as Mr. Manning was talking to another teacher at a bar that some of the teachers went to on Fridays after school was closed. I was with the group of teachers socializing.

48. The quote was taken shorthand as Ms. Banks was talking to another teacher in the teachers' conference room between classes. I was in the conference room sitting at the table next to them.

49. The quote was taken shorthand as Mr. Kaliki was talking to three other teachers as they walked to catch the subway after school. I was walking with them to catch the same train.

50. The quote was taken shorthand as Elvia was talking to two of her friends during lunch period. I was seated at the table immediately to the left of her.

51. The quote was taken shorthand while Emmet and two other teachers were talking during an after-school meeting. I was among the group of teachers at the meeting.

52. See the work of Lewis Anthony Dexter, *The Tyranny of Schooling,* 43–44, who argues that often it is the "gifted" who are underserved by an educational system constructed to bring competence up to some average point in order to maximize education for the most students. As I found in the present study, this tendency for the system to focus on some "average" level (mean or medium) affects each regimen / track in the same way because within each regimen / track there is variation. Thus, students in each of the regimen / tracks must find ways to manage this situation if they are intent on progressing to the next level successfully.

53. The quote was taken shorthand as Mr. Zim was talking to another math teacher during both of their "preparation periods." I was in the room as they were conversing.

54. See David Harding, *Living the Drama: Community, Conflict, and Culture among Inner-City Boys* (Chicago: University of Chicago Press, 20), chap. 7, who found that students had differing cultural takes on schooling and that these positions could change throughout the high school years. While it might be difficult, if not impossible, to have completely different cultural orientations, small issues concerning one's attitude toward schooling could change if they were in line with the more dominant cultural orientation of the person.

55. See Tyson, "Tracking, Segregation and the Opportunity Gap."

56. The quote was taken shorthand as Nancy was talking to a fellow student before her English class. I was standing at the back of the room behind them waiting for the teacher to begin class.

57. See Barnett Berry, "Good Schools and Teachers for All Students: Dispelling Myths, Facing Evidence, and Pursuing the Right Strategies," in Carter and Welner, *Closing the Opportunity Gap,* 181–94.

58. The quote was taken shorthand as Georgia was talking to the dean of her class. I was in the dean's office observing how the deans in the schools being studied carried out their duties. When Georgia came into the dean's office, the dean introduced me to her, described what I was doing at the school as well as why I was sitting in the dean's office, and asked her if she wanted me to leave to make their meeting more private. Georgia said that I could stay.

59. The statement was taken shorthand as Cynthia was talking with a friend in the local convenient grocery store after school. I was standing next to the owner as they were talking and getting ready to pay for their sodas and chips.

60. The quote was taken shorthand as Roberto was talking to a friend at a school basketball game. I was seated behind them as they talked.

61. There is a good deal of research within the general educational field, with a few professional journals devoted to research on school counseling (*Professional School Counseling* and *Journal of School Counseling*), but there has been little research in the sociological literature on the impact of counseling on student achievement. For an important exception see M. M. Holland, "Trusting Each

Other: Student-Counselor Relationships in Diverse High Schools," *Sociology of Education* 88, no. 3 (2015): 244–62.

62. Chenoa S. Woods and Thurston Domina, "The School Counselor: Caseload and the High School-to-College Pipeline," *Teachers College Record* 116 (2014): 1–30.

63. The quote was taken shorthand as Darcy and the counselor were discussing his progress to this point and beginning to design an academic plan for the remaining years at the school. I was in the office to observe the interactions between counselors and students and was standing at a coat rack to the right of the counter where they were conversing.

64. The quote was taken shorthand as Casandra and the counselor were talking about her schedule for the current year. I was in the office to observe the interactions between counselors and students and sat at the desk behind them.

65. For research supporting this effort on the part of counselors see Erik M. Hines, James L. Moore, III, Renae D. Mayes, Paul C. Harris, Desireé Vega, Dawn V. Robinson, Crystal N. Gray, and Candice E. Jackson, "Making Student Achievement a Priority: The Role of School Counselors in Turnaround Schools," *Urban Education* 55, no. 2 (2020): 216–37.

66. The quote was taken shorthand as Mr. Dennis was talking to the school's two other counselors while we were eating lunch in the teachers' lounge. I was a member of this group.

67. The quote was taken shorthand as the counselor was talking to Jerry during a scheduled visit. I was in the counselor's office observing their interactions with students. I was introduced to Jerry, who was told what I was doing in the office and asked if he would like me to leave the room to have more privacy with the counselor. He told the counselor that he had no objections to me being there.

68. The quote was taken shorthand as Ms. Conti was talking to one of the school's deans during lunch period. I was walking with them.

69. The quote was taken shorthand as Terrence was talking to his fifth-period math teacher at Oakland's Kaiser High School. I was standing immediately next to them at the teacher's desk.

70. The quote was taken shorthand as Tina was talking to a teacher and another counselor during the lunch period. I was part of the group eating lunch.

71. The quote was taken shorthand as Murray was talking to three teachers during lunch time. I was sitting with the group as they talked.

72. For research showing that students having counselors with small caseloads were more likely to successfully navigate the high school to college transition, see Woods and Domina, "Counselor Caseload."

73. The quote was taken shorthand as Laura was talking to two teachers and a student teacher in the faculty lounge. I am sitting with this group of teachers.

74. The quote was taken shorthand as Jordan was talking to a teacher in the teachers' lounge before classes began for the day. I was sitting at the same table having coffee.

75. Obviously, this is the dark side of an individual's psychology, so how does a researcher determine that this is the motive of an individual counselor as opposed

to one of the other motives previously mentioned? In cases where an individual counselor was identified with this motive, I observed them making statements in which they voiced the thought that students got better treatment today than during the counselor's generation and yet they were not as good as the students of the counselor's generation. They would also make statements that they (the counselors) were better students than nearly all of the students in the present high school. Following these statements, I would focus on whether they provided advice concerning what courses a student should take that was inconsistent with the student's grades or what the student declared were their goals. Finally, after they had advised the student, these same counselors had been observed making statements that they believed the students they just interacted with thought they were better academically than they actually were, and / or they had been overrated by teachers. Thus, my assessment was based on individuals who engaged in each of these practices.

76. The quote was taken shorthand as Carol was having coffee and talking to another counselor before school began. I was sitting at the table next to them.

77. The quote was taken shorthand as Ada was talking to two other students during the morning nutrition program. I was sitting at the table immediately to their left.

78. For evidence as to the positive impact of counselors in students going on to college see A. S. Belasco, "Creating College Opportunity: School Counselors and Their Influence on Postsecondary Enrollment," *Research in Higher Education* 54 (2013): 781–804.

79. See Stephen Vaisey, "What People Want: Rethinking Poverty, Culture, and Educational Attainment," *Annals of the American Academy of Political and Social Science* 629, no. 1 (2010): 75–101.

CHAPTER 4. THE IMPACT OF CULTURAL AND SOCIAL CAPITAL

1. For a description of the human capital concept see Gary S. Becker, *Human Capital: A Theoretical and Empirical Analysis with Special Reference to Education* (Chicago: University of Chicago Press, 1993).

2. See the theoretical work of Pierre Bourdieu, "Forms of Capital," in *Handbook of Theory and Research for the Sociology of Education*, ed. John G. Richardson (Westport, CT: Greenwood Press, 1986); Ronald S. Burt, *Structural Holes: The Social Structure of Competition* (Cambridge, MA: Harvard University Press, 1992); James S. Coleman, "Social Capital in the Creation of Human Capital," *American Journal of Sociology* 94 (supplemental issue, 1988): S95–S121; Nan Lin, *Social Capital: A Theory of Social Structure and Action* (Cambridge: Cambridge University Press, 2001); Alejandro Portes, "Social Capital: Its Origins and Applications in Modern Sociology," *Annual Review of Sociology* 98 (1998): 1320–50; and Bonnie Erickson, "Culture, Class and Connections," *American Journal of Sociology* 102 (1996): 217–51.

3. Annette Lareau and Elliot B. Weininger, "Cultural Capital in Education Research: A Critical Assessment," *Theory and Society* 32, nos. 5/6 (2003): 567–606.

4. See Mark Granovetter, *Getting a Job: A Study of Contacts and Careers*, 2nd ed. (Chicago: University of Chicago Press, 1995); Luis M. Falcon, "Social Networks and Employment for Latinos, Blacks, and Whites," *New England Journal of Public Policy* 11, no. 1 (1995): 17–28; Roberto Fernandez and Isabel Fernandez-Mateo, "Networks, Race, and Hiring," *American Sociological Review* 71, no. 1 (2006): 42–71; Roberto Fernandez and Nancy Weinberg, "Sifting and Sorting: Personal Contacts and Hiring in a Retail Bank," *American Sociological Review* 62, no. 6 (1997): 883–902; and Sandra Susan Smith, *Lone Pursuit: Distrust and Defensive Individualism among the Black Poor* (New York: Russell Sage Foundation, 2007).

5. There is a great deal of literature focused on the adolescent period of psychological and physical development. Nearly all of the works point to the importance of this stage in bringing about the character of adult life. I shall simply list a few of the many studies along these lines. See Sarah-Jayne Blakemore and Kathryn L. Mills, "Is Adolescence a Sensitive Period for Sociocultural Processing?," *Annual Review of Psychology* 65 (January 2014): 187–207; Dennis P. Hogan and Nan Marie Astone, "The Transition to Adulthood," *Annual Review of Sociology* 12 (1986): 109–30; and Laurence Steinberg and Amanda Sheffield Morris, "Adolescent Development," *Annual Review of Psychology* 52 (February 2001): 83–110. As for the issues of social and cultural capital see Annette Lareau, "Cultural Knowledge and Social Inequality," *American Sociological Review* 80, no. 1 (February 2015): 1–27; and Annette Lareau and Elliot B. Weininger, "Class and Transition to Adulthood," in *Social Class: How Does It Work?*, ed. Annette Lareau and Dalton Conley (New York: Russell Sage Foundation, 2008).

6. Pierre Bourdieu, *Distinction: A Social Critique of the Judgement of Taste* (Cambridge, MA: Harvard University Press, 1984; Ricardo Stanton-Salazar, "A Social Capital Framework for the Study of Institutional Agents and Their Role in the Empowerment of Low-Income Students and Youth," *Youth and Society* 43, no. 3 (2010): 1066–109; Annette Lareau, *Unequal Childhoods: Class, Race, and Family Life* (Berkeley: University of California Press, 2003); and the classic of Pierre Bourdieu and Jean-Claude Passeron, *Reproduction in Education, Society, Culture* (Beverly Hills, CA: Sage, 1977).

7. See *The MIT Dictionary of Modern Economics*, 4th ed. (Cambridge, MA: MIT Press, 1992), 49–50.

8. Of course, Bourdieu uses the concept of "capital" to analyze how a social system reproduces inequality, but using it this way can lead a researcher to miss the most important point—that some individuals and groups in a society have larger amounts of various forms of capital than others and this (re)creates inequality. Thus, some individuals have it and they use it to be more prestigious and powerful while others do not; but it is only reasonable to expect those who have a high level want to hold on to it and those who have a lower level want to procure more of it. See Bourdieu, "Forms of Capital," 84–85.

9. See George Farkas, *Human Capital or Cultural Capital: Ethnicity and Poverty Groups in an Urban School District* (Hawthorne, NY: Aldine de Gruyter, 1996); Bourdieu and Passeron, *Reproduction in Education, Society, Culture*; Paul Willis, *Learning to Labor: How Working Class Kids Get Working Class Jobs* (New York: Columbia University Press, 1977); Jay MacLeod, *Ain't No Making It: Aspirations and Attainment in a Low-Income Neighborhood* (Boulder, CO: Westview Press, 1995); Paul DiMaggio, "Cultural Capital and School Success: The Impact of Status Culture Participation of the Grades of US High School Seniors," *American Sociological Review* 47, no. 2 (April 1982): 189–201; and David J. Harding, *Living the Drama: Community, Conflict and Culture among Inner-City Boys* (Chicago: University of Chicago Press, 2010), 204–38.

10. For a critique see John H. Goldthorpe, "Cultural Capital: Some Critical Observations," *Sociologica* 2 (2007): 1–24.

11. See Bourdieu and Passeron, *Reproduction in Education, Society, Culture;* and Farkas, *Human Capital or Cultural Capital?*, 10–19.

12. There are geographic accents associated with New York and New England, the Deep South, the eastern mountains of Appalachia, the Plains, and the Southwest that are colloquially represented in such descriptions as nasal, drawls, and twangs.

13. This particular situation was highlighted in the late twentieth century when there was an intense debate as to whether children from African American families should be taught in what was described as "Black English" or that of the dominant White middle class. The issue was not that there were two distinct languages, but that there existed two significant variations in syntax and idiom. See Lisa J. Green, *African American English: A Linguistic Introduction* (Cambridge: Cambridge University Press, 2002); John U. Ogbu, "Beyond Language: Ebonics, Proper English, and Identity in Black-American Speech Community," *American Education Research Association* 36, no. 2 (1998): 147–74; and Walt Wolram, "Language Ideology and Dialect: Understanding the Oakland Ebonics Controversy," *Journal of English Linguistics* 26, no. 2 (1998): 108–21.

14. There is a great deal of research on code-switching and thus I will just mention a couple of works: Carol Myers-Scotten, "Code-Switching," in *Handbook of Sociolinguistics* (Oxford: Blackwell, 1997), 217–37; and Peter Auer, ed., *Code-Switching in Conversation: Language, Interaction and Identity* (London: Routledge, 1998). Code-switching is not easy and requires a great deal of work to develop the skills to smoothly make the switch in different situations.

15. This can be seen in the United Kingdom. There, social class idioms (e.g., the described "cockney" accent) are so strong because of both preference and competency reasons that have the power to stigmatize individuals throughout their educational, social, and employment lifetimes. For education see Willis, *Learning to Labor*, 11–58.

16. See Gilberto Q. Conchas, *The Color of Success: Race and High Achieving Urban Youth* (New York: Teachers College Press, 2006).

17. The quote was taken shorthand while listening to Ms. Evans and two other teachers talking during lunch in the faculty lounge. I was sitting with them as they were talking.

18. The quote was taken shorthand as Mr. Raines was talking to two other teachers during a preparation period. I was sitting with them as they were talking.

19. The quote was taken shorthand as Mrs. Lawrence was talking to a new faculty member after school. I was sitting at a table next to theirs.

20. The quote was taken shorthand as Mr. Thompson was talking to a new teacher during a "teacher preparation period" in the faculty lounge. I was sitting at the table next to them.

21. The quote was taken shorthand as Mr. Larsen was talking to two other teachers during lunch hour in the faculty lounge. I was with their group.

22. The quote was taken shorthand as Ms. Fitzgerald was talking to another teacher as they were driving to attend a varsity football game at another high school. I was in the car with them.

23. The quote was taken shorthand as Ms. Jardeen was meeting with the student outside the main office. Ms. Jardeen met with Eric outside the main office because she needed to wait for the custodians to show up to fix a broken fuse box. I was standing with a group of students next to Mrs. Jardeen as she was talking to Eric.

24. See John U. Ogbu, *Black American Students in and Affluent Suburb: A Study of Academic Disengagement* (Mahwah, NJ: Lawrence Erlbaum Associates, 2003), 42–44.

25. In addition, it is important that even in liberal democratic states there are efforts to remove religious garb while attending public schools. For the controversies concerning the wearing of religious garb in public places see Pew Research Center, "Restrictions on Women's Religious Attire," Religion and Public Life, April 5, 2016; Jonathan Fox, *Political Secularism, Religion, and the State: A Time Series Analysis* (Cambridge: Cambridge University Press, 2015); and Christian Joppke, *Veil: Mirror of Identity* (London: Polity Press, 2009).

26. This finding differs from Bourdieu's vision of cultural capital, which is monolithic. See Corey M. Abramson, "From 'Ether-Or' to 'When and How': A Context-Dependent Model of Culture in Action," *Journal for the Theory of Social Behavior* 42, no. 2 (May 2012): 155–80; and John R. Hall, "The Capital(s) of Cultures: A Nonholistic Approach to Status Situations, Class, Gender, and Ethnicity," in *Cultivating Boundaries: Symbolic Boundaries and the Making of Inequality*, ed. Michèle Lamont and Marcel Fournier (Chicago: University of Chicago Press, 1992), 257–85.

27. The quote was taken shorthand as Dennis was sitting in the office waiting for the counselor to come and discuss the allegation of misconduct. He was talking to another student he knew who was also waiting for the counselor. I was in class when the incident occurred, and after Dennis left I followed a few minutes later to the counselor's office and was standing about ten feet away from where he and the other student were sitting and talking.

28. The quote was taken shorthand as Sharlene was talking to two friends during lunch hour. I was at the table next to them eating lunch.

29. The quote was taken shorthand as Ms. Calison was talking to two new teachers in the faculty lounge. I was in the lounge with another teacher sitting immediately next to them.

30. A conclusion that can be drawn is that one cannot readily predict how kids are going to do based on test scores because their presentation of "self" influences some teachers to give them (or not give them) special breaks.

31. The quote was taken shorthand as Ms. Leary was talking to another teacher in the teachers' lounge during their preparation period. I was in the lounge with another teacher.

32. The quote was taken shorthand as Mr. Daniels was talking to a teacher and an assistant principal in the faculty cafeteria during lunch. I was one of the members of the group.

33. See Tina Wildhagen, "Why Does Cultural Capital Matter for High School Academic Performance?: An Empirical Assessment of Teacher-Selection and Self-Selection," *Sociological Quarterly* 50, no. 1 (Winter 2009): 173–200.

34. There has been research on aspects of culture existing in lower-class communities and much of this has taken on the image of being a subculture. Sometimes these cultural images are referred to as "street culture" for African Americans, "cholo culture" (gang or delinquent) for Mexicans, or "slum culture" for White ethnicities, but they all share a perspective that inhabitants in low-income communities develop a cultural orientation directly related to their socioeconomic condition.

35. See Mario Small, David Harding, and Michèle Lamont, "Reconsidering Culture and Poverty," *Annals of the American Academy of Arts and Social Sciences* 629 (2010): 6–27; and Harding, *Living the Drama*, 204–38. The cultural frames conceptual framework in which a multiplicity of frames exist within and across individuals misses that the origins of cultures are the moral, values, and worldviews that have been socialized in individuals over a sustained period during their early lives and become dominant. It is possible to change a cultural orientation, but it takes a considerable amount of work and time, and when completed, the new orientation replaces the old one and becomes dominant. In brief, cultural frames exist, but they are associated with specific sociological groupings (e.g., social class, ethnicity, religion, gender) or subgroupings (e.g., sects within religions, drug consumption groups, military, etc.). Finally, it may be possible for the individual at any one time to have elements of other cultural orientations within their dominant framework, but these orientations will be integrated into their present dominant framework and not act independently, nor be available as the "cultural frames conceptual framework" suggests to be utilized in multiple behavior patterns.

36. See Stephen Vaisey, "What People Want: Rethinking Poverty, Culture, and Educational Attainment," *Annals of the American Academy of Arts and Social Sciences* 629 (2010): 75–101.

37. This quote was taken shorthand as Brian was talking to a friend while waiting for a bus to take them home. I was behind them waiting in line for the bus.

38. This quote was taken shorthand as Alicia was talking to the students in her homeroom. I was in the room sitting four desks from her while she was talking.

39. The quote was taken shorthand as Jamie was talking to his friend Alex before their math course began. I was standing immediately to their right waiting to enter the classroom with them.

40. I was in the counselor's office when Terrence came to talk. I also would try to observe him at various times in the day including the times he left school to go home. I lived a few blocks from where Terrence lived so as I walked by his apartment, I would often see Terrence there studying, and on four occasions I by chance rode with him on the subway as he went to his sister's apartment for the weekend. As regards his grades, since he and I had a good relationship, he shared them with me.

41. This was documented in the earlier work of Paul Willis in his *Learning to Labor*, 11–88, which described this for England. See also MacLeod, *Ain't No Making It*; and the more recent work of Prudence L. Carter, "Black Cultural Capital, Status Positioning and the Conflict of Schooling for Low-Income African American Youth," *Social Problems* 50, no. 1 (2003): 136–55; L. Janelle Dance, *Tough Fronts: The Impact of Street Culture on Schooling* (New York: Routledge-Fulmer, 2002); and Martín Sánchez-Jankowski, *Cracks in the Pavement: Social Change and Resilience in Poor Neighborhoods* (Berkeley: University of California Press, 2008), 299–342.

42. See Carter, "Black Cultural Capital"; Dance, *Tough Fronts*, 33–43, 51–70; Sánchez-Jankowski, *Cracks in the Pavement*, 299–342.

43. The concept of sociability was advanced by Georg Simmel. See his "Sociability" in *Georg Simmel: On Individuality and Social Forms,* ed. Donald E. Levine (Chicago: University of Chicago Press, 1971), 127–40. For the low-income community, it was utilized by Elijah Anderson in *A Place on the Corner* (Chicago: University of Chicago Press, 1978), 179–206.

44. See Dance, *Tough Fronts*, 51–70; and it is also described by Joseph C. Krupnick and Christopher Winship, "Keeping Up the Front: How Disadvantaged Black Youths Avoid Street Violence in the Inner City," in *The Cultural Matrix: Understanding Black Youth*, ed. Orlando Patterson (Cambridge, MA: Harvard University Press, 2015); and Elijah Anderson, *Streetwise: Race, Class and Change in an Urban Community* (Chicago: University of Chicago Press, 1992), and his *Code of the Street: Decency, Violence and the Moral Life of the Inner City* (New York: Norton, 1999).

45. Harding, *Living the Drama*, 204–38; Small, Harding, and Lamont, "Reconsidering Culture and Poverty," 6–29.

46. See Willis, *Learning to Labor*, 11–51; MacLeod, *Ain't No Making It*, 25–43; Dance, *Tough Fronts*, 73–75; Sánchez-Jankowski, *Cracks in the Pavement*, 299–342; and Tommie Shelby, "Liberalism, Self Respect, and Troubling Cultural Patterns in Ghettos," in Patterson, *The Cultural Matrix*, 498–532. The discussion of culture permeates most of the books I have just mentioned, but I simply identify pages that address the impact of culture.

47. This quote was taken shorthand as Drew was talking to a friend during study period. I was sitting at a desk that was in back of them.

48. This is one of the points made by Annette Lareau in *Unequal Childhoods*.

49. For the importance of dispositions see Pierre Bourdieu, "Cultural Reproduction and Social Reproduction," in *Knowledge, Education, and Cultural Change,*

ed. Richard Brown (London: Tavistock, 1973). See Lareau, *Unequal Childhoods,* 277–78, who describes how a disposition worked for a family in the American context.

50. Many scholars have been critiquing Bourdieu on the singularity of the concept, so I will only cite two examples. The first is an older paper, but still one of the best at articulating this point. William Sewell, Jr., "A Theory of Structure: Duality, Agency, and Transformation," *American Journal of Sociology* 98, no. 1 (July 1992): 1–29; and Goldthorpe, "Cultural Capital."

51. Lin, *Social Capital,* 24–25.

52. Bourdieu, "Forms of Capital," 51–52.

53. For the economic concept of "human capital" see Theodore W. Schultz, *Investment in Human Capital: The Role of Education and Research* (New York: Free Press, 1971); and Becker, *Human Capital.*

54. There is a great deal of literature that is focused on social capital and its use by various elements within the socioeconomic spectrum of societies throughout the world. For example, see Frank F. Furstenberg, Jr. and Mary Elizabeth Hughes, "Social Capital and Successful Development among At-Risk Youth," *Journal of Marriage and the Family* 57, no. 3 (August 1995): 580–92; Min Zhou and Susan Kim, "Community Focus, Social Capital and Educational Achievement: The Case of Supplementary Education in the Chinese and Korean Immigrant Communities," *Harvard Educational Review* 76, no. 1 (April 2006): 1–29; and Elin Olsson, "Do Disadvantaged Adolescents Benefit More from High-Quality Social Relations?," *Acta Sociologica* 52, no. 3 (2009): 263–86.

55. See Bourdieu and Passeron, *Reproduction in Education, Society and Culture;* and Bourdieu, "Forms of Capital," 241–58. Following the critique of Bourdieu on cultural capital, there has been a parallel critique about the match between social capital and field, i.e., what counts as social capital is dependent on what is being strived for such as getting into college or acquiring the necessary materials for a successful social party. I am using it here as a resource for educational mobility.

56. The quote was taken shorthand as Ellen was talking to four other girls who are waiting for their gym class to begin. I was standing close to them, waiting for the arrival of the teacher.

57. The quote was taken shorthand as Nicolás was talking to Rick and another student during lunch hour. I was at the table immediately to their right.

58. Leticia Oseguera, Giberto Q. Conchas, and Eduardo Mosqueda, "Beyond Ethnicity and Ethnic Culture: Understanding the Preconditions for the Potential Realization of Social Capital," *Youth and Society* 43, no. 3 (2010): 1136–66.

59. I met Corina in her freshman year while she was in the beginning Algebra course. I continued to have discussions with her and her friends throughout her four years at the school. I recorded this statement of hers using shorthand as she and her friends were interacting with each other in front of the school. I was standing with a teacher, but was close enough to hear their conversation.

60. I recorded this statement shorthand as two individuals were talking to another student. I tried to follow up this statement by asking three different indi-

viduals who were part of the conversation what the group was talking about. They confirmed that it was a discussion about whether or not this particular individual would be accepted in the group.

61. I met Elvin in his freshman year and we remained acquainted during his entire high school years. There were times when Elvin would be talking only to me, and other times I would observe him as he talked with others. I was able to follow Elvin's progress and observe that he earned a 3.5 (on a 4.0 scale) grade point average for high school. In an effort to follow Elvin's trajectory after high school, I made a concerted effort to meet and talk with him after he graduated from high school. I followed him through graduating with a BS degree from UCLA and his enrollment in medical school.

62. See Daniel A. McFarland, James Moody, David Diehl, Jeffrey A. Smith, and Reuben J. Thomas, "Network Ecology and Adolescent Social Structure," *American Sociological Review* 79, no. 6 (December 2014): 1088–121.

63. This example came from both a conversation I recorded shorthand that Olivia was having with friends during the school's nutrition period where I was sitting at the table immediately next to the one they occupied, and observing Olivia's interactions with others in the school. Olivia had been a student who I had numerous interactions with over her four years of high school. I observed her as an athlete and student, and conversed with her at school and with her parents at their home.

64. Smith, *Lone Pursuit*, 56–96.

65. The quote was taken shorthand as Debra was talking to two friends at the corner grocery store while they were standing in line waiting to pay for their refreshments. I was standing in line waiting to pay as well.

66. The quote was taken shorthand as Eugene was talking to a student before class. I was standing behind them.

67. The quote was taken shorthand as Kim was talking to her sister on the subway home and I was sitting immediately next to her sister.

68. The quote was taken shorthand as Andrea was talking to another friend while standing in line for lunch. I was also in line next to them.

69. The quote was taken shorthand as Oscar was talking to his brother at the high school basketball game. I was sitting immediately to his left.

70. Mark S. Granovetter, "The Strength of Weak Ties," *American Journal of Sociology* 78, no. 6 (May 1973): 1360–80.

71. These quotes were taken shorthand as Dean was conversing with a friend during lunch period. I was sitting at the table next to them. I did follow Dean throughout his high school years. The last conversation I had with him was during his junior year in college where he was playing football and majoring in cell biology.

72. The data for each individual was accumulated by following them for a week and recording who they interacted with and for how long during the school day over a semester and recording their grade point average in the courses they were taking for that semester. Moving from fieldnotes to the visuals was accomplished by the labor-intensive process of asking the computer program (Folio Views) to identify who the individual interacted with and how many times during the week; and then

drawing out the visuals first by hand and then using the computer to formalize them. The task of visualizing networks with direct observational data has been legitimized and done in other studies. For example, see Corey M. Abramson, Jacqueline Josyln, Katharine A. Rendle, Sarah B. Garrett, and Daniel Dohan, "The Promise of Computational Ethnography: Improving Transparency, Replicability, and Validity for Realist Approaches to Ethnographic Analysis," *Ethnography* 19, no. 2 (June 2018): 254–84.

73. This points to the importance and problems of structural holes as they relate to an individual's network portfolio. For the issue of structural holes see Ronald S. Burt, "Social Capital and Structural Holes," in *The New Economic Sociology: Developments in an Emerging Field*, ed. Mauro F. Guillén, Randall Collins, Paula England, and Marshall Meyer (New York: Russell Sage Foundation, 2002); and Martin Gargiulo and Mario Banassi, "Trapped in Your Own Net? Network Cohesion, Structural Holes, and the Adaptation of Social Capital," *Organization Science* 11, no. 2 (2000): 183–96.

74. The quote was taken shorthand as Sydney was talking to a friend at a small luncheonette they had stopped at on the way home from school. I was standing next to them as they both waited for their order of egg creams. Sydney was one of the students who I was recording network data on.

75. See Bourdieu and Passeron, *Reproduction in Education, Society, Culture;* Bourdieu, "Cultural Reproduction and Social Reproduction," in Brown, *Knowledge, Education, and Culture.*

76. This has also been true within the economics field. There has been a great debate within economics concerning capital theory and how to explain and / or measure its contribution to profits. For a general discussion of the debates see Heinz D. Kurz, "Capital Theory: Debates," in *The New Palgrave Dictionary of Economics*, ed. Steven N. Durlauf and Lawrence E. Blume, 1st ed. (London: Palgrave-Macmillian, 1987).

77. Youth can be in harmful network situations because (a) they don't have many supportive contacts (like academically skilled friends, role models, etc.) and / or (b) they can have the wrong kind of social ties.

78. For an excellent analysis of how social and cultural capital can create success for low-income, non-White youth see Conchas, *The Color of Success.*

CHAPTER 5. SOCIAL TRACKING IN
THE EDUCATIONAL PROCESS

1. There is a wealth of studies that focus on structural issues related to educational outcomes, so I will simply provide a few recent examples. See Prudence L. Carter and Kevin G. Welner, eds., *Closing the Opportunity Gap: What America Must Do to Giver Every Child an Even Chance* (New York: Oxford University Press, 2013); Greg J. Duncan and Richard J. Murnane, eds., *Whither Opportunity? Rising Inequality, Schools, Children's Life Chances* (New York: Russell Sage Foundation,

2012); and Annette Lareau and Kimberly Goyette, eds., *Choosing Homes, Choosing Schools* (New York: Russell Sage Foundation, 2014).

2. The availability and importance of choices for students in high schools is addressed in Michelle Jackson, ed., *Determined to Succeed?: Performance and Choice in Educational Attainment* (Stanford, CA: Stanford University Press, 2013).

3. For students from these low-income families, what I am calling "maximize their social well-being in the future" refers to their desire to gain as many elements of their ideal life as was possible. This could be associated with accumulating and then hoarding the wealth for what might be needed to manage an unforeseen calamity in the future, or simply a sufficient amount of material wealth that could be used instantly to satisfy their desire to enjoy life to the fullest. For a discussion of divergent value-orientations among the poor see Martín Sánchez-Jankowski, *Cracks in the Pavement: Social Change and Resilience in Poor Neighborhoods* (Berkeley: University of California Press, 2008), 20–30.

4. The idea of the "American Dream" was coined by James Truslow Adams, *The Epic of America* (Boston: Little, Brown, 1931). There are differences as to what it means to Americans, but at its basic level it is the belief in the ability of everyone in America to secure economic security. See Michael F. Ford, "Five Myths about the American Dream," *Washington Post,* January 6, 2012, for the survey findings of Xavier University's Center for the Study of the American Dream as to what Americans believe is part of the "American Dream."

5. Congress passed the "No Child Left Behind Act" during the George H. W. Bush administration and the Obama administration initiated the "Every Student Succeeds Act."

6. There are numerous publications about addressing the schools' position via the American Dream. See Jennifer L. Hochschild and Nathan Scovronick, *The American Dream and Public Schools* (New York: Oxford University Press, 2003); Pedro Noguera, *City Schools and the American Dream: Reclaiming the Promise of Public Education* (New York: Teachers College Press, 2003); and Robert D. Putnam, *Our Kids: The American Dream in Crisis* (New York: Simon and Schuster, 2015).

7. The quote was taken shorthand as Ms. Thomas was addressing her American history class. I was sitting in the back of the room observing.

8. See Daniel Katz and Robert Kahn, *The Social Psychology of Organizations* (New York: John Wiley and Sons, 1978).

9. This situation will sound "hegemonic" to some sociologists and political scientists, and as that term has been used, I would agree that when it comes to this general educational belief in the United States, hegemony exists. See Hochschild and Scovronick, *The American Dream and Public Schools;* Noguera, *City Schools and the American Dream;* and Marvin Lazerson, *Higher Education and the American Dream: Success and Its Discontents* (Budapest: Central University Press, 2007).

10. The quote was taken shorthand as Lawrence was talking to another student after school before the start of a school basketball game. I was seated one row behind and to the right of them.

11. The quote was taken shorthand as Dora was talking to her best friend Lydia while waiting for their teacher to arrive to begin class. I was standing in the back of the room about five feet from them.

12. This conversation was taken shorthand as Felton and Nathaniel were talking after having just received their exams and were packing up their materials to go to their next scheduled class. I was standing behind them.

13. This "feeling depressed" quote was taken shorthand as Felton was talking to his friend Warren during lunch hour. I was seated at the table immediately to their right. This small quote was part of a longer conversation that I recorded shorthand.

14. For a discussion of the entrepreneurial concept in sociology see Howard E. Aldrich, "Entrepreneurship," in *Handbook of Economic Sociology*, ed. Neal Smelser and Richard Swedberg, 2nd ed. (Princeton, NJ: Princeton University Press and Russell Sage Foundation, 2005), 451–77.

15. The quote was taken shorthand as Cooper was talking to his cousin while waiting to pay for the soda they had chosen at the local small grocery. I was standing in front of them waiting to pay for a candy bar.

16. The quote was taken shorthand as Cesar was talking to a friend after school while waiting for the bus. I was standing to their right with a small group of students who were also waiting to take the bus.

17. The quote was taken shorthand as Stewart was talking to two friends while he was eating lunch. I was sitting at the table next to his.

18. The quote was taken shorthand as Joaquin was talking to a friend while they were waiting for the teacher to start class. I was standing in the back of the room, one seat from where they were sitting.

19. The quote was taken shorthand as Junior was talking to his friend Felix at the local store after school as they bought some Cheetos and a Coca-Cola. I was sitting, talking to the owner, while they were eating and drinking inside the store as rain began to fall.

20. The quote was taken shorthand as Manny was talking to a friend while he was waiting outside a classroom before his next class begins. I was standing in back of them about five feet away.

21. The quote was taken shorthand as Tremaine was talking to three friends during a designated "study period" at Van Twiller High School. I was sitting three desks from their conversation.

22. The quote was taken shorthand as Lois was talking to four friends during lunch time. I was eating at the table immediately next to them.

23. The quote was taken shorthand as Vilma was talking to a friend in her English class before the teacher arrived. I was sitting two seats behind them waiting for class to begin.

24. This quote was taken shorthand as Erica was talking to a group of five girls as they waited for the bus after school. I was standing just behind them observing.

25. This interaction between Barbara and the teacher was taken shorthand while I was attending this particular English class.

26. The quote was taken shorthand as Dalin was talking to a friend at lunch time. I was at the table right behind them.

27. The quote was taken shorthand as Alex was talking to two friends at a local store after school. I was standing in line behind them waiting to check out.

28. The quote was taken shorthand as Jerry was talking to a friend during lunch time. I was sitting at the table immediately to his left.

29. The quote was taken shorthand as Julia was talking to a friend during lunch time. I was sitting at a table next to her.

30. The quote was taken shorthand as Bryan was sitting talking to his friend at one of the school's basketball games. I was sitting right behind him.

31. It was David Matza in *Delinquency and Drift* (New Brunswick, NJ: Transaction, [1964] 1990), 29, who strategically used the concept of "drift" to elucidate individuals becoming delinquent: "Drift is a gradual process of movement, unperceived by the actor, in which the first stage may be accidental or unpredictable from the point of view of any theoretical frame of reference, and deflection from the delinquent path may be similarly accidental or unpredictable." I am using the concept differently for students in the high schools I studied. In my usage, the student chooses to drift.

32. The quote was taken shorthand as Sally was talking to two other students, one female, the other male in the lunch line. I was also in the lunch line, two persons back.

33. The quote was taken shorthand as Alfredo was talking to a friend as they walked from one class to the other. I was following behind them on my way to their next class.

34. I had chosen Alfredo and Sally to follow while they were in high school and decided to maintain contact after they graduated to see what work trajectory they followed. I lost contact with both after three years.

35. Amaryta Sen, *Development as Freedom* (New York: Anchor Books, 1999), 74–85, 87–110.

36. Those in the Drifting Track are different from those students who are participating in the school's formal extracurricular activities like music, theater, working on the school year book, or sports. The "drifters" participated primarily in fun activities that were more informal than those associated with a school's official extracurricular activities.

37. The literature on tracking has focused on two related problems. The first is to misplace a student in a specific track, and the second is the degree of difficulty for students in changing tracks through their high school careers. See the work of Jeannie Oakes, *Keeping Track: How Schools Structure Inequality*, 2nd ed. (New Haven, CT: Yale University Press, [1989] 2005); Samuel Roundfield Lucas, *Tracking Inequality: Stratification and Mobility in American High Schools* (New York: Teachers College Press, 1999); and Karolyn Tyson, "Tracking, Segregation, and the Opportunity Gap: What We Know and Why It Matters," in Carter and Welner, *Closing the Opportunity Gap*, 167–80.

38. The quote was taken shorthand as Alejandra was talking to two friends in the cafeteria. I was at the table next to them. After this conversation, I observed that

she started to look for something else that she would be interested in. I categorized her as moving from the Bureaucratic Track to the Wandering Track and this was supported by her spending increasing amounts of time with other students who were also wandering in an effort to find something that interested them at school.

39. The quote was taken shorthand as Aurelio was talking to four other friends at a local community club. I was with the group listening to them converse while each of them waited to participate in a volleyball game.

40. The quote was taken shorthand as Damon was talking to two girls who were close friends. I was sitting behind them at their school's basketball game.

41. The quote was taken shorthand as Jackie was talking to a friend before her class in English started. I was standing in the back waiting for class to begin and they were a short distance from me.

42. The quote was taken shorthand as Evron was talking to a security guard after school and I was standing next to him.

43. The quote was taken shorthand as Adriana was talking to one of the janitors while waiting for her brother to pick her up from the front of the school. I was standing with a group of students next to her who were also waiting to be picked up.

44. I questioned the English, Math, and History teachers who knew each of these students. The quote, which was taken shorthand, was from the History teacher, but the other two made similar comments.

45. The quote was taken shorthand as Victor was talking to a classmate before their science class started. I was standing three desks behind them.

46. I questioned the English, Math, and Social Studies teachers who knew each of them. The quote, which was taken shorthand, was from the Math teacher, but the other two made very similar statements.

47. The quote was taken shorthand as Reynaldo was talking to two friends while working on a project during his woodshop class. I was at the worktable next to them.

48. The quote was taken shorthand as Norma was talking to three friends at the intermission of a school boys' basketball game. I was sitting in the row behind her.

49. The quote was taken shorthand as Dario was talking with a friend at a small grocery store a block from the school. I was in the store eating some snacks while listening to him.

50. I am using the concept of "personal agency" in the following manner: the ability to act on the choices one wants to pursue.

CONCLUSION

1. See Annette Lareau, *Unequal Childhoods: Class, Race and Family Life* (Berkeley: University of California Press, 2003); Stephen J. Ball, *Class Strategies and the Education Market: Middle Classes and Social Advantage* (London: Routledge, 2003); Ellen Brantlinger, *Dividing Classes: How the Middle Class Negotiates and Rationalizes School Advantage* (New York: Routledge, 2003); and Fiona Devine,

Class Practices: How Parents Help Their Children Get Good Jobs (Cambridge: Cambridge University Press, 2004), 95–119.

2. It would be particularly useful for schools to know who the most vulnerable students are so they could provide interventions to increase these students' chances of making a successful transition. This could require an estimate of the probability for each student successfully transitioning to the next educational level. The current study is a participant-observation study, and scholars engaged in such studies generally do not address statistical probability, but estimating the probability of a student successfully transitioning to the next educational stage could be beneficial for both scholars utilizing quantitative analyses of educational outcomes and professionals engaged in direct services to students. Using the findings from the present study, a rather elementary form (and I emphasize *elementary*) of estimating the probability for each student successfully transitioning to the next educational level within high school might appear as:

$$P = f(X_1, X_2, X_3, X_4 \ldots)$$

Where P is the probability of an individual successfully transitioning, X_1 is the number of obstacles encountered by the individual while attending high school; X_2 is the number of obstacles successfully overcome while attending high school; X_3 is the amount of determination indicated by the individual to be academically successful in high school, which is the function of the number of statements indicating a desire to succeed (d_1) minus the number of statements indicating doubt that they can overcome the obstacle(s) and succeed (d_2), i.e., $f d_1 - d_2$; and X_4 is the number of "lucky" interventions aiding the individual in overcoming obstacles. Finally, as specified, the present equation allows for the addition of other predictors.

3. See Gama Zamarro, Collin Hitt, and Ildefonso Mendez, "When Students Don't Care: Reexamining International Differences in Achievement and Student Effort," *Journal of Human Capital* 13, no. 4 (Winter 2019): 519–52. There are more individuals from low-income families who participate in the illicit economy and experience varying amounts of time being incarcerated. Once involved in this type of economic activity and being incarcerated, it is more difficult to successfully reintegrate into the legal economy. See David J. Harding, Anh P. Nguyen, Jeffrey D. Morenoff, and Shawn D. Bushway, "Effects of Incarceration on Labor Market Outcomes among Young Adults," in *Youth, Jobs, and the Future: Problems and Prospects,* ed. Lynn S. Chancer, Martín Sánchez-Jankowski, and Christine Trost (New York: Oxford University Press, 2019), 160–88. Also see Bruce Western, *Punishment and Inequality in America* (New York: Russell Sage Foundation, 2006), especially figure 1.4 on page 27 that shows the probability of going to prison based on educational level.

4. Max Weber, *Economy and Society* (Berkeley: University of California Press, [1921] 1978), 969–71.

5. This formula of politics as to who gets what, when, and how was advanced by Harold Lasswell, *Politics: Who Gets What, When and How* (New York: Whittlesey House, 1936).

6. See Meredith Phillips and Tiffani Chin, "School Inequality: What Do We Know?," in *Social Inequality*, ed. Kathryn M. Neckerman (New York: Russell Sage Foundation, 2004), 479–89. They discuss issues surrounding teacher quality in providing educational equity.

7. See Michelle Jackson, *Manifesto for a Dream: Inequality, Constraint, and Political Reform* (Stanford, CA: Stanford University Press, 2021), who also calls for a broad change in the way the US manages education and the constraints that leave some individuals more unequal than others.

8. School administrators and teachers generally recognize this, but it is specifically at the theoretical, not the practical, level. This is a result of teachers and administrators having to focus on the everyday operations of their duties in each classroom, which compartmentalizes their efforts. Further, there is the issue of finite amounts of time and energy to provide the necessary follow-up procedures to reinforce learning throughout a year and from year to year.

9. Michelle Jackson also discusses the problems associated with this way of measuring student achievement and constraint. See her *Manifesto for a Dream*, 6–17.

10. Personal insecurities as opposed to academic competence are often the source of students not doing well on standardized tests. Previous research has found this to be the case particularly when it comes to racial stereotypes and their impact on students doing well on standardized tests. On the importance of stereotypes in negatively impacting scores on standardized tests, see Claude Steele, *Whistling Vivaldi and Other Clues to How Stereotypes Affect Us* (New York: Norton, 2010).

11. For Weber's point about such tests see Max Weber, *Economy and Society*, 1000. There is a great deal of research on the pros and cons of standardized testing in the US. See, for example, Linda Croker, "Teaching For the Test: How and Why Test Preparation Is Appropriate," in *Defending Standardized Testing*, ed. Richard P. Phelps (Mahwah, NJ: Lawrence Erlbaum Associates, 2005), 159–74; Eric Grodsky, John Robert Warren, and Erika Felts, "Testing and Social Stratification in American Education," *Annual Review of Sociology* 34 (2008): 385–404; Hani Morgan, "Relying on High-Stakes Standardized Tests to Evaluate Schools and Teachers: A Bad Idea," *Clearing House: A Journal of Educational Strategies, Issues and Ideas* 89, no. 2 (2016): 67–72; and Mathew Knoester and Wayne Au, "Standardized Testing and School Segregation: Like Tinder for Fire," *Race, Ethnicity and Education* 20, no. 1 (2017): 1–14.

12. Standardized tests have been particularly problematic in certifying competence and determining if a student should be retained in their current grade. It is also possible that standardized "exit exams" could encourage students who feel they are likely to do poorly on them to drop out of school. See Robert Houser, "Progress in Schooling," in Neckerman, *Social Inequality*, 271–318. However, they could be used for purposes of establishing remedial assistance within a particular grade so that retention would not be necessary and students could continue to grow academically toward graduation.

13. See Claude Fischer and Michael Hout, *A Century of Difference: How America Changed in the Last One Hundred Years* (New York: Russell Sage Foundation,

2006), 9–22. Also, see Samuel Bowles and Herbert Gintis, *Schooling in Capitalist America: Educational Reform and the Contradictions of Economic Life* (New York: Basic Books, 1976), who argue that historically the education system found in the US is at the service of the economy.

14. See Jason Fletcher, "Intergenerational Mobility in Education: Variation in Geography and Time," *Journal of Human Capital* 13, no. 4 (Winter 2019): 585–634; James J. Heckman, John Eric Humphries, and Gregory Veramendi, "The Nonmarket Benefits of Education and Ability," *Journal of Human Capital* 12, no. 2 (Summer 2018): 282–304; and Seik Kim, "Uncertainty in Human Capital Investment and Earnings Dynamics," *Journal of Human Capital* 4, no. 1 (Spring 2010): 62–83.

15. See Michael Hout, "Social and Economic Returns to Higher Education in the United States," *Annual Review of Sociology* 38 (2012): 379–400.

16. See Mike Hout, "The Employment Patterns of Young Adults, 1989–2014," in Chancer et al., *Youth, Jobs, and the Future*, 19–34; and Arne L. Kalleberg, "Precarious Work and the Young Workers in the United States," in Chancer et al., *Youth, Jobs, and the Future*, 35–52. There is the question as whether education can ever create social mobility for all as there will always be someone who is at the bottom. A discussion of education and upward mobility can be found in Claude Fischer's *Made in America* blog at https://madeinamericathebook.wordpress .com/2016/06/07/doe-education-work/.

17. Prudence L. Carter and Kevin G. Welner, eds., *Closing the Opportunity Gap: What America Must Do to Give Every Child an Even Chance* (New York: Oxford University Press, 2013); and Greg J. Duncan and Richard J. Murnane, eds., *Whither Opportunity?: Rising Inequality, Schools and Children's Life Chances* (New York: Russell Sage Foundation, 2011).

18. The work by scholars stressing structural inequities as the source of the ongoing problem of improving the educational and economic opportunities for youth from low-income families is quite large. See, for example, the early work of Jonathan Kozol, *Savage Inequalities: Children in America's Schools* (New York: Crown, 1991); and more recent work by Linda Darling-Hammond, "Inequality and School Resources: What It Will Take to Close the Opportunity Gap," in Carter and Welner, *Closing the Opportunity Gap*, 77–97; Elizabeth O. Ananat, Anna Gassman-Pines, and Christina M. Gibson-Davis, "The Effects of Local Employment Losses on Children's Educational Achievement," in Duncan and Murnane, *Whither Opportunity?*, 299–314; and Kathryn M. Neckerman, *Schools Betrayed: Roots of Failure in Inner-City Education* (Chicago: University of Chicago Press, 2007).

19. See Stephen L. Morgan, Michael W. Spiller, and Jennifer J. Todd, "Class Origins, High School Graduation, and College Entry in the United States," in *Determined to Succeed: Performance Versus Choice in Educational Attainment*, ed. Michelle Jackson (Stanford, CA: Stanford University Press, 2013), 34–55.

20. See Rucker C. Johnson, "Can Schools Level the Intergenerational Playing Field? Lessons from Equal Educational Opportunity Policies," in *Economic Mobility: Research and Ideas on Strengthening Families, Communities and the Economy,*

ed. Federal Reserve Bank of St. Louis (St. Louis: Federal Reserve Bank of St. Louis, 2017), 291–324.

21. There is a great deal of literature concerning this debate, so I will simply provide a few examples. There is evidence that historical progress was being made in reducing disparities in education finance—see Sean Corcoran, William N. Evans, Jennifer Godwin, Sheila E. Murray, and Robert M. Schwab, "The Changing Distribution of Education Finance, 1972 to 1997," in Neckerman, *Social Inequality*, 433–66; although even with finance changes, the gains were limited, and on this finding see W. Norton Grubb, *Money Myth: School Resources, Outcomes, and Equity* (New York: Russell Sage Foundation, 2009); and William M. Evers and Paul Clopton, "High Spending, Low-Performing Schools Districts," in *Courting Failure: How School Finance Lawsuits Exploit Judges' Good Intentions and Harm Our Children*, ed. Eric A. Hanushek (Stanford, CA: Hoover Institution Press, 2006).

22. See the older work of Paul Willis, *Learning to Labour: How Working Class Kids Get Working Class Jobs* (New York: Columbia University Press, 1977); and, more recently, Jay MacLeod, *Ain't No Making It: Aspirations and Attainment in a Low-Income Neighborhood*, 3rd ed. (Boulder, CO: Westview Press, 2009); L. Janelle Dance, *Tough Fronts: The Impact of Street Culture on Schooling* (New York: Routledge, 2002); Prudence L. Carter, "Black Cultural Capital, Status Positioning, and the Conflict of Schooling for Low-Income African American Youth," *Social Problems* 50, no. 1 (2004): 136–55; Martín Sánchez-Jankowski, *Cracks in the Pavement: Social Change and Resilience in Poor Neighborhoods* (Berkeley: University of California Press, 2008), chaps. 10 and 11; David Harding, *Living the Drama: Community, Conflict and Culture among Inner-City Boys* (Chicago: University of Chicago Press, 2010); and John Ogbu, *Black American Students in an Affluent Suburb: A Study of Academic Disengagement* (New York: Routledge, [2003] 2009).

23. There are two sources of culture that have been identified and discussed. One has to do with the impact of school (i.e., organizational) cultures on educational process, as seen in the article by Prudence Carter, "Student and School Cultures and the Opportunity Gap: Paying Attention to Academic Engagement and Achievement," in Carter and Welner, *Closing the Opportunity Gap*. The second has to do with the impact of social culture on educational outcomes, which is discussed in Orlando Patterson, ed., *The Cultural Matrix: Understanding Black Youth* (Cambridge, MA: Harvard University Press, 2015), 84–86.

24. See the historical work of Joel Perlman, *Ethnic Differences: Schooling and Social Structure among the Irish, Italians, Jews and Blacks in an American City, 1880–1935* (Cambridge: Cambridge University Press, 1988), 213–19. Among others who have addressed the issue of culture in educational outcomes, see Jennifer Lee and Min Zhou, *The Asian American Achievement Paradox* (New York: Russell Sage Foundation, 2015); Gilbert Q. Conchas, *The Color of Success: Race and High Achieving Urban Youth* (New York: Teachers College Press, 2006); and Leticia Oseguera, Giberto Q. Conchas, and Eduardo Mosqueda, "Beyond Ethnicity and Ethnic Culture: Understanding the Preconditions for the Potential Realization of Social Capital," *Youth and Society* 43, no. 3 (2010): 1136–66.

25. See Lee and Zhou, *The Asian American Achievement Paradox;* Claude S. Fischer, Michael Hout, Martín Sánchez Jankowski, Samuel R. Lucas, Ann Swidler, and Kim Voss, *Inequality by Design: Cracking the Bell Curve Myth* (Princeton, NJ: Princeton University Press, 1996), 201; Scott Jaschick, "The Numbers and Arguments on Asian Admissions," *Inside Higher Ed,* August 7, 2017; and for some examples of other immigrant groups see Richard Alba and Nancy Foner, "The Children of Low-Status Immigrants and Youth Unemployment in the United States and Western Europe," in Chancer et al., *Youth, Jobs, and the Future,* 119–40; and Van C. Tran, "More Than Just Black: Cultural Perils and Opportunities in Inner-City Neighborhoods," in Patterson, *The Cultural Matrix,* 252–81.

26. Some sociologists might argue that the success seen among these groups is the result of an increase in the opportunity structure and not values. However, such an argument would be insufficient in accounting for variance among and within groups that involve variations in values placed on educational attainment. Some examples include Appalachian Whites who are of Scotch-Irish ethnic descent, and for this group see Constance Elam, "Culture, Poverty and Education in Appalachian Kentucky," *Education and Culture* 18, no. 1 (Spring 2002): 10–13; and Erica Chenoweth and Renee Galliber, "Factors Influencing College Aspirations of a Rural West Virginia High School," *Journal of Research in Rural Education* 19, no. 2 (2004): 1–14. There are also cultural issues related to some urban Irish groups in the Northeast; see Michael Patrick MacDonald, *All Souls: A Family Story from Southie* (Boston: Beacon Press, 1999); and MacLeod, *Ain't No Making It.* There are also differences in success seen among Asian American groups, which suggests that, in addition to increased opportunities, differences in cultural value orientations has a significant impact on the degree of educational success seen among different Asian ethnic groups. For values affecting educational aspirations and attainment among the Hmong from Laos, see Christopher T. Vang, "Hmong-American K–12 Students and Academic Skills Needed for a College Education: A Review of the Existing Literature and Suggestions for the Future," *Hmong Studies Journal* 5 (2004–5): 1–35.

27. See Jack Citrin, Amy Lerman, Michael Murakami, and Kathryn Pearson, "Testing Huntington: Is Hispanic Immigration a Threat to American Identity?," *Perspectives on Politics* 1 (March 2007): 31–48.

28. An excellent description of this dynamic is reported in Daniel Dohan, *The Price of Poverty: Money, Work, and Culture in the Mexican American Barrio* (Berkeley: University of California Press, 2003).

29. On the issue of there being educational improvement for Mexican, Central American, and Haitians from the first generation of immigration to the second, and then this improvement stalling, see Mary Waters and Marisa Gerstein Pineau, eds., *The Integration of Immigrants into American Society* (Washington, DC: National Academies Press, 2015), chap. 6. Also see Edward E. Telles and Vilma Ortiz, *Generations of Exclusion: Mexican Americans, Assimilation, and Race* (New York: Russell Sage Foundation, 2009), chap. 5.

30. See David Harding, "Rethinking the Cultural Context of Schooling Decisions in Disadvantaged Neighborhoods: From Deviant Subculture to Cultural Heterogeneity," *Sociology of Education* 84, no. 4 (2011): 322–39.

31. Although a participant-observation study is unable to accurately assess the number of students who believe this way, the evidence in chapter 5 indicates that there are students who do not value the education they are receiving, and are prepared to suspend their study activity to pursue what they do value. In terms of the rationality of these students' beliefs, current evidence would support that the economic return on education has become more stunted. See Kalleberg, "Precarious Work and Young Workers," in Chancer et al., *Youth, Jobs, and the Future,* 40–45.

32. See Marshall Sahlins, *Islands of History* (Chicago: University of Chicago Press, 1985): 136–56, who forcefully argues that culture, like structure, is not chosen by individuals. They inherit culture and adapt as a result to its structuring effects, meaning that history and structure coexist.

33. See Perlman, *Ethnic Differences,* 213–19. For Asian and Jewish success in academic achievement see Fischer et al., *Inequality by Design,* 172–74, 190–94; and Lee and Zhou, *The Asian American Achievement Paradox.*

34. General Richard Henry Pratt was the founder of Carlisle Indian Industrial School and author of the motto "Kill the Indian and Save the Man" for the mission of the Indian Boarding Schools. By 1926 there had been a total of 357 Indian Boarding Schools throughout thirty states. On the American Indian social policy experiment of boarding schools see David Wallace Adams, *Education for Extinction: American Indians and the Boarding School Experience* (Lawrence: University Press of Kansas, 1995); and Ward Churchill, *Kill the Indian, Save the Man: The Genocidal Impact of American Indian Residential Schools* (San Francisco: City Lights, 2005).

35. This has been the tendency in much of the research on minorities of color in the US, although it has been based on sociological fallacious assumptions and not the empirical research that has been done on the middle classes of these groups. For empirical work on African Americans that empirically challenges these assumptions, see Mary Patillo-McCoy, *Black Picket Fences: Privilege and Peril among the Black Middle-Class* (Chicago: University of Chicago Press, 1999); and for Mexican Americans see Jody Agius Vallejo, *Barrios and Burbs: The Making of the Mexican American Middle Class* (Stanford, CA: Stanford University Press, 2012).

36. This point has been consistently made by other researchers. For example, see Telles and Ortiz, *Generations of Exclusion*; and for a description of the values associated with lower-class African Americans see Kathryn Edin, Peter Rosenblatt, and Queenie Zhu, " 'I Do Me': Young Black Men and the Struggle to Resist the Street," in Patterson, *The Cultural Matrix,* 229–51; and Sánchez-Jankowski, *Cracks in the Pavement,* 299–342.

37. There was a time during the twentieth century where there was a considerable amount of research on lower-class culture. For example see Walter B. Miller, "Lower Class Culture as a Generating Milieu for Gang Delinquency," *Journal of Social Issues* 14, no. 3 (1958): 4–19; Lee Rainwater, "The Problem of Lower Class Culture," *Journal of Social Issues* 26, no. 2, (1970): 133–48; Edward Banfield, *The Unheavenly City*

Revisited (Boston: Little, Brown, 1974): 52–75; and Marc Fried, *The World of the Working Poor* (Cambridge, MA: Harvard University Press, 1973).

38. See Stephen Vaisey, who leveled the same critique in "What People Want: Rethinking Poverty, Culture, and Educational Attainment," *Annals of the American Academy of Political and Social Science* 629, no. 1 (2010): 75–101. As for the issue of changing the fundamental concept of culture, it is best seen in the work of Michèle Lamont and associates. For example, see Michèle Lamont and Mario Small, "How Culture Matters for Understanding Poverty: Enriching Our Understanding," in *Color of Poverty: Why Racial and Ethnic Disparities Exist*, ed. David Harris and Ann Lin (New York: Russell Sage Foundation, 2006); Harding, *Living the Drama;* and Mario Small, David Harding and Michèle Lamont, "Reconsidering Culture and Poverty," *Annals of the American Academy of Political and Social Science* 629 (2010): 6–27.

39. See Oscar Lewis, *Five Families: Mexican Case Studies in the Culture of Poverty* (New York: Basic Books, 1959); Daniel P. Moynihan, "The Culture of Poverty," in *On Understanding Poverty: Perspectives from the Social Sciences*, ed. Daniel P. Moynihan (New York: Basic Books, 1969), 187–220; and Oscar Lewis, *La Vida: A Puerto Rican Family in the Culture of Poverty—San Juan and New York* (New York: Random House, 1965).

40. This particular criticism may have started with a focus on Oscar Lewis, but it has remained. For an example see Jennifer C. Ng and John L. Rury, "Poverty and Education: A Critical Analysis of the Ruby Payne Phenomenon," *Teachers College Record,* July 18, 2006. In the past, the focus was on Oscar Lewis and his studies of the culture of poverty, but there would be criticisms of others who utilized the concept of "lower-class culture" like Miller, "Lower Class Culture as a Generating Milieu"; Daniel Patrick Moynihan, "The Negro Family: The Case for National Action," US Department of Labor, 1965; and see the discussion in Alice O'Connor, *Poverty Knowledge: Social Science, Social Policy, and the Poor in Twentieth-Century America* (Princeton, NJ: Princeton University Press, 2001), 117–23, 196–210.

41. See, for example, William Ryan, *Blaming the Victim* (New York: Vintage, 1976); Charles A. Valentine, *Culture of Poverty: Critique and Counter Proposal* (Chicago: University of Chicago Press, 1968); and Lee Rainwater and William Y. Yancy, *The Moynihan Report and the Politics of Controversy* (Cambridge: MIT Press, 1967).

42. Max Weber in the *Protestant Ethic and the Spirit of Capitalism* (New York: Penguin, [1905] 2002) noted these two responses, but associated them with differences in the theologies of Roman Catholics and Protestants. Although these two responses may have been present among these two religious groups, over time it has also been present in different social classes. On the social class front, see the work of Lee Rainwater, "The Problem of Lower Class Culture," *Journal of Social Issues* 26, no. 2 (1970): 133–48; and Miller, "Implications of Urban Lower-Class Culture." Much of this work is older, as issues related to lower-class culture have been either thought to be documented, or avoided as being politically too sensitive to academically pursue; however, on the contemporary front see Elijah Anderson, *Code of the*

Street: Decency, Violence and the Moral Life of the Inner City (New York: Norton, 1999); Sánchez-Jankowski, *Cracks in the Pavement,* 18–53; and Joseph C. Krupnick and Christopher Winship, "Keeping Up the Front: How Disadvantaged Black Youth Avoid Street Violence in the Inner City," in Patterson, *The Cultural Matrix,* 311–50.

43. This is often reported in lower-income groups that are both immigrant and native. See Van C. Tran, "More Than Just Black: Cultural Perils and Opportunities in Inner-City Neighborhoods," in Patterson, *The Cultural Matrix,* 270–73; and Mary Waters and Jennifer Sykes, "Spare the Rod, Spoil the Child?: First and Second Generation West Indian Child Rearing Practices," in *Across Generations: Immigrant Families in America,* ed. Nancy Foner (New York: New York University Press, 2009), 101–32.

44. There is a vast literature on the subjugation of working-class people to the physical roles associated with their tasks, and the use of physical force to enforce the rules associated with the perpetuation of their socioeconomic condition. I will simply mention a few: Karl Marx, *Capital,* vol. 1 (New York: International, [1867] 1967); Peter Kolchin, *Unfree Labor: American Slavery and Russian Serfdom* (Cambridge, MA: Harvard University Press, 1987): 195–240; David Montejano, *Anglos and Mexicans in the Making of Texas, 1836–1986* (Austin: University of Texas Press, 1987); Jacob Riis, *How the Other Half Lives: Studies among the Tenements of* New York (New York: Dover [1890] 1971); Dan Georgakas and Marvin Surkin, *Detroit: I Do Mind Dying* (New York: St. Martin's Press, 1975); and Michael Burawoy, *The Politics of Production* (London: Verso, 1985), 63–117.

45. The issue of time orientation and aspirations among different social classes has been reported over a long period. More recently see Sánchez-Jankowski, *Cracks in the Pavement,* 20–23; Joke Simmons, Maarten Vansteenkiste, Will Lens, and Marlies Lacante, "Placing Motivation and Future Time Perspective," *Educational Psychology* 16, no. 3 (2004): 121–39; MacLeod, *Ain't No Making It,* 107; and older works by Marc Fried, *The World of the Working Poor,* 177–258, and Banfield, *The Unheavenly City,* 52–75.

46. The quote was taken shorthand as an English teacher at Los Angeles's Chester Himes High School was talking to a group of four other teachers during the lunch period. I was also part of the group, though not directly engaged in the conversation.

47. See Zamarro, Hitt, and Mendez, "When Students Don't Care."

48. There are a considerable amount of studies that have identified significant numbers of students from low-income families not believing education is important or saying it is important but not acting in a way that suggests they wanted—or knew how—to be successful in their educational activities. See Willis, *Learning to Labor;* MacLeod, *Ain't No Making It;* Dance, *Tough Fronts;* Prudence L. Carter, *'Keepin' It Real: School Success beyond Black and White* (New York: Oxford University Press, 2005), and Carter, "Student and School Cultures and the Opportunity Gap"; Harding, *Living the Drama;* and Signithia Fordham and John U. Ogbu, "Black Students' School Success: Coping with the Burden of 'Acting White,'" *Urban Review* 18, no. 3 (1986): 176–206.

49. There is evidence that there has been a decline among US youth in general as to the economic value of obtaining a college degree. See Kalleberg, "Precarious Work and Young Workers"; and Josh Douglas and Douglas Belkin, "Americans Losing Faith in College Degrees Poll Finds," *Wall Street Journal,* September 7, 2017.

50. See Stanley S. Litow and Grace Suh, "Transforming High School and Addressing the Challenge of America's Competitiveness," in Chancer et al., *Youth, Jobs, and the Future,* 191–218, for an example of potential curricular changes in high schools that could make a positive impact on students' lives after graduation.

51. See the work of Annette Larue, *Unequal Childhoods,* who identifies clearly different cultures but does not carry it forward to the issue of high school achievement levels and differing rates of acceptance to colleges.

52. For social class differences in attending college see Thomas J. Kane, "College-Going and Inequality," in Neckerman, *Social Inequality,* 319–54. For theoretical and interpretive perspectives on social class culture in American life see Robert K. Merton, one of the important sociological theorists of the twentieth century who thought cultural elements were shared by members throughout a society, and thus a subculture related to any subgroup was theoretically problematic. See his *Social Theory and Social Structure* (Glencoe, IL: Free Press, [1949] 1968), 185–213. Subsequent research has tended not to support his theoretical position; see Rainwater, "The Problem of Lower Class Culture"; Miller, "Lower Class Culture as a Generating Milieu."

53. Orlando Patterson began to discuss the importance of cultural issues related to African Americans in "Taking Culture Seriously: A Framework and an African American Illustration," in *Culture Matters: How Values Shape Human Progress,* ed. Lawrence E. Harrison and Samuel P. Huntington (New York: Basic Books, 2000), 202–30. More recently he has edited a book that analyzes the impact of culture on the various aspects of the lives of African American youth. See Patterson, ed., *The Cultural Matrix,* chap. 1.

54. In an effort to improve the economic prospects of African Americans Tommie Shelby has seen the need for cultural reform, and presented some suggestions along these lines. See his "Liberalism, Self-Respect, and Troubling Cultural Patterns in Ghettos," in Patterson, *The Cultural Matrix,* 507–32.

55. In addition to skill (knowledge) impediments to college success there remain cultural ones as well. See James E. Rosenbaum, Jennifer Stephan, Janet Rosenbaum, Amy E. Foran, and Pam Shuetz, "Beyond BA Blinders: Cultural Impediments to College Success," in Patterson, *The Cultural Matrix,* 471–98; and Richard Arum and Josipa Roksa, *Academically Adrift: Limited Learning on College Campuses* (Chicago: University of Chicago Press, 2011).

56. Tiffany M. Estep, "The Graduation Gap and Socioeconomic Status: Using Stereotype Threat to Explain Graduation Rates," *SES Indicator,* American Psychological Association, October 2016; and Emily Tate, "Graduation Rates and Race," *Inside Higher Ed,* April 26, 2017.

57. The Pew 2020 Survey of American Adults found that within each income category of those who see too much income inequality, 70 percent think that some

amount of inequality is acceptable (see Survey of U.S. Adults, September 16–29, 2020, Pew Research Center). What is more, for the last thirty-five years the General Social Survey administered by the University of Chicago's National Opinion Research Center (NORC) has found that under 50 percent of Americans favor government action to reduce income inequality. The only exceptions to this finding were in 1989, 1990, and 1991, when the number reached 50 percent. What is important is that the questions usually ask Americans if they are in favor of government intervening to *reduce* inequality and not *eliminate* inequality.

58. For the idea that there are and will always be social inequalities in a society see Charles Tilly, *Durable Inequalities* (Berkeley: University of California Press, 1999); and for the position that US society has chosen to structure its inequalities in a particular way see Fischer et al., *Inequality by Design.*

59. Clearly there is discrimination at work in the education process. See Samuel Roundfield Lucas, *Theorizing Discrimination in a Time of Contested Prejudice*, vol. 1, *Discrimination in the United States* (Philadelphia: Temple University Press, 2009), 28–35; Lucas, *Just Who Loses?*, vol. 2, *Discrimination in the United States* (Philadelphia: Temple University Press, 2012), 138–74; and Kevin Lang, *Discrimination and Poverty* (Princeton, NJ: Princeton University Press, 2007), 317–33.

60. Claude Fischer et al., *Inequality by Design,* 130.

61. See Hout, "Social and Economic Returns to Higher Education," for the consistent finding that individual income has the tendency to rise in relation to the number of years of schooling, although in the first part of the twenty-first century there seems to be a decline in this trend. See Patrick J. Carr and Maria Kefalas, "Real Jobs and Redshirting: Job-Seeking Strategies for College-Educated Youth," and Yasemin Besen-Cassino, "Part-Time Employment and Aesthetic Labor among Middle-Class Youth," both in Chancer et al., *Youth, Jobs, and the Future.*

62. It should be remembered that in one of the more comprehensive studies of American inequality, Christopher Jencks et al., *Inequality: A Reassessment of the Effects of Family and Schooling in America* (New York: Basic Books, 1972), addressed the question of what factors predicted socioeconomic success and found "chance" to be particularly salient, though to be specific, it was the unexplained variance in assessing the two that he decided to call "chance." In a subsequent study Christopher Jencks et al., *Who Gets Ahead?: The Determinants of Economic Success in America* (New York: Basic Books, 1979), found education to be important but could not definitively determine whether it was the skills accumulated or the credentials given by the educational institution that was more important in economic success.

63. Michelle Jackson has argued that the American Dream has two incarnations: one established during the eighteenth and nineteenth centuries and another that she describes as being a "phantom" of the first that came to full fruition in the early part of the twenty-first century. The first was based on sociological arrangements and the latter on individual psychological elements. See her *Manifesto for a Dream,* 1–23.

64. There are a host of examples so I will simply provide a few: Carter and Welner, eds., *Closing the Opportunity Gap*; and Duncan and Murnane, eds., *Whither Opportunity?*.

65. For a discussion of educational reform implications see Lang, *Discrimination and Poverty*, 211–42.

66. Michelle Jackson, in *Manifesto for a Dream,* has similarly argued for radical change in not only education but all of America's social institutions.

67. See the various research articles in Carter and Welner, eds., *Closing the Opportunity Gap*, and Duncan and Murnane, eds., *Whither Opportunity?*.

68. See Gary Orfield, "Housing Segregation Produces Unequal Schools: Causes and Solutions," in Carter and Welner, *Closing the Opportunity Gap,* 40–60; Jacob L. Vigdor, "School Desegregation and the Black-White Test Score Gap," in Duncan and Murnane, *Whither Opportunity,* 443–63; and Douglas Massey and Nancy Denton, *American Apartheid: Segregation and the Making the American Underclass* (Cambridge, MA: Harvard University Press, 1993).

69. This was vividly the case when White parents—knowing that racial educational inequity was associated with racial and socioeconomic discrimination in the nation's housing markets—opposed the policy of school busing to integrate all the schools in the district. There is a great deal of controversy in the literature on Whites' opposition to busing as to whether it was based on "self-interest" or some form of prejudice related to "symbolic" or "traditional" racism. It would be hard to analytically separate them as each could work to reinforce the other. See David O. Sears, Carl P. Hensler, and Leslie K. Speer, "White Opposition to Busing: Self-Interest or Symbolic Politics?," *American Political Science Review* 73 (1973): 369–84; Donald R. Kinder and David O. Sears, "Symbolic Racism Versus Threats to the Good Life," *Journal of Personality and Social Psychology* 40 (1981): 414–21; Larry Bobo, "White Opposition to Busing: Symbolic Racism or Realistic Group Conflict?," *Journal of Personality and Social Psychology* 45 (1983): 1196; and McKee McClendon, "Rational Choice and White Opposition to Racial Change," *Public Opinion Quarterly* 49 (Summer 1985): 214–33.

70. See Orfield, "Housing Segregation Produces Unequal Schools"; Vigdor, "School Desegregation and the Black-White Test Score Gap"; and Phillips and Chin, "School Inequality."

METHODOLOGICAL APPENDIX

1. See Martín Sánchez-Jankowski, *Cracks in the Pavement: Social Change and Resilience in Poor Neighborhoods* (Berkeley: University of California Press, 2008), 355–65.

2. See Martín Sánchez-Jankowski, *Burning Dislike: Ethnic Violence in High Schools* (Oakland: University of California Press, 2016), 203–13.

3. For a detailed discussion of the principles and practices to this approach to participant observation see Martín Sánchez Jankowski and Corey M. Abramson, "Foundations of the Behavioral Approach to Comparative Participant Observation," and Corey M. Abramson and Martín Sánchez-Jankowski, "Conducting Comparative Participant Observation: Behavioralist Procedures and Techniques,"

in *Beyond the Case: The Logics and Practices of Comparative Ethnography*, ed. Corey M. Abramson and Neil Gong (New York: Oxford University Press, 2020), 31–87.

4. I used the earliest version of askSam and the periodically upgraded new versions through Version 3, which was the last upgrade before the project on neighborhood change ended in 1999. For Folio Views, I have continued to use any upgrades from the time that my original research on ethnic violence in schools began in 2000.

BIBLIOGRAPHY

Abdulghani, Hanza M., Norah A. Alrowis, Norah S. Ben-Saad, Nourah M. Al-Subaie, Alhan M.A. Haji, and Ali I. Alhaqwi. "Sleep Disorder among Medical Students: Relationship to Their Academic Performance." *Medical Teacher* 34 (2012): 37–41.

Abramson, Corey M. *The End Game: How Inequality Shapes Our Final Years.* Cambridge, MA: Harvard University Press, 2015.

———. "From 'Either-Or' to 'When and How': A Context-Dependent Model of Culture in Action." *Journal for the Theory of Social Behavior* 42, no. 2 (2012): 155–80.

Abramson, Corey M., Jacqueline Josyln, Katharine A. Rendle, Sarah B. Garrett, and Daniel Dohan. "The Promise of Computational Ethnography: Improving Transparency, Replicability, and Validity for Realist Approaches to Ethnographic Analysis." *Ethnography* 19, no. 2 (June 2018): 254–84.

Abramson, Corey M., and Martín Sánchez-Jankowski, "Conducting Comparative Participant Observation: Behavioralist Procedures and Techniques." In *Beyond the Case: The Logic and Practice of Comparative Ethnography*, edited by Corey Abramson and Neil Gong, 31–56. New York: Oxford University Press, 2020.

Adams, David Wallace. *Education for Extinction: American Indians and the Boarding School Experience.* Lawrence: University Press of Kansas, 1995.

Adams, James Truslow. *The Epic of America.* Boston: Little, Brown, 1931.

Alba, Richard, and Nancy Foner. "The Children of Low-Status Immigrants and Youth Unemployment in the United States and Western Europe." In *Youth, Jobs, and the Future: Problems and Prospects,* edited by Lynn S. Chancer, Martín Sánchez-Jankowski, and Christine Trost, 119–40. New York: Oxford University Press, 2019.

Aldrich, Howard E. "Entrepreneurship." In *Handbook of Economic Sociology,* edited by Neal Smelser and Richard Swedberg, 2nd ed., 451–77. Princeton. NJ: Princeton University Press and Russell Sage Foundation, 2005.

Ananat, Elizabeth O., Anna Gassman-Pines, and Christina M. Gibson-Davis. "The Effects of Local Employment Losses on Children's Educational Achievement." In

Whither Opportunity? Rising Inequality and the Uncertain Life Chances of Low-Income Children, edited by Greg J. Duncan and Richard J. Murnane, 299–314. New York: Russell Sage Foundation, 2011.

Anderson, Elijah. *Code of the Street: Decency, Violence and the Moral Life of the Inner City.* New York: Norton, 1999.

———. *A Place on the Corner.* Chicago: University of Chicago Press, 1978.

———. *Streetwise: Race, Class and Change in an Urban Community.* Chicago: University of Chicago Press, 1992.

Archibald, Doug, and Elizabeth N. Farley-Ripple. "Prediction of Placement in Lower Level Versus Higher Level High School Mathematics." *High School Journal* 96, no. 1 (October 2012): 33–55.

Archibald, Doug, Joseph Glutting, and Xiaoyu Qian. "Getting into Honors or Not: An Analysis of the Relative Influence of Grades, Test Scores and Race on Track Placement in a Comprehensive High School." *American Secondary Education* 37, no. 2 (Spring 2009): 65–81.

Arum, Richard, and Josipa Roksa. *Academically Adrift: Limited Learning on College Campuses.* Chicago: University of Chicago Press, 2011.

Auer, Peter, ed. *Code-Switching in Conversation: Language, Interaction and Identity.* London: Routledge, 1998.

Ball, Stephen J. *Class Strategies and the Education Market: Middle Classes and Social Advantage.* London: Routledge, 2003.

Banfield, Edward. *The Unheavenly City Revisited.* Boston: Little, Brown, 1974.

Beck, Frederick A. G. *Greek Education: 450–350 B. C.* London: Methuen, 1964.

Becker, Gary S. *Human Capital: A Theoretical and Empirical Analysis with Special Reference to Education.* Chicago: University of Chicago Press, 1993.

Belasco, Andrew S. "Creating College Opportunity: School Counselors and Their Influence on Postsecondary Enrollment." *Research in Higher Education* 54 (2013): 781–804.

Berry, Barnett. "Good Schools and Teachers for All Students: Dispelling Myths, Facing Evidence, and Pursuing the Right Strategies." Chap. 13 in *Closing the Opportunity Gap: What America Must Do to Give Every Child an Even Chance,* edited by Prudence L. Carter and Kevin G. Welner. New York: Oxford University Press, 2013.

Besen-Cassino, Yasemin. "Part-Time Employment and Aesthetic Labor among Middle-Class Youth." In *Youth, Jobs, and the Future: Problems and Prospects,* edited by Lynn S. Chancer, Martín Sánchez-Jankowski, and Christine Trost, 97–118. New York: Oxford University Press, 2019.

Blakemore, Sarah-Jayne, and Kathryn L. Mills. "Is Adolescence a Sensitive Period for Sociocultural Processing?" *Annual Review of Psychology* 65 (January 2014): 187–207.

Bobo, Larry. "White Opposition to Busing: Symbolic Racism or Realistic Group Conflict?" *Journal of Personality and Social Psychology* 45 (1983): 1196.

Bonner, Stanley F. *Education in Ancient Rome.* Berkeley: University of California Press, 1977.

Bourdieu, Pierre. "Cultural Reproduction and Social Reproduction." In *Knowledge, Education, and Cultural Change*, edited by Richard Brown, 71–112. London: Tavistock, 1973.

———. *Distinction: A Social Critique of the Judgement of Taste*. Cambridge, MA: Harvard University Press, 1984.

———. "Forms of Capital." In *Handbook of Theory and Research for the Sociology of Education*, edited by John G. Richardson, 78–92. Westport, CT: Greenwood Press, 1986.

———. "Le Capital Social: Notes Provisoires." *Actes de la Recherche Science Social* 31 (1980): 2–3.

Bourdieu, Pierre, and Jean-Claude Passeron. *Reproduction in Education, Society, Culture*. Beverly Hills, CA: Sage, 1977.

Bowles, Samuel, and Herbert Gintis. *Schooling in Capitalist America: Educational Reform and the Contradictions of Economic Life*. New York: Basic Books, 1976.

Bradbury, Bruce, Miles Corak, Jane Waldfogel, and Elizabeth Washbrook. *Too Many Children Left Behind: The U.S. Achievement Gap in Comparative Perspective*. New York: Russell Sage Foundation, 2015.

Brantlinger, Ellen. *Dividing Classes: How the Middle Class Negotiates and Rationalizes School Advantage*. New York: Routledge, 2003.

Breen, Richard, and Jan O. Jonsson. "Inequality of Opportunity in Comparative Perspective: Recent Research on Educational Attainment and Social Mobility." *Annual Review of Sociology* 31 (2005): 223–43.

Burawoy, Michael. *The Politics of Production*. London: Verso, 1985.

Burt, Ronald S. "Social Capital and Structural Holes." In *The New Economic Sociology: Developments in an Emerging Field,* edited by Mauro F. Guillén, Randall Collins, Paula England, and Marshall Meyer, 148–90. New York: Russell Sage Foundation, 2002.

———. *Structural Holes: The Social Structure of Competition*. Cambridge, MA: Harvard University Press, 1992.

Cameron, Steven V., and James Heckman. "Life Cycle Schooling and Dynamic Selection Bias: Models and Evidence for Five Cohorts." *Journal of Political Economy* 106, no. 2 (April 1998): 262–333.

Carr, Patrick J., and Maria Kefalas. "Real Jobs and Redshirting: Job-Seeking Strategies for College-Educated Youth." In *Youth, Jobs and the Future: Problems and Prospects,* edited by Lynn S. Chancer, Martín Sánchez-Jankowski, and Christine Trost, 75–96. New York: Oxford University Press, 2019.

Carter, Prudence L. "Black Cultural Capital, Status Positioning and the Conflict of Schooling for Low-Income African American Youth." *Social Problems* 50, no. 1 (2003): 136–55.

———. *Keepin' It Real: School Success beyond Black and White*. New York: Oxford University Press, 2005.

———. *Stubborn Roots: Race, Culture, and Inequality in the US and South African Schools*. New York: Oxford University Press, 2012.

————. "Student and School Cultures and the Opportunity Gap: Paying Attention to Academic Engagement and Achievement." Chap. 10 of *Closing the Opportunity Gap: What America Must Do to Give Every Child an Even Chance,* edited by Prudence L. Carter and Kevin J. Welner. New York: Oxford University Press, 2013.

Carter, Prudence L., and Kevin G. Welner, eds. *Closing the Opportunity Gap: What America Must Do to Give Every Child an Even Chance.* New York: Oxford University Press, 2013.

Chenoweth, Erica, and Renee Galliber. "Factors Influencing College Aspirations of a Rural West Virginia High School." *Journal of Research in Rural Education* 19, no. 2 (2004): 1–14.

Chetty, Raj, David Grusky, Maximilian Hell, Nathaniel Hendren, Robert Manduca, and Jimmy Narang. "The Fading American Dream: Trends in Absolute Income Mobility since 1940." *Science* 356, no. 6336 (December 2016): 398–406.

Chetty, Raj, Nathaniel Hendren, Maggie R. Jones, and Sonya R. Porter. "Race and Economic Opportunity in the United States: An Intergenerational Perspective." *Quarterly Journal of Economics* 134, no. 2 (2019): 647–713.

Churchill, Ward. *Kill the Indian, Save the Man: The Genocidal Impact of American Indian Residential Schools.* San Francisco: City Lights, 2005.

Ciotti, Paul. "Money and School Performance: Lessons From the Kansas City Desegregation Experiment." *Policy Analysis* no. 298, Cato Institute, March 16, 1998.

Citrin, Jack, Amy Lerman, Michael Murakami, and Kathryn Pearson. "Testing Huntington: Is Hispanic Immigration a Threat to American Identity?" *Perspectives on Politics* 1 (March 2007): 31–48.

Clark, William A. V. "Residential Patterns: Avoidance, Assimilation, and Succession." In *Ethnic Los Angeles,* edited by Roger Waldinger and Mehdi Bozorgmehr, 109–38. New York: Russell Sage Foundation, 1996.

Coleman, James S. "Social Capital in the Creation of Human Capital." *American Journal of Sociology* 94 (supplemental issue, 1988): S95–S121.

Collins, Kathleen M. *Ability Profiling and School Failure: One Child's Struggle to Be Seen as Competent.* New York, Routledge: 2013.

Conchas, Gilbert Q. *The Color of Success: Race and High Achieving Urban Youth.* New York: Teachers College Press, 2006.

Corcoran, Sean, William N. Evans, Jennifer Godwin, Sheila E. Murray, and Robert M. Schwab. "The Changing Distribution of Educational Finance, 1972–1997." In *Social Inequality,* edited by Kathryn M. Neckerman, 433–66. New York: Russell Sage Foundation, 2004.

Croker, Linda. "Teaching For the Test: How and Why Test Preparation Is Appropriate." In *Defending Standardized Testing,* edited by Richard P. Phelps, 159–74. Mahwah, NJ: Lawrence Erlbaum Associates, 2005.

Dance, L. Janelle. *Tough Fronts: The Impact of Street Culture on Schooling.* New York: Routledge, 2002.

Darling-Hammond, Linda. "Inequality and School Resources: What It Will Take to Close the Opportunity Gap." In *Closing the Opportunity Gap: What America Must Do to Give Every Child an Even Chance,* edited by Prudence L. Carter and Kevin G. Welner, 77–97. New York: Oxford University Press, 2013.

Devine, Fiona. *Class Practices: How Parents Help Their Children Get Good Jobs.* Cambridge: Cambridge University Press, 2004.

Dexter, Lewis Anthony. "On the Politics and Sociology of Stupidity in Our Society." In *The Management of Purpose: Lewis Anthony Dexter,* edited by Martín Sánchez-Jankowski and Alan J. Ware, 65–74. New Brunswick, NJ: Transaction, 2010.

———. "The Sociology of the Exceptional Person." In *The Management of Purpose: Lewis Anthony Dexter,* edited by Martín Sánchez-Jankowski and Alan J. Ware, 75–80. New Brunswick, NJ: Transaction, 2010.

———. *The Tyranny of Schooling: An Inquiry into the Problem of "Stupidity."* New York: Basic Books, 1964.

DiMaggio, Paul. "Cultural Capital and School Success: The Impact of Status Culture Participation of the Grades of US High School Seniors." *American Sociological Review* 47, no. 2 (April 1982): 189–201.

DiMaggio, Paul, Eszter Hargittai, Coral Celeste, and Steven Shafer. "Digital Inequality: From Unequal Access to Differentiated Use." In *Social Inequality,* edited by Kathryn M. Neckerman, 355–400. New York: Russell Sage Foundation, 2004.

Dinnerstein, Leonard, and David M. Reimers. *Ethnic Americans: A History of Immigration.* New York: Columbia University Press, 2009.

Dohan, Daniel. *The Price of Poverty: Money, Work, and Culture in the Mexican American Barrio.* Berkeley: University of California Press, 2003.

Dohan, Daniel, and Martín Sánchez-Jankowski. "Using Computers to Analyze Ethnographic Field Data: Theoretical and Practical Considerations." *Annual Review of Sociology* 24 (1998): 477–98.

Domina, Thurston, Andrew McEachen, Paul Hanselman, Prijanka Agarwal, NaYoung Hwang, and Ryan W. Lewis. "Beyond Tracking and Detracking: The Dimensions of Organizational Differentiation in Schools." *Sociology of Education* 92, no. 3 (2019): 293–322.

Douglas, Josh, and Douglas Belkin. "Americans Losing Faith in College Degrees, Poll Finds." *Wall Street Journal,* September 7, 2017.

Duncan, Greg J., and Ricard J. Murnane. "Introduction: The American Dream Then and Now." In *Whither Opportunity?: Rising Inequality, Schools, and Children's Life Chances,* edited by Greg J. Duncan and Richard J. Murnane, 3–8. New York: Russell Sage Foundation, 2011.

———. "Rising Inequality in Family Incomes and Children's Educational Outcomes." *Russell Sage Foundation Journal of the Social Sciences* 2, no. 2 (May 2016): 142–58.

———, eds. *Whither Opportunity?: Rising Inequality, Schools, and Children's Life Chances.* New York: Russell Sage Foundation, 2011.

Durlauf, Steven N., and Lawrence E. Blume, eds. *The New Palgrave Dictionary of Economics*, 1st ed. London: Palgrave-Macmillian, 1987.

Edin, Kathryn, Peter Rosenblatt, and Queenie Zhu. " 'I Do Me:' Young Black Men and the Struggle to Resist the Street." In *The Cultural Matrix: Understanding Black Youth,* edited by Orlando Patterson, 229–25. Cambridge, MA: Harvard University Press, 2020.

Elam, Constance. "Culture, Poverty and Education in Appalachian Kentucky." *Education and Culture* 18, no. 1 (Spring 2002): 10–13.

Erickson, Bonnie. "Culture, Class and Connections." *American Journal of Sociology* 102 (1996): 217–51.

Erikson, Erik H. *Identity: Youth and Crisis.* New York: Norton, 1968.

———. *Identity and the Life Cycle.* New York: Norton, 1980.

Erlanger, Howard S. "Social Class and Corporal Punishment in Childrearing: A Reassessment." *American Sociological Review* 39 (1974): 68–85.

Estep, Tiffany M. "The Graduation Gap and Socioeconomic Status: Using Stereotype Threat to Explain Graduation Rates." *SES Indicator.* American Psychological Association, October 2016.

Evers, William M., and Paul Clopton. "High Spending, Low-Performing Schools Districts." In *Courting Failure: How School Finance Lawsuits Exploit Judges' Good Intentions and Harm Our Children,* edited by Eric A. Hanushek. Stanford: Hoover Institution Press, 2006.

Ewisch, John, and Marco Francesconi. "Family Matters: Impact of Family Background on Educational Achievements." *Economica* 68, no. 270 (May 2001): 137–56.

Falcon, Luis M. "Social Networks and Employment for Latinos, Blacks, and Whites." *New England Journal of Public Policy* 11, no. 1 (1995): 17–28.

Farkas, George. *Human Capital or Cultural Capital: Ethnicity and Poverty Groups in an Urban School District.* Hawthorne, NY: Aldine de Gruyter, 1996.

Farkas, George, Christy Lleras, and Steve Maczuga. "Does Oppositional Culture Exist in Minority and Poverty Peer Groups." *American Sociological Review* 67, no. 1 (February 2002): 148–55.

Fernandez, Roberto, and Isabel Fernandez-Mateo. "Networks, Race, and Hiring." *American Sociological Review* 71, no. 1 (2006): 42–71.

Fernandez, Roberto, and Nancy Weinberg. "Sifting and Sorting: Personal Contacts and Hiring in a Retail Bank." *American Sociological Review* 62, no. 6 (1997): 883–902.

Fischer, Claude S. *Made in America* (blog). https://madeinamericathebook.wordpress.com/2016/06/07/doe-education-work/.

Fischer, Claude S., and Michael Hout. *A Century of Difference: How America Changed in the Last One Hundred Years.* New York: Russell Sage Foundation, 2006.

Fischer, Claude S., Michael Hout, Martín Sánchez-Jankowski, Samuel R. Lucas, Ann Swidler, and Kim Voss. *Inequality by Design: Cracking the Bell Curve Myth.* Princeton, NJ: Princeton University Press, 1996.

Fletcher, Jason. "Intergenerational Mobility in Education: Variation in Geography and Time." *Journal of Human Capital* 13, no. 4 (Winter 2019): 585–634.

Ford, Michael F. "Five Myths about the American Dream." *Washington Post*, January 6, 2012.

Fordham, Signithia, and John Ogbu. "Black Students' School Success: Coping with the Burden of 'Acting White.'" *Urban Affairs* 18, no. 3 (1986): 176–206.

Fosse, Ethan. "The Values and Beliefs of Disconnected Black Youth." In *The Cultural Matrix: Understanding Black Youth,* edited by Orlando Patterson, 139–66. Cambridge, MA: Harvard University Press, 2015.

Fox, Jonathan. *Political Secularism, Religion, and the State: A Time Series Analysis.* Cambridge: Cambridge University Press, 2015.

Fried, Marc. *The World of the Working Poor.* Cambridge, MA: Harvard University Press, 1973.

Friedman, Lawrence S. "Adolescence." In *The Child: An Encyclopedic Companion,* edited by Richard A. Shweder, 18–21. Chicago: University of Chicago Press, 2009.

Frisvold, David E. "Nutrition and Cognitive Achievement: An Evaluation of the School Breakfast Program." *Journal of Public Economics* 124 (April 2008): 91–104.

Furstenberg, Jr., Frank F., and Mary Elizabeth Hughes. "Social Capital and Successful Development among At-Risk Youth." *Journal of Marriage and the Family* 57, no. 3 (August 1995): 580–92.

Gándara, Patricia, and Frances Contreras. *The Latino Education Crisis.* Cambridge, MA: Harvard University Press, 2009.

Gargiulo, Martin, and Mario Banassi. "Trapped in Your Own Net? Network Cohesion, Structural Holes, and the Adaptation of Social Capital." *Organization Science* 11, no. 2 (2000): 183–96.

Georgakas, Dan, and Marvin Surkin. *Detroit: I Do Mind Dying.* New York: St. Martin's Press, 1975.

Glock, Sabine, Sabine Krolak-Schwerdt, Florian Klapproth, and Mathias Böhmer. "Beyond Judgement Bias: How Students' Ethnicity and Academic Profile Consistency Influences Teachers' Tracking Judgements." *Social Psychology of Education* 16, no. 4 (December 2013): 555–73.

Goldthorpe, John H. "Cultural Capital: Some Critical Observations." *Sociologica* 2 (2007): 1–24.

Gomes, Ana Allen, José Tavares, and Maria Heena P. de Azenvedo. "Sleep and Academic Performance in Undergraduates: A Multi-Measure, Multi-Predictor Approach." *Chronobiology International* 28 (2011): 786–801.

Gordo, Blanca Esthela. "What Planning Crisis? Reflections on the 'Digital Divide' and the Persistence of Unequal Opportunity." *Berkeley Planning Journal* 16 (2002): 4–23.

Gorski, Paul. *Reaching and Teaching Students in Poverty.* New York: Teachers College Press, 2017.

Granovetter, Mark S. *Getting a Job: A Study of Contacts and Careers*, 2nd ed. Chicago: University of Chicago Press, 1995.

———. "The Strength of Weak Ties." *American Journal of Sociology* 78, no. 6 (May 1973): 1360–80.

Green, Lisa J. *African American English: A Linguistic Introduction.* Cambridge: Cambridge University Press, 2002.

Grodsky, Eric, John Robert Warren, and Erika Felts. "Testing and Social Stratification in American Education." *Annual Review of Sociology* 34 (2008): 385–404.

Grubb, W. Norton. *Money Myth: School Resources, Outcomes, and Equity.* New York: Russell Sage Foundation, 2009.

Gruber, Reut, Gail Somerville, Lana Bergane, Laura Fontil, and Saukaina Paquin. "Sleep-Based Sleep Education Program Improves Sleep and Academic Performance of School-Age Children." *Sleep Medicine* 21 (May 2016): 93–100.

Haenfler, Ross. *Goths, Gamers & Grrrls: Deviance and Youth Subcultures.* London: Oxford University Press, 2015.

Hall, John R. "The Capital(s) of Cultures: A Nonholistic Approach to Status Situations, Class, Gender, and Ethnicity." In *Cultivating Boundaries: Symbolic Boundaries and the Making of Inequality,* edited by Michele Lamont and Marcel Fournier, 257–85. Chicago: University of Chicago Press, 1992.

Hanushek, Eric A., Paul E. Peterson, Laura M. Talpey, and Ludger Woessman. "The Unwavering SES Achievement Gap: Trends in US Student Performance." Working Paper 25648, National Bureau of Economic Research, 2019.

Harding, David. *Living the Drama: Community, Conflict, and Culture among Inner-City Boys.* Chicago: University of Chicago Press, 2010.

———. "Rethinking the Cultural Context of Schooling Decisions in Disadvantaged Neighborhoods: From Deviant Subculture to Cultural Heterogeneity." *Sociology of Education* 84, no. 4 (2011): 322–39.

Harding, David J., Anh P. Nguyen, Jeffrey D. Morenoff, and Shawn D. Bushway. "Effects of Incarceration on Labor Market Outcomes among Young Adults." In *Youth, Jobs, and the Future: Problems and Prospects,* edited by Lynn S. Chancer, Martín Sánchez-Jankowski, and Christine Trost, 160–88. New York: Oxford University Press, 2019.

Harris, David, and Ann Lin, eds. *Color of Poverty: Why Racial and Ethnic Disparities Exist.* New York: Russell Sage Foundation, 2006.

Hauser, Robert M. "Progress in Schooling." In *Social Inequality,* edited by Katrhryn M. Neckerman, 271–318. New York: Russell Sage Foundation, 2004.

Hauser, Robert, and Megan Andrew. "Another Look at the Stratification of Educational Transition: The Logistic Response Model and Partial Proportionality Constraint." *Sociological Methodology* 36 (2006): 1–26.

Heckman, James J., John Eric Humphries, and Gregory Veramendi. "The Nonmarket Benefits of Education and Ability." *Journal of Human Capital* 12, no. 2 (Summer 2018): 282–304.

Herrnstein, Richard, and Charles Murray. *The Bell Curve: Intelligence and Class Structure in American Life.* New York: Free Press, 1996.

Hines, Erik M., James L. Moore, III, Renae D. Mayes, Paul C. Harris, Desireé Vega, Dawn V. Robinson, Crystal N. Gray, and Candice E. Jackson. "Making Student

Achievement a Priority: The Role of School Counselors in Turnaround Schools." *Urban Education* 55, no. 2 (2020): 216–37.

Hinrichs, Peter. "The Effects of the National School Lunch Program on Education and Health." *Journal of Policy and Management* 29, no. 3 (Summer 2010): 479–505.

Hochschild, Jennifer L. *Facing Up to the American Dream: Race, Class, and the Soul of America.* Princeton, NJ: Princeton University Press, 1995.

Hochschild, Jennifer L., and Nathan Scvronick. *The American Dream and Public Schools.* New York: Oxford University Press, 2003.

Hogan, Dennis P., and Nan Marie Astone. "The Transition to Adulthood." *Annual Review of Sociology* 12 (1986): 109–30.

Holland, Megan M. "Trusting Each Other: Student-Counselor Relationships in Diverse High Schools." *Sociology of Education* 88, no. 3 (2015): 244–62.

Horn, Ivor Braden, Jill G. Joseph, and Tina L. Cheng. "Non-Abusive Physical Punishment and Child Behavior among African American Children: A Systematic Review." *Journal of the National Medical Association* 96, no. 9 (2004): 1162–68.

Houser, Robert. "Progress in Schooling." In *Social Inequality,* edited by Kathryn M. Neckerman, 271–318. New York: Russell Sage Foundation, 2004.

Hout, Michael. "The Employment Patterns of Young Adults, 1989–2014." In *Youth, Jobs, and the Future: Problems and Prospects,* edited by Lynn S. Chancer, Martín Sánchez-Jankowski, and Christine Trost, 19–34. New York: Oxford University Press, 2019.

———. "Social and Economic Returns to Higher Education in the United States." *Annual Review of Sociology* 38 (2012): 379–400.

Hudley, Cynthia, and Sandra Graham. "Stereotypes of Achievement Striving among Early Adolescents." *Social Psychology of Education* 5 (June 2001): 201–21.

Ispa-Landa, Simone. "Effects of Affluent Suburban Schooling: Learning Skilled Ways of Interacting with Educational Gatekeepers." In *The Cultural Matrix: Understanding Black Youth,* edited by Orlando Patterson, 393–414. Cambridge, MA: Harvard University Press, 2015.

Jackson, Michelle. *Determined to Succeed?: Performance Versus Choice in Educational Attainment.* Stanford, CA: Stanford University Press, 2013.

———. *Manifesto For a Dream: Inequality, Constraint, and Political Reform.* Stanford, CA: Stanford University Press, 2021.

Jackson, Michelle, and Brian Holzman. "A Century of Educational Inequality in the United States." *Proceedings of the National Academy of Sciences of the United States of America,* July 27, 2020.

Jaeger, Mads Meir, and Kristian Karlson. "Cultural Capital and Educational Inequality: A Counterfactual Analysis." *Sociological Science* 5 (2018): 775–95.

Jaschick, Scott. "The Numbers and Arguments on Asian Admissions." *Inside Higher Ed,* August 7, 2017.

Jencks, Christopher, et al. *Inequality: A Reassessment of the Effects of Family and Schooling in America.* New York: Basic Books, 1972.

Jencks, Christopher, et al. *Who Gets Ahead?: The Determinants of Economic Success in America*. New York: Basic Books, 1979.

Johnson, Heather Beth. *The American Dream and the Power of Wealth: Choosing Schools and Inheriting Inequality in the Land of Opportunity*. New York: Routledge, 2015.

Johnson, Rucker C. "Can Schools Level the Intergenerational Playing Field? Lessons from Equal Educational Opportunity Policies." In *Economic Mobility: Research and Ideas on Strengthening Families, Communities and the Economy*, edited by Federal Reserve Bank of St. Louis, 289–324. St. Louis: Federal Reserve Bank, 2017.

Joppke, Christian. *Veil: Mirror of Identity*. London: Polity Press, 2009.

Kalleberg, Arne L. "Precarious Work and Young Workers in the United States." In *Youth, Jobs, and the Future: Problems and Prospects*, edited by Lynn S. Chancer, Martín Sánchez-Jankowski, and Christine Trost, 40–45. New York: Oxford University Press, 2019.

Kane, Thomas J. "College-Going and Inequality." In *Social Inequality*, edited by Kathryn M. Neckerman, 319–54. New York: Russell Sage Foundation, 2004.

Karnig, Albert K., and Susan Welch. *Black Representation and Urban Policy*. Chicago: University of Chicago Press, 1980.

Kartsonaki, Christiana, Michelle Jackson, and David R. Cox. "Primary and Secondary Effects: Some Methodological Issues." In *Determined to Succeed?: Performance Versus Choice in Educational Attainment*, edited by Michelle Jackson, 34–55. Stanford, CA: Stanford University Press, 2013.

Katz, Daniel, and Robert Kahn. *The Social Psychology of Organizations*. New York: John Wiley and Sons, 1978.

Kellow, T. Thomas, and Brett D. Jones. "The Effects of Stereotypes on the Achievement Gap: Reexamining the Academic Performance of African Americans High School Students." *Journal of Black Psychology* 34 (February 2008): 94–120.

Kim, Seik. "Uncertainty in Human Capital Investment and Earnings Dynamics." *Journal of Human Capital* 4, no. 1 (Spring 210): 62–83.

Kinder, Donald R., and David O. Sears. "Symbolic Racism Versus Threats to the Good Life." *Journal of Personality and Social Psychology* 40 (1981): 414–21.

Klimstra, Theo. "Adolescent Personality Development and Identity." *Child Development Perspective* 7, no. 2 (June 2013): 80–84.

Knoester, Mathew, and Wayne Au. "Standardized Testing and School Segregation: Like Tinder for Fire." *Race, Ethnicity and Education* 20, no. 1 (2017): 1–14.

Kohn, Melvin. *Class and Conformity: A Study of Values*. New York: John Wiley and Sons, 1969.

Kolchin, Peter. *Unfree Labor: American Slavery and Russian Serfdom*. Cambridge, MA: Harvard University Press, 1987.

Kozol, Jonathan. *Death at an Early Age*. New York: Plume, 1985

———. *Savage Inequalities: Children in America's Schools*. New York: Crown, 1991.

Krupnick, Joseph C., and Christopher Winship. "Keeping Up the Front: How Disadvantaged Black Youth Avoid Street Violence in the Inner City." In *The Cultural*

Matrix: Understanding Black Youth, edited by Orlando Patterson, 311–50. Cambridge, MA: Harvard University Press, 2015.

Kurz, Heinz D. "Capital Theory: Debates." In *The New Palgrave Dictionary of Economics,* edited by Steven N. Durlauf and Lawrence E. Blume, 1st ed. London: Palgrave-Macmillian, 1987.

Lamont, Michèle, and Mario Small. "How Culture Matters for Understanding Poverty: Enriching Our Understanding." In *Color of Poverty: Why Racial and Ethnic Disparities Exist,* edited by David Harris and Ann Lin. New York: Russell Sage Foundation, 2006.

Lang, Peter. *Discrimination and Poverty.* Princeton, NJ: Princeton University Press, 2007.

Lareau, Annette. "Cultural Knowledge and Social Inequality." *American Sociological Review* 80, no. 1 (February 2015): 1–27.

———. "Social Class Differences in Family-School Relationships: The Importance of Cultural Capital." *Sociology of Education* 60 (1978): 73–85.

———. *Unequal Childhoods: Class, Race, and Family Life.* Berkeley: University of California Press, 2003.

Lareau, Annette, and Kimberly Goyette, eds. *Choosing Homes, Choosing Schools.* New York: Russell Sage Foundation, 2014.

Lareau, Annette, and Elliot B. Weininger. "Class and Transition to Adulthood." In *Social Class: How Does It Work?,* edited by Annette Lareau and Dalton Conley. New York: Russell Sage Foundation, 2008.

Lareau, Annette, and Elliot B. Weininger. "Cultural Capital in Education Research: A Critical Assessment." *Theory and Society* 32, nos. 5 / 6 (2003): 567–606.

Lasswell, Harold Dwight. *Politics: Who Gets What, When, How.* New York: Wittlesey House, 1936.

Lazerson, Marvin. *Higher Education and the American Dream: Success and Its Discontents.* Budapest: Central University Press, 2007.

Lee, Jennifer, and Min Zhou. *The Asian American Achievement Paradox.* New York: Russell Sage Foundation, 2015.

Lehrmann, Paul G., Timothy Z. Keith, and Thomas M. Reimers. "Home Influence on School Learning: Direct and Indirect Effects of Parental Involvement on High School Grades." *Journal of Educational Research* 80, no. 6 (1987): 330–37.

Lewis, Oscar. *Five Families: Mexican Case Studies in the Culture of Poverty.* New York: Basic Books, 1959.

———. *La Vida: A Puerto Rican Family in the Culture of Poverty—San Juan and New York.* New York: Random House, 1965.

Lin, Nan. *Social Capital: A Theory of Social Structure and Action.* Cambridge: Cambridge University Press, 2001.

Litow, Stanley S., and Grace Suh. "Transforming High School and Addressing the Challenge of America's Competitiveness." In *Youth, Jobs, and the Future: Problems and Prospects,* edited by Lynn S. Chancer, Martín Sánchez-Jankowski, and Christine Trost, 191–218. New York: Oxford University Press, 2019.

Lucas, Samuel Roundfield. *Just Who Loses?*, vol. 2, *Discrimination in the United States.* Philadelphia: Temple University Press, 2013.

———. *Theorizing Discrimination in a Time of Contested Prejudice*, vol. 1, *Discrimination in the United States.* Philadelphia: Temple University Press, 2009.

———. *Tracking Inequality: Stratification and Mobility in American High Schools.* New York: Teachers College Press, 1995.

MacDonald, Michael Patrick. *All Souls: A Family Story from Southie.* Boston: Beacon Press, 1999.

MacLeod, Jay. *Ain't No Making It: Aspirations and Attainment in a Low-Income Neighborhood*, 3rd ed. Boulder, CO: Westview Press, 2009.

Mare, Robert D. "Social Background and School Continuation Decisions." *Journal of the American Statistical Association* 75 (1980): 295–305.

———. "Statistical Models of Educational Stratification: Hauser and Andrew's Models of School Transitions." *Sociological Methodology* 36 (2006): 27–37.

Marx, Karl. *Capital,* vol. 1. New York: International, [1867] 1967.

Massey, Douglas, and Nancy Denton. *American Apartheid: Segregation and the Making the American Underclass.* Cambridge, MA: Harvard University Press, 1993.

Matza, David. *Delinquency and Drift.* New Brunswick, NJ: Transaction [1964] 1990.

———. "Poverty and Disrepute." In *Contemporary Social Problems,* edited by Robert K. Merton and Robert A. Nisbet, 2nd ed. New York: Harcourt, Brace & World, 1966.

McClendon, McKee. "Rational Choice and White Opposition to Racial Change." *Public Opinion Quarterly* 49 (Summer 1985): 214–33.

McFarland, Daniel A., James Moody, David Diehl, Jeffrey A. Smith, and Reuben J. Thomas. "Network Ecology and Adolescent Social Structure." *American Sociological Review* 79, no. 6 (December 2014): 1088–121.

McWhorter, John. *Losing the Race: Self-Sabotage in Black America.* New York: Harper Perennial, 2001.

Merton, Robert K. *Social Theory and Social* Structure. Glencoe, IL: Free Press, [1949] 1968.

Meyers, Marcia K., Dan Rosenbaum, Christopher Ruhm, and Jane Waldfogel. "Inequality in Early Childhood Education and Care: What Do We Know?" In *Social Inequality,* edited by Kathyrn M. Neckerman, 223–69. New York: Russell Sage Foundation, 2004.

Miller, Walter B. "Implications of Urban Lower-Class Culture for Social Work." *Social Services Review* 33, no. 3 (1959): 219–36.

———. "Lower Class Culture as a Generating Milieu for Gang Delinquency." *Journal of Social Issues* 14, no. 3 (1958): 4–19.

Ming, Xue, Rebecca Koransky, Victor Kang, Sarah Buchman, and Christina E. Sarris. "Sleep Insufficiency, Sleep Health Problems and Performance in High School Students." *Clinical Medicine Insights: Circulatory, Respiratory, and Pulmonary Medicine* 5 (May 2011): 71–79.

Montejano, David. *Anglos and Mexicans in the Making of Texas, 1836–1986.* Austin: University of Texas Press, 1987.

Morgan, Hani. "Relying on High-Stakes Standardized Tests to Evaluate Schools and Teachers: A Bad Idea." *Clearing House: A Journal of Educational Strategies, Issues and Ideas* 89, no. 2 (2016): 67–72.

Morgan, Stephen L., Michael W. Spiller, and Jennifer J. Todd. "Class Origins, High School Graduation, and College Entry in the United States." In *Determined to Succeed: Performance Versus Choice In Educational Attainment,* edited by Michelle Jackson, 279–305. Stanford, CA: Stanford University Press, 2013.

Morgan, Teresa. *Literate Education in Hellenistic and Roman Worlds.* Cambridge: Cambridge University Press, 1998.

Moynihan, Daniel P. "The Culture of Poverty." In *On Understanding Poverty: Perspectives from the Social Sciences,* edited by Daniel P. Moynihan, 187–220. New York: Basic Books, 1969.

———. "The Negro Family: The Case for National Action." U.S. Department of Labor, 1965.

Murry, Velma McBride, Cady Berkel, Noni K. Gaylord-Harden, Nikeea Copeland-Linder, and Maury Nation. "Neighborhood Poverty and Adolescent Development." *Journal of Research on Adolescence* 21, no. 1 (March 2011): 114–28.

Myers-Scotten, Carol. "Code-Switching." In *Handbook of Sociolinguistics,* 217–37. Oxford: Blackwell, 1997.

Neckerman, Kathryn M. *Schools Betrayed: Roots of Failure in Inner-City Education.* Chicago: University of Chicago Press, 2007.

———, ed. *Social Inequality.* New York: Russell Sage Foundation, 2004.

Ng, Jennifer C., and John L. Rury. "Poverty and Education: A Critical Analysis of the Ruby Payne Phenomenon." *Teachers College Record,* July 18, 2006.

Noguera, Pedro. *City Schools and the American Dream: Reclaiming the Promise of Public Education.* New York: Teachers College Press, 2003.

O'Connor, Alice. *Poverty Knowledge: Social Science, Social Policy, and the Poor in Twentieth-Century America.* Princeton, NJ: Princeton University Press, 2001.

Oakes, Jeannie. *Keeping Track: How Schools Structure Inequality,* 2nd ed. New Haven, CT: Yale University Press, 2005.

Ochoa, Gilda L. *Latinos, Asian-Americans and the Achievement Gap.* Minneapolis: University of Minnesota Press, 2013.

Ogbu, John U. "Beyond Language: Ebonics, Proper English, and Identity in Black American Speech Community." *American Education Research Association* 36, no. 2 (1998): 147–74.

———. *Black American Students in an Affluent Suburb: A Study of Academic Disengagement.* Mahwah, NJ: Lawrence Erlbaum Associates, 2003.

———. "Collective Identity and the Burden of 'Acting White' in Black History, Community, and Education." *Urban Review* 36, no. 1 (2004): 1–35.

Olsson, Elin. "Do Disadvantaged Adolescents Benefit More from High-Quality Social Relations?" *Acta Sociologica* 52, no. 3 (2009): 263–86.

Orfield, Gary. "Housing Segregation Produces Unequal Schools: Causes and Solutions." In *Closing the Opportunity Gap: What America Must Do to Give Every Child an Even Chance,* edited by Prudence L. Carter and Kevin G. Welner, 40–60. New York: Oxford University Press, 2013.

Oseguera, Leticia, Giberto Q. Conchas, and Eduardo Mosqueda. "Beyond Ethnicity and Ethnic Culture: Understanding the Preconditions for the Potential Realization of Social Capital." *Youth and Society* 43, no. 3 (2010): 1136–66.

Owens, Jayanti, and Douglas Massey. "Stereotype Threat and College Academic Performance: A Latent Variable Approach." *Social Science Research* 40, no. 1 (January 2011): 150–66.

Pastor, Manuel. "Keeping It Real: Demographic Change, Economic Conflict, and Interethnic Organizing for Social Justice in Los Angeles." In *Black and Brown in Los Angeles: Beyond Conflict and Coalition,* edited by Josh Kun and Laura Pulido, 3–66. Berkeley: University of California Press, 2014,

Patillo-McCoy, Mary. *Black Picket Fences: Privilege and Peril among the Black Middle-Class.* Chicago: University of Chicago Press, 1999.

Patterson, James T. *America's Struggle against Poverty in the Twentieth Century.* Cambridge, MA: Harvard University of Press, [1981] 2000.

Patterson, Orlando. "Taking Culture Seriously: A Framework and an African American Illustration." In *Culture Matters: How Values Shape Human Progress,* edited by Lawrence E. Harrison and Samuel P. Huntington, 202–30. New York: Basic Books, 2000,.

Patterson, Orlando, with Ethan Fosse, eds. *The Cultural Matrix: Understanding Black Youth.* Cambridge, MA: Harvard University Press, 2015.

Perlman, Joel. *Ethnic Differences: Schooling and Social Structure among the Irish, Italians, Jews and Blacks in an American City, 1880–1935.* Cambridge: Cambridge University Press, 1988.

Pew Research Center. "Restrictions on Women's Religious Attire." Religion and Public Life, April 5, 2016.

Phillips, Meredith, and Tiffani Chin. "School Inequality: What Do We Know?" In *Social Inequality,* edited by Kathryn M. Neckerman, 467–520. New York: Russell Sage Foundation, 2004.

Portes, Alejandro, "Social Capital: Its Origins and Applications in Modern Sociology." *Annual Review of Sociology* 98 (1998): 1320–50.

Portes, Alejandro, and Rubén G. Rumbaut. *Immigrant America: A Portrait,* 4th ed. Berkeley: University of California Press, 2014.

———. *Legacies: The Story of the Immigrant Second Generation.* Berkeley: University of California Press, 2001.

Putnam, Robert D. *Our Kids: The American Dream in Crisis.* New York: Simon and Schuster, 2015.

Rainwater, Lee. "The Problem of Lower Class Culture." *Journal of Social Issues* 26, no. 2 (1970): 133–48.

Rainwater, Lee, and William Y. Yancy. *The Moynihan Report and the Politics of Controversy* Cambridge, MA: MIT Press, 1967.

Reardon, Sean. "The Widening Academic Achievement Gap between the Rich and Poor: New Evidence and Possible Explanations." In *Whither Opportunity? Rising Inequality, Schools, and Children's Life Chances,* edited by Greg J. Duncan and Richard J. Murnane, 91–116. New York: Russell Sage Foundation, 2011.

Riis, Jacob. *How the Other Half Lives: Studies among the Tenements* of New York. New York: Dover [1890] 1971.

Rosenbaum, James E., Jennifer Stephan, Janet Rosenbaum, Amy E. Foran, and Pam Shuetz. "Beyond BA Blinders: Cultural Impediments to College Success." In *The Cultural Matrix: Understanding Black Youth,* edited by Orlando Patterson. 471–98. Cambridge, MA: Harvard University Press, 2015.

Ryan, William. *Blaming the Victim.* New York: Vintage, 1976.

Sabagh, Georges, and Mehdi Bozorgmehr. "Population Change: Immigration and Ethnic Transformation." In *Ethnic Los Angeles,* edited by Roger Waldinger and Mehdi Bozorgmehr, 79–107. New York: Russell Sage Foundation, 1996.

Saegert, Susan, J. Phillip Thompson, and Mark R. Warren, eds. *Social Capital and Poor Communities.* New York: Russell Sage Foundation, 2001.

Sahlins, Marshall. *Islands of History.* Chicago: University of Chicago Press, 1985.

Saltman, Kenneth J. *The Politics of Education: A Critical Introduction.* New York: Routledge, 2014.

Samuel, Lawrence R. *The American Dream: A Cultural History.* Syracuse, NY: Syracuse University Press, 2012.

Sánchez-Jankowski, Martín. *Burning Dislike: Ethnic Violence in High Schools.* Oakland: University of California Press, 2016.

———. *Cracks in the Pavement: Social Change and Resilience in Poor Neighborhoods.* Berkeley: University of California Press, 2008.

Sánchez-Jankowski, Martín, and Corey M. Abramson, "Foundations of the Behavioralist Approach to Comparative Participant Observation." In *Beyond the Case: The Logics and Practices of Comparative Ethnography,* edited by Corey M. Abramson and Neil Gong, 31–56. New York: Oxford University Press, 2020.

Schultz, Theodore W. *Investment in Human Capital: The Role of Education and Research.* New York: Free Press, 1971.

Sears, David O., Carl P. Hensler, and Leslie K. Speer. "White Opposition to Busing: Self-Interest or Symbolic Politics?" *American Political Science Review* 73 (1973): 369–84.

Sen, Amaryta. *Development as Freedom.* New York: Anchor Books, 1999.

Sewell, William, Jr. "A Theory of Structure: Duality, Agency, and Transformation." *American Journal of Sociology* 98, no. 1 (July 1992): 1–29.

Shavit, Yossi, and Hans-Peter Blossfeld, eds. *Persistent Inequality: A Comparative Study of Educational Attainment in Thirteen Countries.* Boulder, CO: Westview Press, 1993.

Shelby, Tommie. "Liberalism, Self-Respect, and Troubling Cultural Patterns in Ghettos." In *The Cultural Matrix: Understanding Black Youth,* edited by Orlando Patterson, 498–532. Cambridge, MA: Harvard University Press, 2015.

Shinn, Marybeth, and Hirokazu Yoshikawa, eds. *Toward Positive Youth Development: Transferring Schools and Community Programs.* New York: Oxford University Press, 2018.

Simmel, Georg. "Sociability." In *Georg Simmel: On Individuality and Social Forms,* edited by Donald E. Levine, 127–40. Chicago: University of Chicago Press, 1971.

Simmons, Joke, Maarten Vansteenkiste, Will Lens, and Marlies Lacante. "Placing Motivation and Future Time Perspective." *Educational Psychology* 16, no. 3 (2004): 121–39.

Skiba, Russell J., Kavitha Medirata, and M. Karega Rausch, eds. *Inequality in School Discipline: Research and Practice to Reduce Disparities.* New York: Oxford University Press, 2012.

Small, Mario, David Harding, and Michèle Lamont. "Reconsidering Culture and Poverty." *Annals of the American Academy of Political and Social Science* 629 (May 2010): 6–27.

Smith, Sandra Susan. *Lone Pursuit: Distrust and Defensive Individualism among the Black Poor.* New York: Russell Sage Foundation, 2007.

Sonenshein, Raphael J. *Politics in Black and White: Race and Power in Los Angeles.* Princeton, NJ: Princeton University Press, 1993.

Sowell, Thomas. *Black Rednecks and White Liberals.* San Francisco: Encounter Books, 2005.

Stanton-Salazar, Ricardo. "A Social Capital Framework for the Study of Institutional Agents and Their Role in the Empowerment of Low-Income Students and Youth." *Youth and Society* 43, no. 3 (2010): 1066–109.

Steele, Claude. *Whistling Vivaldi and Other Clues to How Stereotypes Affect Us.* New York: Norton, 2010.

Steele, Claude, and Joshua Aronson. "Stereotype Threat and the Intellectual Test Performance of African Americans." *Journal of Personality and Social Psychology* 69, no. 5 (November 1995): 797–811.

Steele, Shelby. *The Content of Our Character: A New Vision of Race.* New York: Harper Perennial, 1991.

Steinberg, Laurence, and Amanda Sheffield Morris. "Adolescent Development." *Annual Review of Psychology* 52 (February 2001): 83–110.

Szatrowski, Alisa. "Pathways to Graduation and Beyond: Practices From Two High Schools for Low-Income Students." PhD diss., University of California, 2019.

Tate, Emily. "Graduation Rates and Race." *Inside Higher Ed,* April 26, 2017.

Tate, Katherine. *From Protest to Politics: The New Black Voters in American Elections.* Cambridge, MA: Harvard University Press, 1993.

Telles, Edward E., and Vilma Ortiz. *Generations of Exclusion: Mexican Americans, Assimilation, and Race.* New York: Russell Sage Foundation, 2009.

The MIT Dictionary of Modern Economics, 4th ed. Cambridge, MA: MIT Press, 1992.

Thomson, Anne. *Critical Reasoning: A Practical Introduction,* 2nd ed. New York: Routledge, 2002.

Tilly, Charles. *Durable Inequalities.* Berkeley: University of California Press, 1999.

Tran, Van C. "More Than Just Black: Cultural Perils and Opportunities in Inner-City Neighborhoods." In *The Cultural Matrix: Understanding Black Youth,* edited by Orlando Patterson, 252–81. Cambridge, MA: Harvard University Press, 2015.

Tyson, Karolyn. *Integration Interrupted: Tracking Black Students and Acting White after Brown.* New York: Oxford University Press, 2011.

———. "Tracking, Segregation, and the Opportunity Gap: What We Know and Why It Matters." Chap. 12 in *Closing the Opportunity Gap: What Americans Must Do to Give Every Child an Even Chance,* edited by Prudence L. Carter and Kevin G. Welner. New York: Oxford University Press, 2013.

Vaca, Nicolás C. *The Presumed Alliance: The Unspoken Conflict between Latinos and Blacks and What It Means for America.* New York: HarperCollins, 2004.

Vaisey, Stephen. "What People Want: Rethinking Poverty, Culture, and Educational Attainment." *Annals of the American Academy of Political and Social Science* 629, no. 1 (2010): 75–101.

Valentine, Charles A. *Culture and Poverty: Critique and Counter-Proposals.* Chicago: University of Chicago Press, 1968.

Valenzuela, Angela. *Subtractive Schooling: US-Mexican Youth and the Politics of Caring.* Albany: State University Press of New York, 1999.

Vallejo, Jody Agius. *Barrios and Burbs: The Making of the Mexican American Middle Class.* Stanford, CA: Stanford University Press, 2012.

Vang, Christopher T. "Hmong-American K–12 Students and Academic Skills Needed for a College Education: A Review of the Existing Literature and Suggestions for the Future." *Hmong Studies Journal* 5 (2004–5): 1–35.

Victora, Cesar, Caroline Fall, Pedro C. Hallal, Reynaldo Martorell, Linda Richter, and Harshpal Singh Sachdev. "Maternal and Child Undernutrition: Consequences for Adult Health and Human Capital." *Lancet* 371 (2008): 340–57.

Vigdor, Jacob L. "School Desegregation and the Black-White Test Score Gap." In *Whither Opportunity: Rising Inequality, Schools, and Children's Lives,* edited by Greg J. Duncan and Richard J. Murnane, 443–63. New York: Russell Sage Foundation, 2011.

Waldinger, Roger. *Still the Promised City? African Americans and New Immigrants in Postindustrial New York.* Cambridge, MA: Harvard University Press, 1999.

Waldinger, Roger, and Mehdi Bozorgmehr, eds. *Ethnic Los Angeles.* New York: Russell Sage Foundation, 1996.

Waters, Mary, and Jennifer Sykes. "Spare the Rod, Spoil the Child?: First and Second Generation West Indian Child Rearing Practices." In *Across Generations: Immigrant Families in America,* edited by Nancy Foner, 101–32. New York: New York University Press, 2009.

Waters, Mary, and Marisa Gerstein Pineau, eds. *The Integration of Immigrants into American Society.* Washington, DC: National Academies Press, 2015.

Weber, Max. *Economy and Society.* Berkeley: University of California Press, [1921] 1978.

———. *Protestant Ethic and the Spirit of Capitalism.* New York: Penguin, [1905] 2002.

Western, Bruce. *Punishment and Inequality in America.* New York: Russell Sage Foundation, 2006.

Wildhagen, Tina. "Why Does Cultural Capital Matter For High School Academic Performance: An Empirical Assessment of Teacher-Selection and Self-Selection Mechanisms as Explanations of the Cultural Capital Effect." *Sociological Quarterly* 50, no. 1 (2009): 173–200.

Willis, Paul. *Learning to Labor: How Working Class Kids Get Working Class Jobs.* New York: Columbia University Press, 1977.

Wilson, William Julius. *The Declining Significance of Race: Blacks and Changing American Institutions.* Chicago: University of Chicago Press, 1978.

Woessman, Ludger. "How Equal Are Educational Opportunities? Family Background and Student Achievement in Europe and the US." Center for Economic Research–Munich Working Paper Series, no. 1162 (April 2004).

Wolram, Walt. "Language Ideology and Dialect: Understanding the Oakland Ebonics Controversy." *Journal of English Linguistics* 26, no. 2 (1998): 108–21.

Woods, Chenoa S., and Thurston Domina. "The School Counselor: Caseload and the High School-to-College Pipeline." *Teachers College Record* 116 (2014): 1–30.

Zamarro, Gama, Collin Hitt, and Ildefonso Mendez. "When Students Don't Care: Reexamining International Differences in Achievement and Student Effort." *Journal of Human Capital* 13, no. 4 (Winter 2019): 519–52.

Zhou, Min, and Susan Kim. "Community Focus, Social Capital and Educational Achievement: The Case of Supplementary Education in the Chinese and Korean Immigrant Communities." *Harvard Educational Review* 76, no. 1 (April 2006): 1–29.

INDEX

addiction, 70

administrators: overview of, 16–21; appointment of, 16, 21, 26; authority and, 18, 19, 25, 29; culture of, 17, 42–43; ethnicity and, 19–23, 26; evaluation of, 179; public image and, 17–19, 24–25, 29; review boards and, 175; social control and, 17, 19; standardized tests and, 18, 35; status quo and, 30. *See also* principals; superintendents

advanced placement, 80, 82–85, 89–91, 99, 102

advancing, definition of, 3, 172

African Americans: administration and, 21–23; civil rights movement and, 22; culture and, 119, 188; identity and, 210n42, 217n23; language and, 119, 224; networks and, 129; segregation and, 204; stigma and, 211n46

agency: definition of, 234n50; culture and, 184; human capital and, 3; social tracking and, 151, 168–69

aggression, 54, 71, 213n71

alcohol, 70

American Dream, 1–2, 146–47, 191–92, 244n63

American Indian Schools Program, 185, 188, 240n34

antipathy, 183–84, 187

anxiety, 69, 73, 99

aptitude, 81–84

Aristotle, 113

Asian Americans, 239n26

athletes. *See* sports

attention deficit disorder (ADD), 74–75

attention deficit hyperactivity disorder (ADHD), 74–75

Aurelius, Marcus, 145

authority: administration and, 18, 19, 25, 29; student dislike of, 152; teachers and, 40, 78

Bacon, Francis, 170

Baldwin, James, 1, 44

boards of education, 16–17, 23

boredom, 92, 100, 157, 161

Bourdieu, Pierre, 113, 125–26, 223n8

budgets, 17–18, 181

Bureaucratic Track, 147–50, 163–66

Bush, George W., 2, 26, 231n5

capitalism, 190

Central Americans, 22, 183

centralization, 192

cheating, 130

Cicero, Marcus Tillius, 78

civil rights movement, 22

classical educators, 218n34

class participation, 62, 70

Clinton, Bill, 2, 26

clubs, 56

code switching, 124, 224n14

cognitive disabilities, 64–65, 75

community college, 83, 128, 162

participant observation, 7–8, 10–11, 196–97

participation, 62, 70

Patterson, Orlando, 188

peer groups, 61, 85, 101, 115

physicality, 71–75, 186

poverty, 9, 39, 186, 188

Pratt, Richard Henry, 185, 240n34

pregnancy, 58

prejudice, 24, 41, 62, 76, 97, 108

principals: appointment of, 26–27, 35; demographics and, 23; evaluation of, 35; instructional policy and, 33–34; public image and, 25, 31, 41; reforms and, 27–29, 31–32, 36–42; school discipline and, 32; teachers and, 30, 35–42

problem-solving, 39, 91

promotions, 16, 19–20, 27, 148

Quintilianus, Marcus Fabius, 44, 113

reading: curiosity and, 156; disorders and, 74; home environment and, 52; language and, 156; parents and, 67; remedial interventions and, 65, 73; sitting and, 72–73; teaching styles and, 94; underdevelopment of, 63–64

recruiters, 128

regulations, 3, 6

remedial interventions: budgets and, 182; parents and, 64; reading and, 65, 73; social tracking and, 149

reputation, 118, 120, 121

research methods, 7–12, 195–97

responsibility, 68–69, 184

review boards, 175

role models, 39, 230n77

SAT, 27, 40

scholarships, 153

segregation, 22, 192–93, 204n16, 245n69

self-discipline, 49, 57, 61, 66

self-employment, 152

Sen, Amartya, 159

sibling care, 68–69

sitting, 72–73

sleep, 53–54, 208n24

Small, Mario, 121

Smith, Sandra, 129

social capital, 3, 113–14, 125–26, 142–44, 228n55

social etiquette, 115, 118–19

socialism, 190

social networks. *See* networks

social tracking: overview of, 145–46; Bureaucratic Track, 147–50, 163–66; changing tracks, 146, 160–68; counselors and, 165; Drifting Track, 158–60, 163, 165–68; Entrepreneurial Track, 150–55, 160–61, 163, 165–68; gender and, 151; remedial interventions and, 149; standardized tests and, 150; Wandering track, 155–60, 162–64, 166–67

special programs, 76, 103

sports, 56, 64, 154, 191

standardized tests: administrators and, 18, 35; aptitude and, 82; college admission and, 2; construction of, 180; curriculum and, 180; insecurities and, 236n10; learning disabilities and, 64–65; SAT, 27, 40; social tracking and, 150; teachers and, 38–39, 178

stigma, 64, 76, 211, 214n79, 224n15

study habits, 50, 55, 61, 71, 123

subcultures, 87, 182–83, 217n29, 226n34

superintendents, 16–19, 23–25

suspension, 59–60, 76

talent, 1, 34, 161–62

teachers: overview of, 35–42; authority of, 40, 78; code enforcement and, 40; cultural capital and, 39; dismissal of, 177; evaluation of, 34, 177–79; grading and, 120, 150; homework and, 49–51; in-class discipline and, 54; instructional policy and, 32–34, 38; language skills and, 116–20, 156; principals and, 30, 35–42; reassignment of, 30–31; review boards and, 175; salaries and, 176; standardized tests, 38–39, 178; teaching styles and, 89–98, 100–102; transfer of, 30–31, 34, 36, 98, 176

teachers' unions: administration and, 20, 25, 29, 30, 34, 41; curriculum reform and, 177; instructional policy and, 34; teacher evaluations and, 178

textbooks, 42, 89, 93, 96, 97, 102

Founded in 1893,
UNIVERSITY OF CALIFORNIA PRESS
publishes bold, progressive books and journals
on topics in the arts, humanities, social sciences,
and natural sciences—with a focus on social
justice issues—that inspire thought and action
among readers worldwide.

The UC PRESS FOUNDATION
raises funds to uphold the press's vital role
as an independent, nonprofit publisher, and
receives philanthropic support from a wide
range of individuals and institutions—and from
committed readers like you. To learn more, visit
ucpress.edu/supportus.

www.ingramcontent.com/pod-product-compliance
Lightning Source LLC
Chambersburg PA
CBHW020843270326
41928CB00006B/518